T0090119

PRAISE FOR *THE PROGRESS PARADOX*

"Throughout his clearly written, thought-provoking book, Gregg Easterbrook summons a broad range of social scientists as witnesses. He gives us facts and figures galore to remind us how very well our nation is doing as the richest and strongest on the earth. Pages of good, telling reportage remind the reader of how fortunate we Americans have become with respect to our standard of living. . . . At times his writing connects with that of two others: a Danish theologian and social observer, Kierkegaard, who took sharp moral aim at nineteenth-century Copenhagen's comfortable but self-preoccupied bourgeoisie; and our own twentieth-century novelist and philosophical essayist Walker Percy, who mused long and hard about the irony that goes with having everything except a sense of purpose—of life's meaning."
—Robert Coles, *The Boston Globe*

"Marvelous . . . [a] gem of a book . . . Easterbrook, a fellow at the Brookings Institution who writes for both *The Atlantic Monthly* and *The New Republic* (and may actually be best known for Tuesday Morning Quarterback, his wildly popular blog about professional football), is a graceful prose stylist with a long history of endorsing controversial, and contrarian, ideas. He is not easy to pin down politically. (In his other work, he has supported national health insurance, for example, but skewered the environmental movement for its excesses.) But what is always useful in his work is that, unlike so many who write to stir up controversy, he likes to propose practical solutions."
—Stephen L. Carter, *Christianity Today*

"Page after well-researched page, Easterbrook lays out his case. . . . His book is strongest when documenting the unobvious, when it gives reasons for reexamining our pessimism and contemplating the actual goodness of our day-to-day lives. You're unlikely to look at the world, or even a television commercial, in quite the same way again, and by that metric the book is a success."
—*San Francisco Chronicle*

"Easterbrook . . . has a knack for bringing to light little-considered facts and collating them toward sometimes surprising conclusions."
—*The Washington Post Book World*

"This important book lays out exactly why we should all quit whining. . . . [Easterbrook's] scientifically backed optimism is a rare and eye-opening treat."

—*People*

"[Easterbrook's] view is refreshing. . . . The unexpectedness of the argument, the sense of surprise in the book, and the deft way Easterbrook makes you think will keep a reader with this book and looking for his other works."

—*The Hartford Courant*

"If there is a more stylistically sound liberal-moderate writer in the United States right now than Gregg Easterbrook, his name eludes me. . . . *The Progress Paradox* is, as a purely literary experience, a tremendous pleasure."

—*The American Spectator*

"Thought-provoking . . . an insightful and accessible work presented in clear, concise language often tinged with irony."

—*Library Journal*

"[An] absorbing, far-ranging tome—which people from all walks of life would benefit from reading . . . [Easterbrook's] astute observations place *The Progress Paradox* among the best and most important books of the year."

—Fort Worth *Star-Telegram*

"Gregg Easterbrook in *The Progress Paradox* observes that people in the West 'live in a favored age yet do not feel favored.' Probing the causes of the paradox . . . he point[s] out that our society is undergoing a fundamental shift from 'material want' to 'meaning want.' And, as he points out, finding meaning is a lot harder than finding a car to buy."

—Ellen Heltzel and Margo Hammond, "The Book Babes"

"An important, timely, and well-reasoned book that is sure to have people talking."

—*Booklist*

ABOUT THE AUTHOR

GREGG EASTERBROOK is a senior editor of *The New Republic*, a contributing editor of *The Atlantic Monthly*, a visiting fellow in economics at the Brookings Institution and a columnist for NFL.com. He is the author of six books, including *A Moment on the Earth*, a *New York Times* and American Library Association Notable Book. He has also been a contributing editor at *Newsweek* and an editor of *The Washington Monthly*. He lives in Maryland and can be reached via the Internet at www.greggeasterbrook.com.

BY GREGG EASTERBROOK

The Here and Now

Beside Still Waters

Tuesday Morning Quarterback

A Moment on the Earth

This Magic Moment

The Leading Indicators

Sonic Boom

The Progress Paradox

THE PROGRESS PARADOX

THE
PROGRESS
PARADOX

*How Life Gets Better
While People Feel Worse*

GREGG EASTERBROOK

RANDOM HOUSE TRADE PAPERBACKS / NEW YORK

2004 Random House Trade Paperbacks Edition
Copyright © 2003 by Gregg Easterbrook

This work was originally published in hardcover by Random House in 2003.

Library of Congress Cataloging-in-Publication Data
Easterbrook, Gregg.
The progress paradox : how life gets better while people feel worse / by Gregg
Easterbrook.
p. cm.
Includes index.
ISBN 978-0-8129-7303-7
1. Progress.   2. Quality of life.   3. Discontent.   4. Pessimism.   I. Title.
HM891.E27   2003   303.44—dc21   2003046611

Random House website address: www.atrandom.com

Book design by J. K. Lambert

For my mother,

VIMY HOOVER EASTERBROOK

1917–1976

Happiness makes up in height
what it lacks in length.

— ROBERT FROST

CONTENTS

IF THEY COULD SEE US NOW

$\int$uppose your great-great-grandparents, who lived four generations ago, materialized in the United States of the present day.
Surely they would first be struck by the scale and clamor of
present-day life, and might not like these things; neither do we,
necessarily. The physical speed of contemporary life would also
shock our forebears, who considered New York to London in
a week to be a blazing-fast transit, and none of whom ever experienced the velocity now common to everyone on highways.
When newfangled Great Western Railway steam engines left London in 1844 to pull coaches at forty-five miles per hour, commentators expressed horror at such unnatural swiftness, while
physicians urged passengers to avoid the trains on grounds that
anyone moving so rapidly would surely suffocate. Now much
greater speeds go unnoticed in daily events; we live, work, and
try to relax surrounded by steel objects whizzing past, many of
them guided by teenagers. The psychological speeds we must
sustain, and the attendant anxieties, are in their own ways as

hazardous. Add in nuclear bombs, global terrorism, and the inescapable inanity of mass entertainment, and your great-great-grandparents' initial reaction to the present day might be to recoil in dismay and demand to return to their own time.

Yet as your ancestors four generations removed learned more of contemporary life, they would be dazzled. Unlimited food at affordable prices, never the slightest worry about shortage, unlimited variety—strawberries in March!—so much to eat that in the Western nations, overindulgence now plagues not just the well-off but the poor, the poor being more prone to obesity than the population as a whole. Four generations ago, the poor were lean as fence posts, their arms bony and faces gaunt. To our recent ancestors, the idea that today *even the poor* eat too much might be harder to fathom than a jetliner rising from the runway.

Many other aspects of contemporary life, taken for granted by those of us who live it, would dazzle our recent ancestors. At the beginning of the twentieth century, the average American lifespan was forty-one years; now it is seventy-seven years, equating to almost twice as much time on Earth for the typical person. History's plagues—polio, smallpox, measles, rickets—have been defeated, along with a stunning reduction of the infectious diseases that for pre-antibiotics generations instilled terror. Every one of our great-great-grandparents would have known someone who died of a disease that today is shrugged at; many of our recent ancestors themselves departed this life as victims of diseases at which we now shrug. My paternal grandfather died in 1921 of lockjaw—then untreatable, today cured by a few vials of inexpensive chemicals.

Many other aspects of present-day life would strike our recent ancestors as nearly miraculous. The end of backbreaking physical toil for most wage earners. The arrival of leisure, the typical person now engaged in exertion (either for pay or within the household) about half as many hours as in the nineteenth century. The advent of instantaneous global communication and same-day travel to distant cities. The end of formal discrimination against minorities and women, increasing opportunity while allowing those who succeed to feel their achievements are fairly won. Mass home ownership, with heated dwellings everywhere, cooled homes almost everywhere. The entire senior-citizen demographic cared for financially and medically, ending the fear of impoverished old age. Complete, and usually low-cost, access to information, art, and literature. Incredible advances in freedom: political freedom, freedom of expression, sexual freedom, freedom from conscription.

Today we live a long time, in fairly comfortable circumstances; enjoy goods and services in almost unlimited supply; travel where we wish quickly and relatively cheaply; talk to anyone in the world; know everything there is to know; think and say what we please; marry for love, and have sex with whomever will agree; and wail in sorrow when anyone dies young, for this once-routine event has become a wrenching rarity. All told, except for the clamor and speed of society, and for trends in popular music, your great-great-grandparents might say the contemporary United States is the realization of utopia.

....

Yet how many of us feel positive about our moment, or even believe that life is getting better? Today Americans tell pollsters that the country is going downhill; that their parents had it better; that they feel unbearably stressed out; that their children face a declining future—and Americans were telling pollsters this even during the unprecedented boom that preceded the tragedy of September 11, 2001.

The percentage of Americans who describe themselves as "happy" has not budged since the 1950s, though the typical person's real income more than doubled through that period. Happiness has not increased in Japan or Western Europe in the past half-century, either, though daily life in both those places has grown fantastically better, incorporating all the advances noted above plus the end of dictatorships and recovery from general war. On the first day of the twenty-first century, President Bill Clinton declared that Western society had "never before enjoyed, at once, so much prosperity combined with so much social progress." This statement was not just politics; objectively, it is true. Nevertheless the citizens of the United States and the European Union, almost all of whom live better than almost all of the men and women of history, entertain considerable discontent.

Far from feeling better about their lives, many are feeling worse. Throughout the United States and the European Union, incidence of clinical melancholy has been rising in eerie synchronization with rising prosperity: Adjusting for population growth, "unipolar" depression, the condition in which a person simply always feels blue, is today ten times as prevalent as it was half a century ago.

Some modern disaffection may be attributed to auto-grumbling—that no matter how much conditions improve, people will always want to know why things aren't still better. As the French songwriter Jacques Brel phrased this constant: "Sons of the rich, sons of the saint, where is the child without complaint?" Someday if Eden is restored, people may complain about the predictable menu of milk and honey and about the friendly lions purring too loudly.

Widespread incidence of melancholy and pessimism amidst plenty and freedom may hold significance beyond the human proclivity to complain. As Alan Wolfe of Boston University has noted, a leading question of our moment in history is: "Why capitalism and liberal democracy, both of which justify themselves on the grounds that they produce the greatest happiness for the greatest number, leave so much dissatisfaction in their wake."

Perhaps, at some structural level, for every old problem solved, a new problem will always be created, meaning we should not expect a better life to improve happiness. Perhaps Western society has lost its way, producing material goods in impressive superfluity but also generating so much stress and pressure that people cannot enjoy what they attain. Perhaps men and women must reexamine their priorities—demanding less, caring more about each other, appreciating what they have rather than grousing about what they do not have, giving more than lip service to the wisdom that money cannot buy happiness. Perhaps Americans and Europeans also need a lesson in the fundamentals of gratitude. Even considering September 11, nearly all trends in the United States and the European Union are positive and have been positive throughout the lifetimes of most readers of this book. Our forebears worked hard, and sacrificed often, to create the freedom and prosperity that we know. It is past time Americans and Europeans showed some appreciation for this.

The book you are about to read will address topics including:

- The ways in which contemporary American and European life grows steadily better, with nearly every trend line positive.
- The actions, from government policy to individual choices, that have caused nearly every trend line to become positive.

- Why huge numbers of people do not appreciate the fact that Western life grows steadily better, or even deny this is happening.
- Why the prosperous, free, and basically decent societies of the United States and Western Europe produce so many citizens who are unhappy.
- Why rapid progress against "unsolvable" problems, such as pollution and crime, should give us hope that "unsolvable" problems of the present, such as global warming and developing world suffering, can be overcome.
- Why even overcoming every problem that exists might not make us any happier.

In addition, this book will propose a few theories intended to explain the contemporary overlap of sanguine social circumstances and personal unhappiness. They will include:

- That several important new apprehensions have arisen to replace old ones.
  ▲ One is "choice anxiety," the transition from people being so constrained by social forces that they felt trapped to the current situation of having so many options that choice itself becomes a source of anguish.
  ▲ Another is "abundance denial," in which millions of women and men construct elaborate mental rationales for considering themselves materially deprived, and in so doing only succeed in causing their life experiences to be unhappy.
  ▲ Another is "collapse anxiety," a widespread feeling that the prosperity of the United States and the European Union cannot really be enjoyed because the Western lifestyle may crash owing to economic breakdown, environmental damage,

resource exhaustion, terrorism, population growth, or some other imposed calamity.

▲ Another is the "revolution of satisfied expectations," the uneasy feeling that accompanies actually receiving the things that you dreamed of.

- That society is undergoing a fundamental shift from "material want" to "meaning want," with ever larger numbers of people reasonably secure in terms of living standards, but feeling they lack significance in their lives. A transition from "material want" to "meaning want" is not a prediction that men and women will cease being materialistic; no social indicator points to such a possibility. It is a prediction that ever more millions will expect both pleasant living standards and a broad sense that their lives possess purpose. This is a conundrum, as meaning is much more difficult to acquire than material possessions.

- That ultimately we should be glad society is creating the leisure and prosperity that allows people by the millions to feel depressed, for it's better to be prosperous, free, and unhappy than other possibilities.

- That new psychological research, which seeks to explain why some are happy and others not, suggests it is *in your self-interest* to be forgiving, grateful, and optimistic—that these presumptively altruistic qualities are actually essential to personal well-being.

Arriving at this moment, your great-great-grandparents would be surrounded by people who take for granted circumstances our ancestors would view as astonishing progress in the ancient quest to banish privation and establish a Golden Age. But even if the arrow of progress points toward an ever better life, unhappiness persists and is wholly real regardless of whether our recent forebears might find it unbelievable that anyone could be unhappy in an air conditioned house with a refrigerator crammed with food and ambulances on call.

We live in a favored age yet do not feel favored. What does this paradox tell us about ourselves and our future?

THE PROGRESS PARADOX

Chapter 1

THE GREAT STORY OF OUR ERA:
AVERAGE PEOPLE BETTER OFF

Though the airfield does not appear on many charts, its existence is whispered of among pilots. The approach requires skill and timing, and there have been accidents; but when the mission is important, some risks must be accepted. Fliers who have data-pulse receivers of the extraordinarily accurate Global Positioning System satellite network use these devices when inbound, as the runway is only 2,350 feet long—short by the standards of such things—which places a premium on putting the wheels down precisely at the beginning of the field so as not to run out of runway at the end. Pilots exhale with relief when the landing is complete. Once on the ground, planes are directed to taxi to a secluded ramp, where crew and passengers quickly debark to swing into action—because there might be a wait for tables.

The aircraft are not military transports full of commandos but small private planes full of diners landing at McGehee's Catfish House in Marietta, Oklahoma, one of the increasing number of "fly-in" restaurants in the United States. The runway belongs to McGehee's and serves it exclusively. The field is lit for night landings, since the kitchen is open late. Guidance beacons with the aviator's designation Loran T40 can be used to find McGehee's, this being the international locator signal not of an airport or classified facility but a restaurant. At McGehee's, you walk from your airplane to the hostess station. Much of the dinner trade arrives from Dallas, about forty air minutes away, though diners fly in from as far as hundreds of miles distant to savor a menu highlighted by fresh farm-raised catfish, pickled tomatoes, and turtle cheesecake.

Nearly a thousand fly-in restaurants are open for business in America today, according to an organization called Hundred-Dollar Hamburger. (Small private planes cost around $100 an hour to operate.) Most are simply eateries adjacent to general-aviation airports, but an increasing number, like McGehee's, have become fly-in in the complete sense. The advent of such restaurants is exciting to the owners of small planes, many of whom learned to fly as a challenge, or in response to the romance of the air, then discovered that they crave destinations for the kind of one-hour hops that make for recreational aviation. Just imagine trying to explain to the indigent of the developing world that one problem experienced by Americans is finding something to do with their personal aircraft!

So far, fly-in restaurants offer no fly-through windows for takeout; that may only be a matter of time. Regardless of whether the fly-in restaurant is a breakthrough or an absurdity, what is telling is that the aircraft landing at McGehee's are not private jets of the super-rich. Rather, they are one- and two-engine propeller planes of farmers, oil-field workers, mid-career professionals, and others from the middle class: men and women who are scarcely oligarchs, but who can afford to own an airplane and to drop $100 on a whim for a platter of fresh catfish. Today in the United States thousands of private aircraft are owned for personal use by people who are not rich, just as millions of not-rich Americans own two homes or four cars plus a boat, or know other extravagances once reserved for the topmost fraction of the elite.

Fly-in communities have sprung up as well—entire housing developments built around runways for small planes. Spruce Creek, near Daytona Beach, Florida, is a fly-in subdivision which boasts about 1,200 homes and fourteen miles of aircraft taxiway connecting houses with the runway. Pecan Plantation, completed at the turn of the twenty-first century near Fort Worth, Texas, has 125 homes, all served by taxiways. Planes can land, taxi home to the owner's house, and be parked in the drive. Teen pilots can bring airplanes to the front door to pick up their dates. The occupants of Pecan Plantation are well-off but not millionaires. Many houses in the subdivision have hangars rather than garages, a popular option being 4,500-square-foot hangars—sized for two cars and *two* airplanes.

If fly-in dining and runway-based homes aren't your cup of tea, how about golf-course living? Today in the United States there are at least two hundred housing developments built around fairways. At these communities, one sees golf carts scooting along side streets: Many residents own their own carts, park them in the garage, and ride directly from the back porch door to the clubhouse. Golf-course living, with club membership typically included in the home purchase price, has grown so much in popularity that developments are now found not just near big-money cities but in states such as Missouri and Wyoming. Powder Horn, a golf community in Sheridan, Wyoming, looks out on the majestic Bighorn Mountains and offers a well-reviewed eighteen-hole course reached from the porch door via personal cart. The development's realty brochure gives this advice regarding lots: "Select a site on the fairway, one with a river or lake view, nestled in the hillside, close to the clubhouse or walking distance to the practice range." Beautiful, well-appointed homes at Powder Horn cost from about $285,000 to about $425,000—not cheap but not inordinate, within the means of tens of millions of Americans.

Prefer the lake to ducking aircraft or dodging golf carts? In 2000, fully 13 percent of American home purchases were of second homes, mostly in vacation areas of woodland, mountain, or shore. Second-home sales have boomed so much that in many popular rustic retreats—such as the San Juan Islands north of Seattle, Washington, or Deep Creek Lake, Maryland, in the Alleghenies, equidistant from Pittsburgh and Washington, D.C.—vacation homes by the thousands line the desirable riparian acreage, with land parcels growing scarce.

A century ago the very notion of a second home, owned not as a principal dwelling but a place of relaxation, could be contemplated strictly by a minuscule super-elite; now there are millions with a weekend place, and the number keeps rising. Today a leading problem with your dream house by the water is that so many other people also own vacation homes and own powerboats or jet skis—in 2001, Americans spent $25 billion, more than the GDP of North Korea, on recreational watercraft[1]—that the tranquility may be shattered by piston roar. At present many lakeside communities are wrapped up in campaigns to restrict noise from private motor vessels, and the politics of the matter are delicate, because often the factions favoring stillness are arrayed in opposition to boat owners and jet skiers who are working-class women and men, and who feel their privileges are being trampled.

But imagine; the boat owners are working-class. Merely the concept of the "pleasure" boat possessed by an average individual rather than by a duke or an industrialist is new to our moment. Now so many average people own pleasure boats that docking space is short in many areas, while marinas have become the "marina industry"—complete with its own lobby group, the International Marina Institute, and with several trade publications, among them *Marina Dock Age* and *Marina and Boatyard Today*. In other battles regarding the great outdoors, such as in the national-monument areas of the California desert or at Yellowstone National Park, the offending machines may be snowmobiles or single-seat all-terrain vehicles, costing $5,000 each or more, owned by average people and opposed by those who dislike the noise. Since 1995, Americans have purchased more than 3 million all-terrain vehicles, which are used almost exclusively for recreation, and continue to snap them up at a rate of about 750,000 per year. But imagine—average people own expensive specialized vehicles just for weekend recreation. And so many of these vehicles exist that they have become a political issue!

Fly-in restaurants, golf-course communities, rustic lakes ringed by second homes, pleasure boats, huge SUVs with heated leather seats and built-in video, custom-painted snowmobiles with GPS: These and many other big-ticket items are now marketed not to the top but to the middle of American society, and increasingly to the middle of European society, too. They serve as well as any examples might to illustrate one of the most fundamental trends in the postwar Western world: namely, the grand increase in living standards for people who *aren't* rich.

Poverty persists in the United States, at lower levels each decade, but its persistence nonetheless is a national outrage; millions live from paycheck to paycheck under nerve-racking financial pressure; millions lack health insurance; runaway materialism simultaneously makes us shallow and fails to give satisfaction; mass culture (the movies, television, pop music) grows stupider by the minute; inequality means some have far more than they could ever need while others have only resentment; global forces cause many to fear job loss. All these are important objections to trends in contemporary American life.

But in the main, Americans are steadily better off, and while the rich are richer, the bulk of the gains in living standards—the gains that really matter—have occurred below the plateau of wealth. Almost every person in the United States and the European Union today lives better than did his or her parents. In the United States and Western Europe, almost everything is getting better for almost everybody: This has been the case for years, and is likely to remain the case.

Consider a few statistics, derived from the 2000 United States Census. Almost 23 percent of households in the United States today have an income of at least $75,000, which equates to some sixty-three million people existing at the material standard of the upper middle class. Sixty-three million people—more than the total population of the United States in the year 1890— now live an "upper" existence in material terms. An upper-or-above life situation hardly ensures happiness, as large numbers of materially favored people today nevertheless feel miserable, a topic this book will explore in some depth. But the notion of sixty-three million people being very well off represents an astonishingly positive trend in standards of living. In 1890, less than 1 percent of American households earned the equivalent of $75,000 in today's dollars; now nearly a quarter of households are at that favored point.

What about the middle? Inflation-adjusted per-capita American income has more than doubled since 1960, meaning that the typical person now commands twice the buying power of his father or mother in the year 1960. This is the adjusted, or "real," comparison, which subtracts the effect of inflation. By some measures, "real" buying power regularly runs well ahead of inflation for the typical person, in part because the prices of many common items, especially food and almost everything electronic, keep falling. As W. Michael Cox, a Federal Reserve Board official, has pointed out, by the measure of how many hours people must work to purchase common goods and services, typical Americans have become steadily better off during the postwar years. In 1956, for example, the typical American had to work sixteen weeks for each 100 square feet of home purchased; today, buying 100 square feet of new home costs the typical person fourteen weeks of work, while the new home itself is significantly swankier. During the 1950s, a cheeseburger at the original McDonald brothers' stand cost half an hour of typical wages; now the typical American can buy a McDonald's cheeseburger for the price of three minutes of work.[2] Cars, furniture, clothing, and other common goods show a steady, ongoing decline in the number of work-hours required for the typical American to purchase them, Cox has found: Of important goods and services, only health care and college education now cost more in work-hours terms than they did in the 1950s.

In 2001, the median U.S. household income was $42,228, while the average household income was $68,000. Average family income has been rising nicely in the United States in recent decades. Median income, the line at which there are equal numbers above and below, has risen only modestly. This means there's a large group stalled at lower incomes: Increases at the top raise average income, while the stalled group at the bottom restrains median income.

Many commentators assert that because in the last quarter century the median U.S. household income has improved only somewhat, rising 15 percent in inflation-adjusted terms between 1973 and 2000, while inflation-adjusted incomes of the top 1 percent of families rose 120 percent in the same period, the typical person must be losing ground.[3] Statistical debate on the question of whether the median is losing ground is excruciating, in part because, if you torture numbers long enough, they will confess to anything. For instance, since 1980 the share of the American population earning $100,000 or more, in today's dollars, has doubled, which sounds like a democratizing trend. Yet entire books[4] have been written lamenting that trends in median incomes are diminishing the typical American's prospects. Certainly it has become an article of faith in gloomy commentary about the United States, and in the talk-show universe, that Americans in the middle are seeing their positions erode and their buying power decline.

....

Has this really happened? As Gary Burtless, an economist at the Brookings Institution, has pointed out, the period of slow growth in median income coincides with the second great wave of immigration into the United States. Through the 1980s and 1990s, America accepted more than a million legal immigrants annually—for each of the last twenty years, the United States has accepted more legal immigrants than *all other nations of the world combined,* along with a huge influx of illegals. Mainly, immigration is a social good; immigrants bring vitality to the economy and to the culture, and, in a troubled world, the United States should take in as many as it can. The result of wide-open borders is that today 11 percent of the United States population is foreign-born, the highest proportion since the 1930s. Immigrants start at the bottom of the income bell curve, and in statistical terms their main impact is to pull down the numbers for the median household. From 1979 to 1999, for example, five million immigrant households below the poverty line were added to the United States. In that same period, the percentage of native-born Americans living in poverty was approximately stable, while the percentage of foreign-born U.S. residents living in poverty rose.[5]

Factor out immigration, and the rise in American inequality diminishes; median-income trends look better. Among the 89 percent of the American population that is native-born, inequality is changing only a small amount—a trend driven in no small part by the rising incomes of African Americans, most of whom are native-born and whose family median incomes are currently rising twice as fast as family median income for the United States as a whole.[6] Immigrants skew inequality figures downward, but take into account that it is in the interest of immigrants that they be allowed to enter the United States—strongly in their interest—and inequality-gap statistics, though always a concern, cease to be an indictment of the American economy. Stated in the opposite way, if the existence of an inequality gap is an indictment of the American economy, then the solution is to forbid immigration. Such a policy would impose grave hardship on poor immigrants. If inequality statistics are bad and the solution is a policy that would impose grave hardships on the poor,[7] the point of absurdity has been reached—which shows how weak the whole inequality-gap objection is in the first place.

Most complaints about rising income inequality in the United States come from the political left, which would be utterly horrified if immigration were restricted. If open borders are to continue, then we must accept slower income gains in the middle. A closed-border U.S. society would produce better statistics about middle-income gain, but be less just in other important ways. Unless you favor the closing of borders, don't complain that the top is pulling away from the middle in income terms.

Also missing from standard complaining about middle-American income is that the typical American household is shrinking. Today, the median American household contains 2.6 people, as an ever increasing proportion of the population lives alone or as pairs of senior citizens with no children under the same roof. Living alone—as about 10 percent of Americans did in 2000—may be good or bad for your mental health and your spirit. Economically, the steady rise of residing alone is a reflection of higher living standards and more buying power for average people, as in previous generations only the rich could afford a dwelling all to themselves.

While today's typical roof shelters 2.6 people, a quarter-century ago the median household held four. This means today's mildly higher typical household income is spread over fewer household members. The result is an effective income gain of about 50 percent in real-dollar terms for middle-class households in the past quarter century. This is not the living-standards stagnation that fashionable commentary likes to suggest. Fifty percent real-dollar gain for average households in the last twenty-five years—during a period of record immigration—speaks of remarkable improvement in the buying power and living standards of the American middle.

....

Missing, as well, from grumbling about trends in standards of living for the typical person is perspective on evolving ways in which national wealth is spent. As Robert J. Samuelson, one of the nation's leading analysts of economics, has written,[9] overall the U.S. standard of living has continued to rise in the last two decades at roughly the same pace as the 1950s and 1960s—it's just that we now take out a considerable share of national wealth in ways that don't directly compare to spending in the 1950s, such as reduced mortality via advanced medical procedures that did not previously exist, less air pollution, the ability to fly anywhere anytime at an affordable price or talk to anyone anywhere anytime, affordably. Unfortunately, Samuelson notes, we also now expend more national wealth on litigation.

The rising medical share of the GDP,[10] often strangely denounced as "waste," is surely money that cannot be spent on other things, but buys for America's citizenry ever longer lives with more vigor and less pain. For instance, Americans regularly complain of the cost of prescription drugs but rarely complain of the benefits. One reason so many American senior citizens are at this writing upset about the costs of prescription drugs is that those drugs have kept them alive long enough that they need more drugs.

Most of the rise in health care spending stems not from the prices of medical goods and services, most of which have been declining in real-dollar terms, but from increased utilization. The population is aging, and the aging require more care than the young. New drugs, medical devices, and procedures have been developed that reduce pain, extend longevity, and enable those who suffer from various conditions to lead better lives; people naturally want to use these new drugs and devices, incurring new costs. A generation ago, a doctor would tell a patient with chronic nonspecific knee pain to take aspirin and avoid strenuous activity first thing in the morning; the standard was that you lived with such things. Today, the notion of living with any treatable discomfort is unthinkable. Patients with knee pain might receive anything from cartilage-growth medication to arthroscopic surgery to a complete artificial knee. Some 200,000 knee replacements were performed in the United States in 2001, at an average cost of $26,000.[11] That's $5.2 billion in health care spending just for artificial knees, a category of treatment that did not even exist a generation ago. Medicare will provide artificial knees at taxpayer expense to patients in their eighties who do not have much longer to live. As available health care technology increases and society feels everyone should have access to the best care under all circumstances, we should expect health care spending to rise even if the prices of individual goods and services are declining. The essential result is that most people are better off.

Medical expenditures have also risen in recent decades because society has decided to spare no expense to fight for the lives of those who, once, would have been quietly allowed to die—among them very premature infants, babies with severe birth defects, and the severely injured victims of accidents. Is this not an important social advance? Typical men and women, not the well-off, constitute the majority of beneficiaries of the new assumption that no expense should ever be spared to extend even a medically problematic life. In 2003, Americans were heartbroken by the tragedy of Jesíca Santillan, a seventeen-year-old who died at Duke University Medical Center after a botched heart-lung transplant, followed by a second heart-lung transplant that failed. Hundreds of thousands of dollars, from government and from private charity, were spent trying to save Santillan, though her prognosis was always poor, and though she was an illegal immigrant. Most nations of the world would have done nothing for Santillan—her native Mexico would not treat her—or even deported her and her parents. The United States spent freely, running up the national GDP figure for health care in the process. Yet if an expense has to rise, health care seems the expense to pick. As the commentator David Wessel has noted,[12] rising medical share of GDP means that "Americans bought 50 percent more health care per person in 2002 than they did in 1982. Isn't that good? We also built 19 percent more cars per person during the same period. Would we really have been better off with even more cars and less health care?"

After the year 2000 Census figures were released, the writer Camille Sweeney interviewed families around the country that were bringing home approximately the median national income.[13] Sweeney's families were hardly living in opulence, but each had recently purchased at least one entry from the following list: a new car, a powerboat, a widescreen TV, a three-bedroom vacation cottage, a swimming pool, an expensive family vacation. Several median-income families had two recent purchases from that list. The median-income Wisconsin dairy-farm family whose members Sweeney interviewed owned two new SUVs, one of them a Ford Expedition, a luxury model. The median-income Louisiana family whose members Sweeney interviewed considered life good in part because they spent weekends cruising aboard their powerboat. Owning a boat or a fancy SUV hardly ensures satisfaction in life, and many families poised at the median national income suffer financial distress, especially regarding health care costs. The point here is simply that, in the United States, people in the middle, which is where most people reside—the middle, after all, dominates all statistics—live favored lives in material terms.

....

Consider other measures of improving material circumstances for the typical person. Two generations ago in the United States, most families lacked a car; by our parents' generation, most families had one car while the two-car lifestyle was a much-sought ideal; today a third of America's families own three cars or more. The United States now contains just shy of one automobile per licensed driver, and is on track to having more cars than licensed drivers. Cars are a mixed blessing, as a future chapter will detail: But there is no doubt they represent convenience, freedom, and, for women, personal security, when compared to standing on street corners waiting for buses or lingering on dark subway platforms. Cars would not be so infuriatingly popular if they did not make our lives easier. Today all but the bottom-most fraction of the impoverished in the United States do most of their routine traveling by car: 100 auto trips in the United States for every one trip on a bus or the subway, according to the American Public Transit Association. The portion of routine trips made in private cars is rising toward overwhelming in the European Union, too. Two generations ago, people dreamed of possessing their own cars. Now almost everyone in the Western world who desires a car has one—and vehicles that are more comfortable, better-equipped, lower-polluting, and much safer than those available only a short time ago.

Averaging out homes and apartments, today the typical American place of dwelling has 5.3 rooms for its average of 2.6 people. This means that a longstanding metric of comfortable living, "a room of one's own," has been gone one better; on average, Americans of today have two rooms of their own. (Most European nations still have slightly fewer dwelling rooms than people, meaning the typical person in Europe does not quite yet have a room of his or her own.) U.S. housing stock took almost two centuries, from the founding of the nation until the early postwar period, to reach the level of an average of one room per person. In just half a century since, the average has zoomed to two rooms per person, this happening during a period of rapid national population growth. While some of this increase comes from the averaged effect of McMansion-style homes with multiple surplus rooms, the bulk of the increase has occurred in the middle.

Today the typical circumstance for an American, even a typical child or teenager, is to have his or her own bedroom—surely the first time in history this has been achieved for an entire large society. Increasingly, the typical American college student has his or her own dorm room. Disappearing is the austere small dorm room of the past, two twin beds and two desks wedged in together, and students stuck every moment with a total stranger. Many U.S. colleges are building well-appointed apartment-style residential centers in which each student has a private bedroom with a telephone, a queen-sized bed, and ample space for computers, stereos, and DVD players, plus access to full kitchens and fitness centers.[14] Overcrowding, defined by most American housing experts as more than one person per dwelling room— almost the entire world lives in conditions that average-income Americans would consider overcrowded—is down to 3 percent of the U.S. population, the lowest level ever. And, in the 2000

Census, the fraction of American dwellings without indoor plumbing dropped below 1 percent for the first time in history; it is now close to unknown even for a poor person to use an outhouse or bathing buckets, both practices being the poor person's lot just two generations ago.

The typical new home now built in the United States is 2,250 square feet, reflecting a steady increase in footage across the years. The postwar Levittowns of Long Island and Pennsylvania, or similar tract suburbs such as Lakewood, California, which rose outside Los Angeles in the 1950s, offered the middle-income buyer a dwelling of about 1,100 square feet, which translated to two bedrooms and a single bath. Today the 2,250-square-foot typical new United States home has three bedrooms and two and a half baths—double the size of a generation ago, more than double per person when smaller families are taken into account. The typical home also now has a garage and, inside it, typically awaits a power mower, or even riding mower. Few buyers today are willing to settle for less than three bedrooms, so builders have essentially stopped constructing smaller homes. (Public housing, apartments for singles, and cooperatives or assisted-living for seniors account for only a minor fraction of total new housing.) And the ever more accommodating American home is designed for, and marketed to, the middle.

Equally significant, as Fareed Zakaria has written, "When an American thinks of the word 'house' today, it is a place that has heat and air conditioning in every room. This would have been considered prohibitively luxurious to the previous generation." Ninety-five percent of American dwellings are now centrally heated, versus about 15 percent in our grandparents' generation; 78 percent have air conditioning, versus essentially zero then. In August 2002, the New York Stock Exchange, which holds brief celebrations of business milestones, brought together officials from heating-and-cooling firms to note the production in the United States of the 130-millionth central air conditioning unit; tens of millions of window air conditioners complement the central units. "Once a luxury for the wealthy, central air conditioning is now included in almost all new single-family homes," the Air Conditioning and Refrigeration Institute declared.

That almost all new American homes have central air conditioning is particularly noteworthy considering that many Americans live at latitudes or elevations where air conditioning is rarely needed. Not long ago, while staying at a house up in the Green Mountains of Vermont, I watched in amazement as trucks and workers arrived to install central air conditioning in a vacation home under renovation nearby. High-altitude Vermont homes might actually need air conditioning ten days per year—perhaps fifteen days, if global warming projections turn out right. But the premise of contemporary American life is that everyone should at all times be as comfortable as physically possible; how could anyone possibly stand a too-warm house ten days per year when calls to air conditioning contractors and to the bank's home-improvement loan office can change this? The goal of being at all times as comfortable as physically possible has long held for the rich. Now, in the Western nations, it holds for almost everybody, led by the hundreds of millions of men and women of the middle.

There is nothing wrong, and much right, with seeking utmost comfort; the only real objection is that billions around the world have far more basic needs that go unmet. We should simply recognize, and feel grateful for, what this reflects about ever higher living standards. Today in the United States even most housing projects are air conditioned at public expense, if with less than certain reliability. This does not mean it is a lark to live in a housing project; it is simply another indicator of the evolution of living standards. A century ago in the tenements of New York and Boston, poor families huddled a dozen to a room in stifling, disease-ridden "inside" apartments that had no ventilation of any kind, not even windows. Now even the poor have their own bedrooms with air conditioning. And they should.

....

While the rich have indeed been getting richer—and engaging in preposterous excess—consider still more ways in which rising well-being for the typical person keeps drawing the average and the elite closer.

A century ago the rich lived in heated houses, rode in carriages, traveled the world, enjoyed unlimited food and wine, had access to physicians, attained college educations, attended the theater for entertainment, and, if engaged in gainful work, did so in a comfortable office. None of these experiences was standard for the typical person. The typical person lived in a tenement, an unheated farmhouse, or a crowded brownstone with no indoor plumbing; worried about the next meal; walked or rode unreliable streetcars; rarely traveled far from the place of his or her birth; if venturing across the ocean, did so in considerable discomfort in steerage accommodations; much of the year ate heavily salted low-quality foodstuffs with few fresh items; received minimal medical care; never completed high school; went to carnivals or saloons for entertainment; and struggled to make a living through pre-tractor-era farming or mining or sweatshop sewing or similar unremitting toil.

These and other indicators meant that a few generations ago the well-off and the average lived in fundamentally different ways—a very small segment of society having education, travel, leisure activities, and health care as well as excellent food and pleasant dwellings, while the majority could not aspire to any of these things. To use a small but revealing example, a century ago many typical people lived out their lives without ever experiencing a hotel stay.

All has changed in an era in which the great story has been the rise in well-being for the typical person. To take one basic but oft-overlooked change, today almost 70 percent of Americans own their places of dwelling, versus less than 20 percent a century ago, when most Americans were tenants. Snobbery looks down on the means by which this grand expansion of ownership was accomplished, namely, the suburban housing tract. But whatever its merits or faults, the suburb should not be denounced as the result of whites fleeing cities, since the early postwar suburban boom was fueled by rural whites moving from the farm *toward* the city, and at any rate increasingly affluent African Americans are now voting with their feet for the suburbs, too. It was the advent of the suburban tract home that allowed the average person to own his or her dwelling, to have four separate walls, none resonating with the next apartment's noise, to have a bit of nature via a lawn and a garden—to own a share, however small, of the nation. Today's intellectual snobs who scorn the suburban existence led by most Americans have forgotten that Progressive Era thinkers initially proposed the suburb, longed for exactly this form of housing in order to bring dignity, and some tranquility, into the lives of the working class.

That most Americans today not only live in suburbs but own the place where they reside suggests a fantastic convergence of the living standards of the average toward those of the wealthy. A few generations ago it was often said, and with considerable force, that the American system was unjust because the wealthy owned land and property while the typical person did not. Now that injustice is no more, since the typical American owns land or property or both, and has begun to hold at least some equity stake in the stock market—U.S. households possessing about $12 trillion worth of stocks in 2001, a figure representing more than a year's GDP for the United States.

....

Lakewood, the postwar tract suburb outside Los Angeles, was built mass-production-style by teams of carpenters moving among poured concrete foundation pads. How it came to be is part of the tale of how typical Americans converged upward toward the wealthy. Some 25,000 people stood in line when the Lakewood sales office opened in April 1950, hoping to sign mortgages at $137 a month ($979 in today's dollars) for a 1,100-square-foot one-bath home with furniture and television set, identical in every respect to every other home. Families moved in so fast that *Life* magazine staged a famous photograph of an entire block with moving vans arriving simultaneously at every house. People were so eager to be housed in Lakewood because it promised the average person the experience of a real home, something the wealthy had long possessed but the typical person only dreamt of. Donald Waldie, whose parents bought one of the first Lakewood tract properties, has lived in that home all his life and now serves as the city's informal historian. He notes, "What towns like Lakewood give most people is, Enough. The town has no exuberance and probably we don't have many witty ironists or exceptional individuals. But probably we don't have many who are racked by inexplicable dissatisfaction either. The town well serves the ordinary person."[15]

All-white at its founding, Lakewood in recent years has enfolded a growing minority population, as Hispanics and African Americans embrace the suburban dream as enthusiastically as whites once did, and with as much care. On a recent drive through the city, I saw nothing but well-kept homes and trimmed lawns, the place by appearances little changed from 1950, except for satellite reception dishes on roofs and enormous SUVs clogging the driveways.

Not too many miles away, in a suburb of San Diego, developers are building Otay Ranch, the modern answer to Lakewood. This 5,300-acre subdivision is laid out as a small town with a main street, back alleys behind homes, playing fields, and pocket parks every few blocks; Otay Ranch is designed so that children walk to school, the project being advertised to buyers as "pedestrian-friendly." Houses cost an average of $400,000, high for the country but close to the local median housing price considering the California cost of living, meaning that Otay Ranch, like Lakewood before it, caters to the typical buyer.

Aspiring owners at Otay Ranch may choose among several home models, for instance the "Mariposa Regent," which sells for about $375,000 and has four bedrooms in 2,407 square feet of space. The price includes a fireplace, marble in the master bathroom, maple cabinets, energy-saving features, built-in Internet wiring, underground lawn sprinklers, and built-in gas lines for outdoor grills. Options include "oversized laundry." Snob critics have assailed the developers of Otay Ranch because, though pedestrian-friendly on the inside, the community can only be reached by car, not public transit; and because many streets are cul-de-sacs, which are hated by design critics but loved by parents who want children to play without being run over.[16] But the average person now moves by car, even the average poor person; so why should not a housing development for average people be reached by car? In 1950, it was seen as a breakthrough that a typical Southern Californian buyer could obtain a 1,100-square-foot home with one bath, a yard, and a television. Today the typical buyer in the same place expects twice the house plus marble inlays, automatic sprinkling, and hidden attachments for the gas grill. It is fabulous that the housing standards of the typical person have converged upward toward the rich in this way. This improvement in the middle, rather than the excess at the top, is the great story of living standards.

The equalizing of education between rich and average is just as striking. Four-fifths of American adults are now high school graduates, and one-quarter hold college degrees. Americans today average 12.3 years of education, the highest figure in the world.[17] The *average* educational achievement for Americans now exceeds the comparable figure for the upper class of a few generations ago.

Today two-thirds of high school graduates go on to at least some college, while fewer than 10 percent drop out of high school, according to the National Center for Education Statistics. The figure for the college-bound is both the highest proportion ever, and amazing in that it means the typical person no longer must start work right after high school. From the nineteenth-century onset of the movement for universal public education to approximately the year 1940, most Americans never completed high school—they dropped out to begin working because their families needed the wages, or because pursuit of the relatively small number of white-collar employment slots seemed too far-fetched.[18] Today there is enough prosperity and income security among average Americans, and a sufficiently huge pool of openings in the white-collar world, that almost everyone finishes high school, while most go on to college. The going-on-to-college proportion places the United States on a fairly short path to becoming the first society in history with more adults who are college graduates than are not.

....

Continuing the equalization of rich and typical, today all but a small portion of the population has on-demand access to the best in high-tech health care, even if that access is mediated by managed-care organizations no one likes. Although about 14 percent of Americans have no medical insurance—a scandalous fault in the American system—this figure is mildly deceptive in that it does not mean 14 percent go without health care. The uninsured nevertheless receive treatment when they arrive at the emergency room, as the case of Jesíca Santillan shows. Medical insurance, bear in mind, did not even exist in any significant sense till after World War I. Just two generations ago it was almost everyone, rather than 14 percent, who lacked health insurance— only the wealthy knew protection against ruinous medical expense, via their wealth. Today, for the majority, medical expenses are often annoying but rarely ruinous.

Today Americans collectively take twenty-five million overseas vacations per year, meaning the majority of holiday trips to France or Brazil are made by someone who is not wealthy. Europeans take international holiday trips at an even greater rate than Americans, with the majority of European holiday trips, often to other continents, taken by those who are not wealthy. Adjusting for population increase, the rate of overseas travel by Americans is now thirty times what it was in 1900: That increase owes its magnitude to distant vacations by the typical person. Air travel, once a preserve of the well-to-do, is now affordable to everyone—Americans took 612 million airline trips in 2002, with the middle class, the working class, even the poor flying. And why shouldn't the poor fly? The convenience of air travel signifies as much to the poor as to anyone else. Originally, the phrase "jet set" meant someone well-heeled enough to travel by air. Now approximately 200 million Americans, 70 percent of the nation, are members of the jet set.[19]

Today the typical American eats four restaurant meals per week, assuming places like McDonald's count. If fast food is excluded, the typical American eats one sit-down restaurant meal per week. For our parents' generation, one restaurant meal per month was the norm, if that. In 1955, our parents' generation spent 25 percent of its food dollars outside the home; today Americans spend 46 percent of their food dollars in restaurants,[20] and the figure continues to rise. In the year 2000, $376 billion was spent in American restaurants: about 4 percent of the nation's GDP, and a figure considerably higher than the defense budget that year. What is notable is not so much the food— Americans are developing poor eating habits based partly on frequency of visits to places that pile on the butter, sugar, and fried items—as the modern, historically unprecedented fact that today the *typical* person has the economic means to pay someone else to prepare his or her meal.

Two more examples of average-rich convergence are the stunning evolution in the way the typical person earns a living, and how much time is left when work is done.

In 1900, as the sociologist Thomas Caplow has shown,[21] 21 percent of men and 20 percent of women were engaged in white-collar work, white-collar here liberally defined as anything a man would do wearing a tie or a woman would do wearing a dress. In 1900, the largest share of men, 42 percent, were involved in "primary labor"—mining, forestry, fishing, and farming—and the next-largest share in factory work. All these forms of toil were backbreaking, dangerous, and low-paying. In 1900, the largest share of wage-earning women, 47 percent, labored as domestic servants, work that was arduous, demeaning, and paid even less.

Today, 58 percent of American men work in white-collar occupations, along with 52 percent of women. White-collar work raises its own set of problems, including stress, while today's borderline white-collar vocations—such as call-center work, where supervisors monitor how many seconds it takes you to get people off the phone—will never be mistaken for fun. But the fact that the typical person now earns his or her living without physical toil, and with at least the moderate dignity inherent in an office setting—and that the typical person's occupational injury concerns are now carpal tunnel syndrome from typing rather than lost limbs from stamping presses or lost eyesight from sewing in low light—numbers among the most impressive social accomplishments in human history.

....

But imagine; there are now more white-collar Americans than blue-collar. This achievement, the release of the majority of society from physical toil, is almost never remarked upon, or, when it is, tends to be spun negatively as some kind of sad decline of farm and factory employment. But it is a good thing when people graduate from farm and factory labor to white-collar occupations—good for their health, if nothing else—and that is exactly what has happened steadily through the postwar period. The well-to-do of history sat at desks. Increasingly, almost everyone sits at desks.

The average have converged with the well-off in another important way, the acquisition of leisure. In 1850, the typical

American man's workweek was sixty-six hours; in 1900, fifty-three hours; today it is forty-two hours. Because wage employment for women was rare a century ago, no comparable figure for women is available. But, a century ago, 90 percent of women spent at least four hours per day doing primary housework: cooking, cleaning. Today ever more women earn wages, with two-thirds of mothers with minor children now working for pay, but women as a group perform ever falling amounts of primary housework, just 14 percent in the year 2000 spending four or more hours per day at this task. (Mothers with infants are of course on call twenty-four-seven; the figure is an average for all adult women.)

Ever falling work hours should mean ever rising hours of leisure—and leisure hours have indeed steadily grown. Many don't believe this, owing to news-magazine covers proclaiming a time-stress epidemic, and to the general sense, widely felt, that time is speeding up. But hour-allocation studies by John Robinson of the University of Maryland and Geoffrey Godbey of Penn State University[22] have shown that "Americans now have more free time than at any point in the nation's history." Since 1960, Robinson and Godbey calculate, the typical American has gained five hours of free time per week, this happening despite the increase in women's employment.[23]

By "free time," Robinson and Godbey mean hours in which you are not under compulsion to perform paid work, to care for infants, or to complete household tasks. Certainly, free time can increase and yet you can still be too busy. In the modern world, many people heavily schedule their free time with trips, sports, shopping, and especially kids' events, and so it may be common to feel time-stressed even when benefiting from additional hours during which no one is compelling you to do any particular thing. Some overachieving Type-A men and women schedule so much, or work so many extra hours, that they hardly have any time to call their own, though in most cases they are living the Type-A lifestyle of their own volition. The point is that the average person has ever more time in which no one is compelling him or her to do anything. Distressingly, Robinson and Godbey estimate, most people use the bulk of their newfound free time to watch more television.

Robert Fogel, a professor at the University of Chicago, estimates that in 1880, between longer work days and the greater time required for routine activities such as shopping or short-distance travel, the typical American adult male spent just eleven hours per week engaged in activities that could be called relaxation. Today, he estimates, the typical adult male has forty hours per week available for relaxation. Fogel further reckons that even with the increase in women's wage-earning, the typical American woman now has about thirty more hours per week available for leisure than in 1880.

More generally, the researchers Jesse Ausubel and Arnulf Grubler of Rockefeller University have found that the typical person's total hours of life spent working has been declining on a more-or-less linear basis for fifteen consecutive decades.[24] In the middle of the nineteenth century, throughout life the typical person spent 50 percent of his or her waking hours engaged in some form of in imposed labor. The number has been falling ever since and today is a little under 20 percent of a person's lifetime waking hours spent in compelled work. The fraction keeps going down, with no end in sight. Some of the rise in percentage of lifetime hours not working comes from ever higher numbers of longer-lived retirees. But even if senior citizenship is factored out, on average people in the Western nations have steadily more free time and steadily less time at wage work or engaged in other imposed time-use.

This means leisure, once an exclusive province of the elite class, now is increasingly available to almost everyone—and, in parallel, the category "recreation and leisure industries" now accounts for a larger share of the GDP than the category "petroleum and utility industries."

That the story of the last century has been the gains made by typical people, rather than the rich, is told most powerfully in health statistics. Until the twentieth century, it was common everywhere in the world for the upper classes to live significantly longer than anyone else, owing to better nutrition, health care, and exemption from physical toil. "As recently as 1870, the average lifespan of the British upper class was 17 years longer than that of the population as a whole, while today the difference between the richest and poorest Briton is less than two years," Christopher DeMuth has said.[25] (Because Great Britain prior to the twentieth century kept better medical records than other nations, its historical data, assumed to be representative, is oft-cited for estimates of past health.) In England in the nineteenth century, the typical adult male from the working class was five inches shorter than the typical male from the upper class, again owing to poor food, poor health care, and a life of toil; today, there is no class distinction in average British height. Nor are there, today, any rich-versus-poor distinctions in lifespan in the United States.[26] Differences of lifespan, height, and other measures of health have disappeared because the great story of Western society has included the extension, to almost everyone, of the kind of nutrition, medical care, education, and exemption from harsh toil that was once known only by the wealthy.

The sum of the social changes detailed above is that, today, the rich and the typical do not live in fundamentally different ways. The well-to-do have the most of everything, have it in higher quality, and their worries are fewer—though this does not necessarily make them happy, as a coming chapter will show. But there is no longer a wall between the basic structure of daily life for the wealthy person and the typical person. Both groups live about the same way, have about the same education, drive on the same roads, visit the same hospitals, and, for good or ill, share the same elemental cultural experiences, namely television and the movies.

Through the past century the inventory of experiences a rich person can have that an average person cannot has shrunk steadily, to the point that there aren't many entries left on such a list. Invitations to exclusive parties, flying on corporate jets, hiring expensive escorts for sex, meeting privately with politicians: There are still a few primary experiences that the rich have and the average person does not. But by the standards of history, these are nothing compared to previous chasms in food, shelter, health care, and education.

Intellectuals and theorists have long expected, almost demanded, that average Americans would develop political antipathy toward the prosperous and vote to confiscate their wealth. Perhaps average Americans do not do this because they know they have spent the last several generations gaining on the well-to-do in significant ways. Whatever faults the United States and the European Union may have—there are many—in recent generations, both have methodically improved daily circumstances for almost everyone.[27] The same social engine that in the United

States and Western Europe is producing spoiled and insufferable billionaires is also producing steady, significant gains for the middle and for the poor.

....

Yet despite steady gains, it is common to hear Americans say, "My parents had it better than I do." Some people say "my parents had it better" as they climb into a luxury SUV to head off for a restaurant meal; yet today huge numbers of Americans truly believe the country is declining and living standards headed down. In one 1996 poll—taken during an economic boom!— 52 percent of respondents said the United States was worse off than when their parents were growing up, 60 percent said they expected their children to live in an even worse country, and a mere 15 percent said they felt overall national conditions were improving.[28]

Such views may seem divorced from the realities that surround most people, but since these views are indisputably common, there must be reasons why they are held. Here are two suggestions why people feel worse as life gets better. One is the "revolution of satisfied expectations," meaning that now we have so much it's hard to look forward to having more. The other is "collapse anxiety."

....

THE REVOLUTION OF SATISFIED EXPECTATIONS. Research conducted by Daniel Kahneman of Princeton University, and by others who have come to approximately the same conclusion, shows that most people judge their well-being not by measuring where they stand but rather based on whether they think their circumstances and income will improve in coming years. For example, in the 1950s, when most American families lived in small houses, owned one car, and few if any family members attended college, people were in good spirits because they expected soon to earn and possess more. Now most families live in larger houses, own at least two cars, and send most children to college—that is, they have what people of the 1950s dreamed of having. But because most now have so much, it's hard to expect that the coming years will bring even more.

For at least a century, Western life has been dominated by a revolution of rising expectations: Each generation expected more than its antecedent. Now most Americans and Europeans already have what they need, in addition to considerable piles of stuff they don't need. "He's/she's so hard to buy for because he/she already has everything!" This was said of the rich in our grandparents' day. Now it can be said of perhaps 500 million people in the United States, Canada, Japan, Australia, and the European Union.

It is good that most people in the West today have most of what they need, at least in material terms. But this brings into play a revolution of satisfied expectations. Americans and Western Europeans live in mainly favorable conditions, yet are experiencing a sense of letdown, as many no longer can dream that the years to come will bring them significantly more than they already possess.

COLLAPSE ANXIETY. Deep-seated in the minds of Americans and Europeans—perhaps in the minds of most—is a fear that the West cannot sustain its current elevated living standards and liberal personal freedom. We fear that the economy will collapse; not just sputter, but cease functioning. We fear that natural resources will run out. We fear that the West's military bulwark will be neutralized by some genetically engineered bio-horror. We fear that anarchy, terrorism, or environmental calamity will overwhelm societies based on freedom and plenty. Anxiety about a coming downturn makes the mostly favorable present hard to appreciate.

Collapse anxiety is essential to understanding why Americans do not seem more pleased with the historically unprecedented bounty and liberty in which most live—and this was true before September 11, 2001, when the physical collapse of the World Trade Center made tangible an inner fear.

Some amount of never-ending anxiety may be rational— keeping us on guard—or even hard-wired into our nature by evolution, as perhaps the most fretful of our ancestors, the ones always warily scanning the horizon, were the ones most likely to survive. And some awful collapse may happen, of course. We can't be sure the arrow of progress will remain pointed forward. For that matter, we can't be sure the earth won't be hit by a comet.

But if a collapse were coming, its signs ought to be some-where. That is not what trends show. Practically everything is getting better: Let's turn to the evidence.

Chapter 2

PRACTICALLY EVERYTHING

GETTING BETTER

Please don't be alarmed, but almost everything about American and European life is getting better for almost everyone.

Public health is improving by nearly every measure, including rising longevity and falling rates of most diseases; even many forms of cancer are in decline. Doomsday claims to the contrary, environmental trends are nearly all positive, with all forms of pollution except greenhouse gases in steady decline in the United States and the European Union. Drinking, smoking, and most forms of drug use are declining. Teen pregnancy is declining. Welfare rolls are shrinking without increase in poverty. Women, immigrants, and minority group members are acquiring ever larger slices of national pies. The divorce rate has stopped increasing. Personal freedom has never been greater. Book sales hit new records almost every year. Movies and television may at times be excruciating, but otherwise art and culture have never been more active, interesting, or diverse. Nearly all forms of deaths due to accident are declining. Crime has declined so rapidly that the fall has been almost eerie. Education levels keep rising, while test scores and public-school performance show guarded improvement. Despite what evening-news carnage suggests, armed conflicts and combat deaths worldwide are in a cycle of decline. Global democracy is rising, military dictatorship and communism are on the run. Each year the number of nuclear warheads in the world declines. The single worst threat to the world—the Cold War—has ended, with complete victory for the West and the hand of friendship extended to former adversaries.

There are disquieting signs regarding terrorism and greenhouse gas accumulation, and there are plenty of the kinds of routine problems societies will always have. In the main, the overwhelming majority of trends in the United States and Western Europe are strongly favorable, while the majority of trends for most of the rest of the world, including for most developing nations, are at least mildly favorable.

Following the heartbreak of September 2001, some analysts said America's "holiday from history" had ended; the 1990s might have been a time of tranquil prosperity, but the course of world events had now turned irreversibly downward.

To a point, it is true that a holiday from history concluded on that horrible morning. America can no longer imagine itself invincible nor shirk engagement with the world, whether that engagement means aggressive attack on terrorists and governments who aid them,[1] or more foreign action to address the injustices of global poverty, or listening more closely to those who hold valid complaints against American policy. But will even an event as awful as September 11 alter the underlying positive arc of Western society? Possibly; chances are it will not.

First, though everyone in the United States was struck emotionally by September 11, only a comparatively tiny number saw their lives altered by the event or its aftermath. In 1941, the Japanese bombing of Pearl Harbor transformed every American life: Almost every family sent sons to the war effort, while those who remained behind knew rationing, overtime labor to increase production, and a country whose customary life nearly ceased. Horrible though it was, September 11 had this sort of direct impact on far less than a thousandth of the American population. One family in a hundred, if even that, will have a son, daughter, or close relative involved in antiterrorism combat. Standards of living are unaffected,[2] while the customary life of the nation continues as usual, except for extra security in airports—something that was needed anyway, as September 2001 unequivocally demonstrated. As Kathleen Tierney, a sociologist at the University of Delaware, has shown, single awful events rarely alter underlying societal trends. Places where things were getting worse before a terror attack or natural disaster will keep getting worse afterward. Places where things were getting better are odds-on to continue getting better.

Next, though people spoke, following September 11, as if all that is good had ended—especially that New York City could never again be a favored or magical place—history suggests otherwise.

When the Nazi air campaign against Britain began in August 1940, commentators spoke of the London of lore as finished forever. Even if England survived the war, it was thought, London could never again be the enchanted, historic place it had been before bombs fell, nor could life in London ever again be as good. Yet it took less than a decade for war damage to London to disappear through rebuilding, and the city's standard of living to exceed its prewar level. Today, six decades later, the average

London dweller is *far* better off, and much healthier, than a counterpart from the days before World War II, with poverty significantly down, senior-citizen poverty nearly eliminated, and average real income more than doubled. The city itself is in its finest-ever physical condition—improvements include a spectacular reduction of air and water pollution, coupled with much higher housing standards—while London's treasured sense of sitting astride history is palpable as before. Arguably, the leading moment in all London's annals is occurring right now: sixty years after it was assumed that the sun had set on the city.

Similar logic applies to the United States. Of course it is possible that some other terrible event, beyond September 11, will occur. Absent that, the underlying societal movements that were in progress before the attacks on New York and Washington should mainly continue, and the arrows show practically everything getting better, for almost everyone. Consider the leading indicators:

CRIME. A slight increase in national crime rates in 2001 followed nine consecutive years of reduction, the longest-ever U.S. drop in crime. During the 1990s, homicides fell by 75 percent in San Diego, 70 percent in New York City, by big margins in Baltimore, Boston, Los Angeles, and other cities.[3] Domestic violence against women fell 21 percent in the 1990s. Robbery and burglary declined; car theft declined. Rape declined by 40 percent in the 1990s, at the same time that extensive efforts were being made to encourage its reporting. Even considering a few horrifying events such as Columbine High, youth violence declined significantly in the 1990s, the "crime offending rate" for teenagers falling an amazing two-thirds. Gun use declined in the 1990s, a big drop in youth-on-youth shootings causing the overall occurrence of adolescent death to decline to the lowest rate ever.[4]

In 1989, New York City streets were so dangerous, and homicides rising at such an awful rate, that New York Governor Mario Cuomo said of the murders, "It's possible you won't be able to solve this problem." Instead New York City homicides peaked in the year 1990 and began to fall backward to the rate of the 1960s. In February 2002, New York had the fewest murders in any month since the city began keeping statistics. The 2002 total for New York City homicides was the same as the 1963 total.[5]

In fact, by 2001 the Big Apple had a lower murder rate than most rural states. Despite the stereotype that big Northeastern cities are the dangerous places, since the onset of crime decline, the Northeast has become the safest region in the nation from the standpoint of homicide. Today the South has the highest murder rate, one per 12,500 people per annum, compared to one per 16,667 people west of the Rockies and one per 25,000 in the Northeast. Note that the regions with more murder tend to vote conservative, those with less murder tend to vote liberal. Rural men and women who vote conservative may be responding to the perceived lawlessness of their regions, while urban voters who favor liberalism may be responding to the perceived stability of their local social order. Who would have guessed that the liberal regions would suffer less crime than the conservative ones? That has been the American pattern in the last decade.

Especially dramatic was the crime drop in the Bronx, New York's poor borough. Rampant lawbreaking there was chillingly depicted in the 1981 Paul Newman movie *Fort Apache: The Bronx*. The film concerned desperate police, based at the Forty-first Precinct station house in the Bronx, nicknamed "Fort

Apache," losing the battle against lawlessness. In the 1970s, the actual Forty-first Precinct averaged 130 homicides, 6,433 burglaries, and 2,632 robberies per year. By 2001, the figures for the Forty-first Precinct had fallen to 12 homicides, 225 burglaries, and 239 robberies—roughly a 95 percent decline, and the population of the precinct rose through this period. Crime in the Forty-first Precinct was down so remarkably, the *Wall Street Journal* reported,[6] that previously besieged officers had started community-outreach programs in order to use their time fully. Needless to say, Paul Newman did not return to make a second movie about how the Forty-first Precinct was getting better. The Bronx going to hell was interesting to Hollywood; the Bronx bouncing back was not a story.

Diminishing crime is associated with the economic revival of inner cities and downtowns, supposedly doomed by irreversible corkscrews of decline. The boarded-up South Bronx neighborhood that Ronald Reagan visited in 1980, in order to denounce urban-renewal programs against a backdrop that seemed a moonscape, is now redeveloped and thriving, offering nice apartments, pleasant cafés, and, yes, Starbucks outlets. The section of inner-city Kansas City used to film the movie *The Day After*—streets that in 1982 looked so decrepit Hollywood felt they could stand in for the debris of a nuclear blast—is now so bustling that residents complain of gentrification. Inner-city Pittsburgh's Hill District neighborhood, boarded up twenty years ago, is reviving with white and black gentrifiers, while Newark, New Jersey, has become a hot destination for young trendies, a development that two decades ago would have seemed to defy the laws of nature. Professional sports teams that in the 1970s and 1980s built stadia in the suburbs to escape the city are moving back to new downtown facilities; Detroit, Washington, D.C., Cleveland, and other cities have seen sports teams return downtown in response to less crime and a copasetic urban feeling. Across most of the United States, inner-city property values, supposedly forever doomed to decline, are instead rising as people rediscover downtowns. The comeback of the cities, led by the fall in crime, is an object lesson in how "irreversible" problems can be thrown into reverse gear surprisingly fast.

That crime has fallen so abruptly can be deceptive, as it fell from the shocking level of the late 1980s, which was the crest of a twenty-year wave. Even after steep decline, many crime statistics remain high: New York City's far-lower homicide rate, for instance, still works out to one murder somewhere in the city each day. But people dread violent crime more than any other civic malfunction—as they should—and now that worst of all problems has shown substantial decline. As Gordon Witkin has written, "It's hard to think of a social trend with greater significance."

THE ENVIRONMENT. Despite the hysterical tone of environmental reporting in the media, in the United States and Europe all environmental trends except for greenhouse-gas accumulation are positive, and in most cases have been positive for decades.

Twenty-five years ago, only one-third of America's lakes and rivers were safe for fishing and swimming; today two-thirds are, and the proportion continues to rise.[7] Puget Sound, Chesapeake Bay, Lake Erie, the Hudson River, and other important water bodies have gone from imperiled to mainly clean. Boston Harbor, whose filth was ridiculed in a political commercial that was pivotal to the 1988 presidential election, now has water so clear that revelers do ceremonial New Year's Day dips, and fishing will soon be legal again. The Potomac—which stank so badly from pollution in the 1960s that when Richard Nixon went cruising on the old presidential yacht, *Sequoia,* he used to sit inside with the windows closed—is now so clean and inviting that swimmers drown in the river annually because no amount of warning signs along the riverbanks will keep people from jumping in. The Chicago River, described in the 1906 Upton Sinclair classic *The Jungle* as so loaded with filth that chickens actually were seen walking across it, and as recently as the 1970s still badly polluted, today hosts art festivals, boat tours, and dinner cruises.

Since 1970 smog has declined by a third, even as the number of cars has nearly doubled and vehicle-miles traveled have increased by 143 percent; acid rain has declined by 67 percent, even though the United States now burns almost twice as much coal annually to produce electric power; airborne soot particles are down, which is why most cities have blue skies again; airborne lead, a poison, is down 97 percent. Emissions of CFCs, which deplete stratospheric ozone, have essentially ended. Denver, which in the 1970s had air almost as bad as Los Angeles of the time, in 2002 became the first major United States city in full compliance with the Clean Air Act. This means that Denver's air is in excellent condition, though the city has entered its fourth straight decade of rapid population growth.[8] Only in Atlanta and a few other cities is smog increasing, by relatively small margins.

During the 2000 presidential campaign, much was made of the fact that Houston had taken over from Los Angeles as the nation's "smog capital." Hardly anyone added that this happened during a period when Houston smog diminished; it's just that L.A. pollution declined even faster, Los Angeles prevailing in a race of positives.[9] During the 1980s, Los Angeles averaged about 150 ozone "health advisory" days per year, and about fifty "stage one" ozone alerts. Figures for the 1970s and 1960s were even higher. By 2000, according to the South Coast Air Quality Management District, advisory days had fallen to about twenty per year, while, at this writing, Los Angeles has had no stage-one ozone alert for four years running[10]—another improvement that, a generation ago, people would have described as prohibited by physical law. The ability of Los Angeles to make fantastic strides against pollution, even during a period when population was shooting up and California car use was increasing, is a remarkable success story. This is why you never hear anything about it.

Other environmental measures are almost uniformly positive. Toxic emissions by industry declined 51 percent from 1988 to 2002, and pollution was not shipped offshore; petrochemical manufacturers, the main industrial source of toxic emissions, increased domestic production during the period. Almost half of Superfund toxic-waste sites are now cleaned up, while none any longer imperil public health. Some Superfund sites are now sufficiently harmless to have been declared National Wildlife Preserves. Rocky Mountain Arsenal, outside Denver, where nerve gas was once made and a location regularly described in heavy-breathing commentary as "the most toxic place on earth," has been a National Wildlife Preserve for ten years; eagles and other biologically delicate species now thrive there.

Total American water consumption has declined 9 percent in the past fifteen years, even as the population expands in the arid Southwest. The wooded acreage of the United States has been expanding for more than a decade. Appalachian forests, expected to be wiped out by acid rain, instead are now "the healthiest they have been since before the industrial era," according to the *Brookings Review*,[11] while deer populations have expanded so much that today this ungulate is more common than when Europeans arrived in North America. Writing in 1854, Thoreau lamented that deer were extinct and he would never see one;[12] now deer wander across suburban lawns from Atlanta to Maine, and border on being a public nuisance. Since the Endangered Species Act reached full implementation in the late 1970s, at most one U.S. animal species has fallen extinct, rather than the thousands predicted, while once-imperiled organisms such as the bald eagle, gray whale, brown pelican, and peregrine falcon have recovered in numbers and been "delisted" from emergency protection.[13]

Environmental trends for Western Europe are also almost entirely positive, though Europe trails America in most categories of improvement. Despite the common perception that Europe is environmentally advanced compared to the United States, U.S. environmental rules are stricter than European Union rules—Paris has worse smog than Houston, for example, and the Mississippi is far cleaner than the Marne. Generally, Europe lags about ten years behind the United States in ecological cleanup, for instance not adopting unleaded gasoline till a decade later; though Europe leads the United States in recycling and energy conservation.

The picture is very different in the developing world, where environmental indicators are as negative as they are positive in the United States and the European Union—a subject this book will return to in a later chapter. But, in the West, where polls show that a majority of the population believes pollution is growing worse,[14] the reality is that all trends other than greenhouse gases are positive and have been positive for decades.

Resource trends are also positive. Prices of most primary commodities, especially metals, coal, and ores, have been falling for two decades as global supply has increased faster than de-mand. At this writing, no important resource other than fresh water in the Middle East and groundwater in China is in short-age or expected to be through the next few decades, not even pe-troleum.[15]

Today the world's "proven reserve" of petroleum—the amount that has been discovered but not taken out of the ground—is larger than in the 1970s, when petroleum-exhaustion forecasts were fashionable. Credible estimates put the world's proven re-serve at about one trillion barrels, a forty-year supply at current rates, while the U.S. Geological Survey estimates there exists at least an additional trillion barrels of petroleum that will become recoverable with improved technology.[16] (The USGS was say-ing this years before the petroleum-loving George W. Bush ad-ministration took office.) Drilling in the deep ocean, just now becoming technologically possible, may also produce new Saudi Arabias' worth of oil.

That there may be decades or even centuries of oil left does not rationalize using petroleum wastefully. The fad for low-mileage SUVs and the misnamed "light" pickup trucks, which inexcusably have received safety, pollution, and fuel-efficiency exemptions, has come back to haunt America in the form of road rage and in political entanglement with the Persian Gulf oil states. And even if petroleum were unlimited, its use releases greenhouse gases, a problem which no nation in the world has faced. But aside from fresh water in the Middle East and ground-water in China, resources themselves do not appear to represent any problem. Managing our use of resources is the problem.

PUBLIC HEALTH. In recent years, it has become common to hear of a cancer epidemic, an endocrine-disruptor epidemic, the "poisoning of America,"[17] and other dire health circumstances. But if we're all being poisoned, our bodies have a strange way of showing it, by living ever longer. Public health in the United States and the European Union has never been better, and continues to improve by almost every measure.

At the beginning of the twentieth century, the average American life expectancy at birth was forty-one years. In 1928, a government study forecast that the "natural" lifespan would ultimately rise to sixty-five years.[18] When the Social Security system was enacted in 1935, this estimate was used as the basis for setting federal retirement age at sixty-five, lawmakers assuming that Social Security would be economical because most people would die without ever receiving a benefit check. Instead, by the beginning of the twenty-first century, the typical American life expectancy at birth had risen to seventy-seven years, meaning people on average were living a decade longer than experts thought would be the maximum.[19] It is easy to overlook this accomplishment, as seventy-seven years has now come to seem the "natural" lifespan—though our recent ancestors, living more naturally (that is, with less technology), did not expect such longevity. The near-doubling of life expectancy has held throughout the Western world and parts of Asia; typical lifespans have risen dramatically even in most poor nations. In 1900, life expectancy in the United States was forty-one years, while today it is sixty-six years for the *entire* world.[20]

The increased life expectancy means twice as much time on earth for the typical person. The economist Julian Simon called the fast rise in life expectancy for typical people "the greatest single achievement in history," and a case can be made for that position.[21] It is ever increasing life expectancy, and surely not birthrates, that caused the population explosion of the late twentieth century, as it took the planet thousands of decades, until the year 1970, to reach a human population of three billion, then just three more decades, from 1970 to 2001, to leapfrog to six billion. Birthrates and fertility declined almost everywhere during the very period when the global census was doubling; steadily, fewer children were being born per woman. But death has declined and longevity improved at even faster rates than fertility decline, the net being ever more people alive. "The population explosion," the analyst Nicholas Eberstadt has written, "is really a health explosion."[22]

More people alive means more crowding and other annoyances; more sprawl, more roads; in the developing world, more competition for employment and resources. More people alive makes us wistfully daydream that the global population would shrink so that life would be quieter and we'd have the roads and the national parks to ourselves. Hardcore environmentalists and, in odd conjunction, hardcore conservatives even speak of rising numbers of men and women as bad. But having been granted the gift of life ourselves, how can we begrudge it to others? "If human life, when some minimal material requirements are satisfied, is a good thing—and it takes a serious pessimist to deny that—then we should be pleased that there are ever-more human beings," the Princeton University ethicist Peter Singer has written.[23] And we must accept ever more people as, barring a comet strike or nuclear war, the global population is fated to keep growing at least until about the year 2050, when, the United Nations projects, today's six billion will have become about nine billion. Eventually global population may decline as the accumulated effects of falling fertility swamp further gains in longevity; the United Nations projects that by the twenty-third century, there will be fewer human beings on earth than today.

For the lifetimes of readers of this book, however, ever more people seems close to cast in stone.

Life-expectancy averages continue to climb, with no limit visible as to what the "natural" lifespan may be. Life expectancy for women in Sweden, a studied topic owing to the preservation of old Swedish health records, has been rising on average by three months per year for almost two centuries, and continues to rise at the same pace.[24] A study by John Wilmoth, a demographer at the University of California at Berkeley, has shown that, for centuries, every passing decade has added one year to the maximum age of death[25]—that is, the age of the oldest person in a society to die. There appears no reason why such longevity advances cannot continue, regardless of whether genetic engineering or similar technologies prove practical. The "natural" lifespan may turn out to be 120 or 150 or even higher.

Life is both steadily longer and the added years blessed with increasing vigor. The notion of the "healthy old"—people in their seventies and even eighties who are in sound health, live independently, travel often, even engage in sports—has gone from pipe dream to standard expectation. As recently as our grandparents' generation, most who reached the seventies would do little more than sit in rocking chairs and be cared for. Today many Americans and Europeans in their seventies live exactly like everyone else, except perhaps for extra naps.

Longevity is increasing, and vigorous aging has become common, because nearly all forms of disease are in decline in the United States and the European Union. Heart disease and stroke have been declining for decades. By the year 2000, U.S. incidence of heart disease death was 60 percent lower, adjusted for population increase, than in 1950; incidence of stroke deaths fell 70 percent in the same period. As recently as the 1960s, it was common for the life of a fifty-year-old man to end as he fell down dead from stroke or heart attack. Now this is rare and shocking. Most heart attacks are survived, and stroke increasingly has become an affliction of late-stage old age.

Most cancers are in retreat for the first time since increasing average age made cancer a general concern. Cancer incidence—the rate compared to population—rose about 1.2 percent per year from 1973 to 1990. The rise stopped around 1993, and since then incidence of most cancers, including breast cancer, has fallen, while for all but a few forms of cancer the increase has ended—this despite the continued aging of the population. (When alarmists say there is "more cancer than ever before" or make similar statements, they mean more total cases—that is, not adjusting for an ever larger population. By this kind of logic there are also now more sneezes than ever before, simply because more people are alive to sneeze.) Most studies by the National Cancer Institute show cancer mortality declining at about 1 percent per year since 1993,[26] again despite overall aging.

Most other health trends are also favorable. Infant mortality has declined 45 percent since 1980, according to the Centers for Disease Control, and is now down to 0.7 percent of live births, the lowest figure ever for the United States. In several European Union nations, infant mortality is lower still, while Iceland has driven the figure down to 0.3 percent, though as recently as a decade ago, neonatologists believed 0.5 percent was the biological minimum, the fraction of newborns fated to die regardless of what anyone did.

AIDS deaths in the West have declined markedly; Africa, obviously, is another story. The rate of suicide is declining, the U.S. rate falling about 5 percent per year during the late 1990s.[27] Surgery has been steadily less invasive and less traumatic in the medical sense, with better results and faster recovery. Drugs and medical devices keep getting better at relieving pain and symptoms, allowing many with diseases or conditions previously viewed as debilitating to lead relatively ordinary lives. Despite the sirens-and-carnage image presented by local newscasts, most forms of accidental death are in long-term decline, as are workplace fatalities. Deaths by fire, especially, have declined, down by 50 percent in the last two decades, as incidence of building fires has fallen sharply owing to smoke alarms, built-in sprinklers, and other advances.[28] Gun deaths have also declined, owing to the crime drop.

Adjusted for miles traveled, traffic deaths have been hitting new lows on an almost annual basis. Even absolute numbers of traffic deaths have fallen in most recent years—for example, 42,850 Americans died in automobile crashes in 2002 versus 52,627 in 1970, though the population rose and auto miles traveled increased about 75 percent through that period.[29]

Of course there are negative measures. The incidence of leukemia has been rising, and researchers don't know why; asthma incidence is rising and the incidence of autism may be increasing, again with exact causes unknown;[30] tuberculosis, once banished from the West, has come back, borne within the lungs of developing-world immigrants; deaths in falling-down accidents have increased among the elderly; and obesity is on a track to replace lung cancer as society's worst self-inflicted medical problem.[31] Overall, the good outweighs the bad in Western health trends by a sizable margin.

VIRTUE. Until the suit-wearing, white-male cohort let America down with the corporate lying scandals of 2002, it could have been argued that nearly all trends related to personal virtue were positive. Setting aside the lack of character exhibited by the liars and privateers discovered to be occupying so many CEO chairs, evidence points to rising virtue among typical Americans. Commentators may claim that today anything goes, that society lacks standards, that Americans no longer fear their God. Except as regards the thieves in corporate boardrooms, statistics say otherwise.

Use of most illegal drugs has been declining for two decades, although drug overdose incidence has been constant. Alcohol consumption per capita has been declining for a generation, including among the young—alcohol use in the United States is down so much that, among Western nations, America is close to the bottom for drinking. Indeed, from some perspectives drinking has declined too much, as moderate consumption—two to three glasses of wine daily, depending on age and body weight—reduces risk of heart disease and other ailments.[32]

Cigarette use continues to decline, especially by the all-important barometer of teen use—smoking habits are often set in the teen years. Today just 10 percent of American tenth-graders smoke, believed to be the lowest number for this age group since packaged cigarettes became common in the 1920s.[33] It is surely worrisome from a health standpoint that overeating and obesity are on the rise, particularly among the young. Since smoking suppresses the appetite, it is likely there is a relationship between the decline in cigarette use and the rise in overweight Americans. But if you had to choose between the two vices—nicotine or sugar—your choice would be easy.

In other important indicators, the divorce rate, which had been climbing seemingly inexorably since the 1950s, flattened out in the 1990s and at present is in shallow decline. It is no longer true that, when you attend a wedding, there is a fifty-fifty chance you are watching people swear vows that will not last; today, in the United States at least, the newly married are odds-on to stay together. (Divorce rates continue to rise in many European Union nations, as do the chances that a person will never marry.)

Of course, some marriages do not work and some women need to escape from dictatorial husbands, but a significant body of academic research, including by the sociologist Linda Waite of the University of Chicago, shows that staying married usually leads to better physical and psychological health for both spouses; in most cases, staying married improves the standard of living in both; and, in nearly all cases, parents staying married is good for children.[34]

The rate of children born outside marriage, climbing seemingly inexorably since the 1950s, like the divorce rate flattened in the 1990s and at present is in shallow decline. In 1980, 18 percent of American children were born to unmarried women; by 1994 the figure had risen to 32 percent, a proportion whose size meant out-of-wedlock birth had become common not just among minorities and the poor but among whites and in the middle class. In 1994, the number peaked and has since been in mild decline; births out of wedlock were down 12 percent in New York state during the late 1990s, for example.[35]

A woman can raise a child without a husband, and of course two committed people can be good parents outside the institution of marriage. But statistics dictate that, on average, those born to married parents live longer, advance farther in school, earn more as adults, and are less likely to have emotional problems or commit crimes.[36] This marriage-is-good-for-kids formula is just as true for white children and middle-class children as it is for children of minorities and the poor. Kids on average simply do better when raised by two parents; dreamy sixties-era claims to the contrary just have not held up under the scrutiny of sociological studies. Thus it is a positive sign for American children that, during the 1990s, according to Census figures, the segment of children who lived with both parents rose from 51 percent to 56 percent. The increase held for African American children as well as for the population as a whole, 39 percent living with both parents at the end of the 1990s versus 35 percent at the beginning.

One reason the share of children without married parents has stopped rising is that teen pregnancy and births to teens fell, by 22 percent and by 15 percent, respectively, during the 1990s. At this writing, U.S. teen pregnancy was at "the lowest rate ever recorded," according to a government study,[37] with fully a third of the teen-births decline having occurred in the supposedly loose-morals environment of the 1990s. Increased use of birth control explains most of the drop in teen pregnancy: Abortion is not the reason, as incidence of teen abortions went down 39 percent from 1995 to 2000, according to the Alan Guttmacher Institute, a birth-control advocacy group.[38] (Total abortions in the United States have been declining steadily for most of the last decade, falling in 2000 to the lowest level since the year 1978, though the population rose during the period.)[39]

Less teen sexual activity explains the rest of the teen-births drop. At the beginning of the 1990s, the typical teenager had had intercourse, 54 percent of boys and girls between sixteen and eighteen years of age being sexually active. By the end of the 1990s, the statistic had dropped to 48 percent, meaning the typical teenager had not yet had intercourse.

Adults who themselves furiously angled for sex when they were teenagers may sound tut-tuttish lauding signs of decline in teen-years sexual activity. So long as birth control is used, sexual activity for teens is in and of itself neither good nor bad—it depends on the person, and the person's beliefs. Though the era of AIDS strengthens the old contention that, when it comes to the first experience of sex, no one has ever been harmed by waiting.

But by resulting in fewer births to teens, declining teen sexual activity benefits thousands of girls and women, since having a child before age twenty is closely associated with ending up impoverished. Statistics show that in order to avoid becoming poor in the United States, you must do three things: graduate from high school, marry after the age of twenty, and marry before having your first child. Only 8 percent of those who do these three things become poor as adults, whereas 79 percent of poor adults have failed to do these three things.[40] Fewer births to teens is also a factor in the crime decline, as boys born to unwed teens are far more likely to commit crimes in later life than boys born to married mothers over the age of twenty, a rule that applies to all races.[41]

Not long ago, family breakup and teen pregnancy were decried as runaway phenomena that could never be reversed, brought about by an irresponsible anything-goes culture. Now these supposedly unstoppable trends have come to a halt, amidst guarded optimism that American culture is increasingly concerned with virtue.

BRAINPOWER. Important indicators are positive in a virtue-related category, studying. Most public-school test scores are either slightly up (math proficiency) or flat (reading proficiency), a study by Thomas Loveless of the Brookings Institution has found—though, with a rising proportion of immigrant children in public schools, test scores would be expected to decline.

Other research detects none of the supposed breakdown in grasp of subjects such as history. "Given the reduced dropout rate and less elitist composition of the 17-year-old student body today, one could argue that students of today know more American history than did their age peers in the past," the educational analyst David Whittington has written.[42] Despite the oft-heard charge that schools are going downhill, "no reliable evidence exists that students as a whole are performing less well than they did 25 years ago," the former Harvard University president Derek Bok has written.[43]

Commentators continue to panic about "declining" SAT scores, but most of the decline happened in the 1970s and was linked to a larger pool of students taking the tests, not to erosion of ability to perform on the tests. The SAT score drop occurred during the period when college was becoming a destination for everyone, not just top students or the rich. Average and even below-average students, a group that previously did not take the SATs, during the 1970s began to sit for this test in large numbers. That almost everyone, not just top students and rich kids, began taking the SAT was a good thing, but did cause a dip in SAT outcomes; the dip ended as soon as the situation stabilized and further groups of low-in-their-class students ceased joining the pool of SAT-takers. Adjust for the fact that today a much higher proportion of high school students take the SAT than during previous decades, and the "decline" in achievement-test scores disappears.[44] Meanwhile, the gap between black and white achievement-test scores has shrunk by about half in the last generation,[45] and this because of African American improvement, not erosion of white scores.

As regards intelligence, since the beginning of the twentieth century, when the Army first started testing for IQ and such tests gradually spread through society, overall IQ scores have risen about 20 percent, and the rate of increase is approximately the same regardless of racial or gender breakdown. Studies by James Flynn, a New Zealand psychologist, have shown that the rise in IQ scores throughout the postwar era applies almost equally to all groups in the United States, European Union, Japan, and Australia and New Zealand.[46] Since genes do not change fast enough to account for a 20 percent IQ boost over just a few generations, to say nothing of the improbability that genes would change so rapidly for all groups, this lays to rest the enduring reactionary notion that intelligence is dictated by DNA. Missing both from the book *The Bell Curve* and the "bell curve" debate it inspired is any explanation of how IQ scores could go up so rapidly worldwide if genetics were determining IQ. Surely genes have something to do with a person's intelligence, just as genes must have something to do with height, coordination, and so on. But genes are only one influence among many; even the most DNA-inclined scientists, such as Steven Pinker of the Massachusetts Institute of Technology, suppose that intelligence and other qualities are only "point five heritable," meaning about half determined by genes.[47]

If our chromosomes cannot change rapidly enough to account for 20 percent higher IQ scores in recent generations, what can? What's changed during the period of higher IQ scores is not genomes but schools and living standards, both of which have improved very rapidly. Better schools, better nutrition, universal education, and other factors made us smarter; probably they will continue to make us smarter. If nutrition, living standards, and schooling are getting better for almost everybody in the Western nations, we might expect this to manifest in people knowing more and scoring higher on IQ tests. That is exactly what is happening.

EQUALITY. Women and minority-group members continue to assume roles once restricted to white males: In 2003, a black man, Colin Powell, was Secretary of State, a black woman, Condoleezza Rice, was National Security Advisor, and a woman, Nancy Pelosi, was Minority Leader of the House of Representatives. Though women and minority-group members remain underrepresented at the top of society, doors have only opened in this generation, and it will take another decade or two to build up a pool of experienced candidates that can be drawn on. Nearly all trend lines in this area are toward increasing female and minority-group success. In 1995, for example, 8 percent of top managers of *Fortune 500* firms were female. The number has risen annually since, in 2002 reaching 16 percent.[48] The gap between women's and men's wages has been shrinking for a generation, and today is the smallest ever, according to the federal Bureau of Labor Statistics; in 1982, women as a group earned 62.5 percent as much as men, and by 2002 that share had risen to 77.5 percent.[49]

Most important are positive trend lines for African Americans, the minority that has suffered most in the United States. As the Harvard University sociologist William Julius Wilson has extensively documented,[50] media fixation on inner-city crime and dysfunction causes us to overlook what history will judge as the big racial story of late-twentieth-century America: the emergence of a black middle class. Through the last generation, the portion of African Americans living in middle-class circumstances has more than doubled. Some kind of watershed was crossed in 1994, when the average income of black families in Queens, New York, long a community treated as symbolic of the working-class-to-middle-class transition, surpassed the average income of white Queens families. Atlanta, Georgia, and Prince George's County, Maryland, near Washington, D.C., now number among several areas with large, economically independent black middle-class populations whose lifestyle is suburban, whose family structures are conventional, and whose values are entirely middle-American.

African American income still lags significantly behind that of whites, but by the end of the twentieth century, black poverty had dropped to "the lowest rate ever recorded," according to a 2002 study by the National Urban League.[51] The decline in black poverty has been aided by the 1996 "workfare" legislation, which caused almost seven million people, slightly more than half of all national welfare recipients, to leave the rolls and start working. (Contrary to the popular perception, the majority of U.S. welfare recipients are white; but a higher proportion of blacks than whites receive welfare, rendering welfare reform of high significance to African Americans.)[52] Welfare reform did not, as was widely predicted, lead to increased black poverty. Instead, during the 1990s, African American poverty went down at the same time welfare poverty compelled many to leave the rolls. Following welfare reform, the percentage of U.S. children living in poverty declined from a peak of 22 percent in 1993, just before reforms were enacted, to 16 percent, the lowest figure in a generation.[53] Surely the strong economy of the 1990s was a factor in the decline of black poverty, but, as the writer Heather MacDonald has noted, there was an economic boom in most of the 1980s, too, and during those pre-welfare-reform years, public-assistance rolls expanded and African American poverty increased.[54]

Minority educational accomplishment continues to rise. In 1996, black high school graduation rates became about the same as white rates—needless to say, for the first time in U.S. history. The black-white math SAT score gap, which was 140 points in 1976, is 110 points now, owing to improved black scores, not erosion of white results. Bok and Bowen noted in *The Shape of the River,* their magnificent 536-page analysis of racial trends in education, that although most African Americans enter college with lower GPAs and SAT scores than white schoolmates, on the real-world test of what they do when they leave the university, top black students now have about the same career achievement as top whites.[55] Income figures back this. While African Americans as a group earn about one-quarter less than whites,[56] black male college graduates now make just 12 percent less than their white counterparts, a much smaller gap than a generation ago, while black female college graduates earn slightly more than white female graduates.[57]

African American home ownership is at record levels, there are four times as many black elected officials today as in 1970, and other indicators are positive. Overall, the African American writer Ellis Cose has written, "It's the best time ever to be black in America."[58]

Obviously problems remain for blacks and for other minority groups, including problems of bias. Yet at the turn of the twentieth century, many African Americans weren't even literate; today, college-completion rates of black Americans exceed the comparable figures for whites in most of Western Europe. If one views African Americans as an immigrant group that "arrived" in the United States with the passage of the Civil Rights Act of 1964, black rates of social progress are little different from those previously displayed by white ethnic immigrant groups, which typically required two to three generations to take their places in the establishment. This suggests African Americans should be beginning to take their places in the establishment right now: exactly what is happening.

DOMESTIC ECONOMICS. When inflation, contraction, and high un-employment all happened simultaneously in the "stagflation" of the 1970s, a negative conjunction that textbooks would have called impossible, economists were at a loss to explain what was happening. Through the 1990s, economists were baffled by a positive conjunction equally impossible according to textbook economics—high growth, low unemployment, and almost no inflation, the conversion of federal deficits to surpluses thrown in to boot.

The "long boom" concluded in 2000, and by 2002 it was known that some of the boom had been illusion, conjured by corporate lying. But though the long boom ended, the economy did not enter a downward spiral. Unemployment rose only somewhat;[59] inflation, the bedeviling problem of the previous decades, stayed too minor for anyone to note; despite the one-two punch of the September 11 attacks and the stock market nosedive that followed the lying-CEO revelations, GDP growth and income continued upward; homes, the main form of equity for the typical person, continued to appreciate in value. Living standards continued to rise for almost everyone. Even the majority of those whose stocks were whacked by the market fall that accompanied the corporate scandals were harmed mainly in the paper sense, losing the figmentary late-nineties Dow runup that had never carried substance anyway.[60]

While market economics have gone global and GDP figures ascended so high into the trillions as to become difficult to comprehend, what has mattered to the typical person in the United States is that there continue to be jobs, including plenty of desirable jobs, and an almost unlimited supply of goods and services at reasonable prices.

From the beginning of the industrial era pretty much to the

present day, policymakers have assumed scarcity of goods to be the leading problem for the typical person, either making possessions unattainable (for example, the prewar period when most Americans did not own a car) or bidding up prices too high. Western society today is almost flooded with goods; anyone can obtain anything, in almost any quantity, and take delivery in a short time if not overnight. Surplus replacing scarcity keeps prices low. Food, housing, clothing, and other essentials cost less in real-dollar terms than a generation ago, despite being higher in quality, while prices of some categories of consumer goods, notably electronics, fall steadily. The whole concept of shortage economics seems to have disappeared from the Western stage, although of course this is no guarantee it will not someday return.

A market flooded with affordable goods is seen in the example of low gasoline prices. A December 2000 poll by the Pew Research Center found that gasoline prices were the number-one issue of public concern—how naïve that would seem ten months later, in September 2001! On the day the 2000 poll was taken, regular gasoline cost less in real-dollar terms than it had in the year 1920. An April 2002 edition of *CBS Evening News* led with a Wisconsin man at a fuel pump announcing himself "outraged!" that gasoline cost $1.35 per gallon self-serve. The newscast then shifted to a report on whether Big Oil was "rigging the market for windfall profits"; Senator Barbara Boxer of California was shown declaring prices "an outrage!" In real-dollar terms, $1.35 was the same as nineteen cents per gallon in the year 1950, the beginning of the period enshrined in our collective nostalgia as Energy Heaven. Since the actual 1950 pump price for gasoline was twenty-one cents, that makes 2002 gasoline prices, complained about as an outrage, lower than the prices our parents considered low a generation ago. And today's gasoline is a superior product to the petrol purchased by our parents in 1950; it has been chemically altered to remove most pollutants (this is one reason smog is declining), while now including substances that improve the longevity of engines. In numerous other areas, real-dollar prices keep declining, accompanied by grumbling that $900 is "too much" for an entire computer or $199 "too much" to fly roundtrip from Miami to San Francisco.

Just as human beings have enjoyed unprecedented improvements in health and longevity during the very period they are supposedly being poisoned by toxins and radiation, typical men and women of the United States and the European Union, including the huge middle class and most of the working class, have enjoyed unprecedented improvements in economic circumstances during the very period in which CEOs have stolen millions and globalization has shifted Western jobs to developing nations. This does not justify CEO rapacity or necessarily rationalize globalization, but does tell us that economic trends are fundamentally good.

GLOBAL ECONOMICS. Globalization must be hurting some at the bottom of the ladder in the Western nations. Half the point of the North American Free Trade Agreement, after all, was to ease the transfer of American factory jobs to Mexico, which is bad for American labor, including for recently arrived immigrant labor, but great for Mexicans. "Any transfer of work from the United States to Mexico can be expected to raise the income of people who are, on average, much worse off than those U.S. workers who lose their jobs," Singer of Princeton University has written.[61] "Those who favor reducing poverty globally, rather than just in their own country, should see this as a good thing." Indeed, NAFTA represents a huge gift from the people of the United States to the people of Mexico, if a gift not all Americans wished to give. Why the globalization debate does not see it this way is hard to fathom, other than that, perhaps, it is simply taboo to say anything positive about trends in international economics.

Since what to American or European workers are rock-bottom wages represents premium pay in dozens of developing nations, those making Nike shoes in Vietnam, or engaged in similar endeavors, by and large are much better off than they would be without the arrival of globalization and Western-financed commerce. Keeping Western production out of the developing world, as some antiglobalizers advocate, would only consign many in developing nations to return to lives of subsistence agriculture—while reducing the chance that their children will escape the factory-labor life, as in the West one generation of factory laborers has usually led to a subsequent generation of educated children entering professional careers.

Hoping to rationalize away the fact most of the developing world is better off with globalization than without it, opponents protest that globalization causes inequity; that "inequality is accelerating everywhere on Earth," according to the antiglobalization International Forum on Globalization.[62] But evidence of rising international inequality is weak; most statistics say otherwise. A 2002 study by the Indian economist and former Brookings Institution fellow Surjit Bhalla found that in 1950, the developing world had 72 percent of the globe's population and commanded 28.8 percent of global income; by 2000, the developing world's share of population had risen somewhat to 81.3 percent, while its share of income had risen at a faster rate, to

42.4 percent. The industrial world's share of global income declined in the same period, from 62.5 percent in 1950 to 52.4 percent in 2000.[63] This hardly seems to represent inequality "accelerating everywhere on Earth," and the trends Bhalla found were about the same after globalization began in earnest, roughly in the 1970s, as before.

That developing-world workers would be harmed if globalization were ended, as surely they would be, is a separate issue from the need to insist they receive safe working conditions, health care, decent housing, and a true living wage. Strict regulations requiring these things of all global industries would both improve lives in developing nations and enable the West to enjoy global imports without guilt. Western prices would rise a little, but Western prices *should* rise a little so that those in developing nations could live better.

Politics in the United States and the European Union has generally favored globalization in part because it is only the Western labor class that feels pain, and in the West the labor class is now a minority, short on clout owing not to industrialist conspiracies but simple lack of numbers at the voting booth. To think that there is now a sizable portion of the world in which the working class is a minority! Imagine trying to tell Karl Marx that wage laborers would become a minority, outnumbered by those with a stake in the status quo.

The politics of globalization might change in the United States and the European Union if it became possible for white-collar jobs, not just production-line work, to take flight overseas. The first step has already been taken, with the movement of some customer-service telephone operations to developing nations. When you call or e-mail Amazon.com, the friendly voice or politely typed reply comes not from Seattle but Bangalore,

India, where the company's customer service department is now located.[64] Jobs there are highly desired, because Amazon.com pays far more than the local prevailing wage and provides clean, safe working conditions. The Call Center Association of India, a trade group, estimates that two million Indians now earn their livings by answering 800 numbers for American and European firms—India is a popular choice for such contracting because its urban population is well-educated and speaks English. If you phone the New Jersey state welfare agency to ask about benefits, your call is taken by a representative sitting in India and speaking by satellite link. The India-based call-taker costs New Jersey about three dollars per hour in wages and benefits, versus the fifteen dollars an hour the state would pay to put a welfare recipient to work answering calls about welfare.

Perhaps if technology makes it possible to move a significant number of Western white-collar jobs to the developing world, Marx's much-predicted and never-realized "iron law of wages" will come into effect and backfire on the West.[65] Yet so far, at least, the era of globalization has been good to almost everyone in the United States and Western Europe, including almost everyone in the working class. Globalization, for instance, is a leading reason Wal-Mart and similar retailers can offer such low prices for essential goods. As the cost of essentials is regressive—prices of jeans, paper towels, and the other sorts of things found at Wal-Mart affect the underprivileged more than the well-to-do—who benefits most from Wal-Mart prices? The leading beneficiaries are the poor and the working class.

The megastores sprouting under globalization may be unsightly, dehumanizing, and may mistreat employees. In 2002, a federal jury found Wal-Mart guilty of requiring hourly employees to perform unpaid "off the clock" work on pain of dismissal. It is outrageous that a big company—Wal-Mart is, in fact, America's largest corporation—would nickel-and-dime struggling minimum-wage laborers in this fashion while lavishing millions on its executives. (For extensive, dismal detail on the mistreatment of hourly workers by American business, see the powerful book *Nickel and Dimed* by Barbara Ehrenreich.)[66] And yet, in the era of Wal-Mart, things have gotten better for almost everyone, including for most of the people who shop at Wal-Mart or work there.

While wage laborers continue in many cases to be mistreated, things keep getting better for the thinkers and writers who refuse to believe that things are getting better. A few generations ago, to be an intellectual or artist required risk and hardship, often combined with a life of penury. Today, the Western nations support tens of thousands of tenured professors—the majority assured of a reasonably comfortable existence and effectively exempt from any political consequences of their words—plus thousands of full-time writers and artists.

Strictly in economic terms, increasing the supply of intellectuals, regardless of how much demand there may be for same, shows the productive power of current market systems. As George Stigler, a Nobel Prize–winning economist, has written, "Since intellectuals are not inexpensive, until the rise of the modern free-enterprise system, no society could afford many." Only a few generations back, the typical national economy produced enough surplus value to support little more than handfuls of writers and artists. Today, the Western economies support huge numbers of professors, thinkers, writers, and artists who devote themselves to denouncing the system that gives them their sinecure and ease. And that's progress! Better to have lots of well-fed disgruntled intellectuals and artists than small numbers of starving crusaders.

A reason Western economies keep performing better may be that capitalism has been supplanted by market economics. Capitalism, as a system, served only those possessing capital; for the typical person, all benefits were trickle-down. Market economics, on the other hand, mainly serves the typical person, as the free exchange of goods and information endlessly pressures corporations to reduce prices and improve quality. Only in the last few decades has it become generally accepted that market economics is good for the typical person, not just for the wealthy. As this message spreads through the developing world— developing nations with market systems have three times the economic growth rate of developing nations with closed systems, and higher living standards for typical people—the term "capitalism" may fade away. "Market democracy" is a much better name for what the Western nations practice today than "capitalism."

These things said, there are many aspects of Western economics that ought to cause concern, chief among them the persistence of poverty amid plenty, which a future chapter will detail. Poverty rates in Western nations have steadily declined during the postwar era, and continue to decline—22 percent of Americans lived in poverty in 1960; by 2001, the figure had fallen to 11.7 percent.[67] But the current situation, in which one person in eight lives in privation in a country as wealthy as the United States, ought to be seen as a national shame.

As the conservative theologian Michael Novak has noted, when the Bible declared, "You always have the poor with you," the context was a feudal agrarian economy that on a physical basis could not produce enough to raise everyone above the level of poverty. Today's high-tech, turbocharged economy produces more than enough—oversupply is a greater issue than scarcity—to grant everyone in the United States and the European Union release from worry over paying the basic bills for food, medicine, clothing, and shelter. Until the day when everyone is released from basic want, a sword will hang over Western abundance.

THE GLOBE. For reasons history will find hard to fathom, during the 1990s it was viewed as inappropriate to rejoice regarding the West's victory in the Cold War. Commentators carped about "triumphalism"—as if there were something wrong with recording a triumph—and denigrated the Cold War result as proof only of Soviet corruption, not of Western goodness.

History will take a clearer view. That the Cold War ended with liberal democracy the winner and without a nuclear shot ever fired is, arguably, the single greatest development ever in international affairs; and the victory came about because democracy was in the right, not because it had more missiles. The result of the Cold War was fabulous not only for the West but for the citizens of the former Soviet nations, who were released from tyranny. The result of the Cold War was fabulous as well for most of the developing world, as the besting of state control by freedom is helping bring liberty and higher living standards to billions of people. Today, as Americans lose sleep over terrorism and its implications, it is well to remember that in the last decade, almost everything in international affairs has gone spectacularly well.

First, consider developing-world conditions. Of course, many signs are distressing, including the heartbreaking fact that more than a billion people live on $1 a day. But to preview a point that will be developed more fully in a later chapter, it is little understood that, even considering all the problems poor countries continue to experience, especially in Africa, for most people in most developing nations, life is mostly getting better. According to the United Nations, in 1975 the average income in developing nations was $2,125 per capita stated in current dollars; today it is $4,000.[68] In 1975, 1.6 billion people lived at what the United Nations classifies as "medium development," meaning with reasonably decent living standards, education, and health care. Today 3.5 billion people do—a stunning increase in the sheer number of human beings who are *not* destitute. Democracy is rising throughout the developing world. Global adult literacy was 47 percent in 1970 and is 73 percent today, while school enrollment for girls has skyrocketed.

Modern communications have become available in some form to most of the world's population, reducing isolation and ignorance. Infant mortality has declined and life expectancy has risen in almost every developing nation. Each year brings more people living on a dollar per day, but this is mainly because population growth means each year brings more people; the percentage of the global community living in such hardship is in steady decline. An estimated eight hundred million people in the world today are malnourished, but the percentage of people who are malnourished is dropping, and the world's average daily caloric intake continues to rise.

Now consider the international military picture. The Cold War never became a hot war, and ended with democracy routing tyranny. Nuclear-bomb factories in the United States and former Soviet Union once turned out doomsday weapons in hideous numbers; today they run in reverse, disassembling warheads in the largest and most important arms-reduction project in history. At the Cold War's peak, each side had approximately 25,000 strategic nuclear warheads aimed at each other's cities— enough to massacre the entire population of both superpowers while bringing wretchedness to the rest of the world via fallout and nuclear-autumn effects. Some old strategic nuclear bombs were monstrosities with the killing power of a small asteroid. Worst among them was the Air Force's nine-megaton B53 warhead, the most powerful explosive device ever built, bearing four hundred times the blast yield of the Hiroshima bomb. Today the United States and Russia are down to six thousand strategic warheads per nation, meaning three-quarters of their Armageddon arsenals have been disassembled. The largest and the worst bombs, such as the B53 and Russia's equivalent high-megaton warheads, were the first ones retired.[69]

In 2002, the United States and the Russian Federation agreed to reduce the number of strategic nuclear warheads still further, to no more than 2,200 per nation. Once this has been accomplished, 90 percent of the Armageddon arsenal will be gone. Newscasts may obsess over pop-starlets' navels and the price of gasoline; historians will view nuclear arms reduction as such an incredible accomplishment that it will seem bizarre in retrospect so little attention was paid while it was happening. Both the United States and Russia are also destroying their entire stockpiles of chemical weapons.[70]

The collapse of Soviet tyranny has been accompanied by a broad-ranging expansion of democracy throughout the world. Twenty-five years ago, only about a third of the globe's nations held true free elections; today, two-thirds do. As the Center for International Development and Conflict Management, at the University of Maryland, said in 2001, that "democratic governments now outnumber autocratic governments two to one" is a situation unprecedented in world history.[71] Democracy has blossomed throughout South and Central America, in parts of Africa. The Chinese monolith is eroding, with this largest of nations starting to move toward openness. And though China is a long way from being free, its rulers now seem shamefaced about that, and to know what direction history is driving them.

Nation after nation in recent decades has changed from various forms of tyranny to democracy, while there has been little traffic in the opposite direction. Since 1980, some eighty countries have moved into the democratic column, in thirty cases replacing military governments with civilian rule. As democracy has expanded, women's rights have been increased in many nations. Only the Arab world has resisted the democracy movement, with the Arab-majority nations still autocratic and backward on women's rights.[72]

In the early 1940s, when the triple tyrannies of German fascism, Soviet communism, and Japanese imperialism were spreading darkness everywhere, the world was down to a dozen or so democracies—including just one free nation left resisting totalitarianism in all of Europe.[73] Now, as Peter Wehner has written, "In every corner of the globe, the tide is with human freedom and dignity." It is not impossible that readers of this book will live to see all nations governed by some form of genuine popular vote, an achievement that would have stood beyond anyone's wildest dreams just two generations ago.

As the number of democracies has grown, the number of armed conflicts in the world has declined, and this may be no coincidence. From the Iraq war and the tenor of the evening news it may seem that fighting is general across the world, but, actually, both declared wars and armed conflicts are declining. According to the Worldwatch Institute, a Washington, D.C., nonprofit group, both declared wars and armed conflicts have steadily declined worldwide in the last decade; there were twenty-eight declared wars and forty-five armed conflicts globally in 2002, for example, versus forty-eight declared wars and sixty-five armed conflicts in 1993.[74] Figures from the World Health Organization show that in 2000, the most recent year for which statistics are available, four times as many people globally died in traffic accidents than in any form of combat—1.3 million traffic deaths versus 300,000 deaths from war.[75] That car crashes currently pose a greater threat to the citizens of earth than combat is surely progress in the right direction.

One reason for the decline of global conflict is that, with the Cold War concluded, neither the United States nor the former Soviet states are arming proxy groups in flashpoint areas. Another reason is that the world spends ever more on peacekeeping, mainly through the United Nations, and peacekeeping is turning out to be an excellent investment.[76] Perhaps most important, historically, democracies have been far less likely to initiate wars than autocratic regimes. Thus as democracies proliferate, war would be expected to decline—exactly what is being observed. Democratic governments respond to the will of their peoples, and people very rarely want war. Citizens of democracies might vote for military actions, such as to protect Kosovar Muslims or hunt down terrorists,[77] but it is hard to imagine people freely voting for war on a regular basis.[78]

Economic interconnectedness will probably, though not certainly, also reduce war. After World War I only begat World War II, European leaders labored to render their nations more interconnected—the Common Market, founded in 1950, helped accomplish this—and the tactic worked, with long-term tensions among England, France, and Germany declining as the nations cooperated economically. Today some fear the United States and China will develop a "Cool War" relationship, pitting the current superpower against the next nation that may acquire such status. But the two nations are already economically inter-connected in a way that no two adversaries ever have been; any military move by one against the other would harm the economies of both. Economic deterrence, in this case, may replace nuclear deterrence.

There's even an economics-of-children analysis that supports the idea that democracy and prosperity will naturally reduce war. For the last century, in every free-market democracy, fertility rates and family sizes have been declining; developing nations that become democracies also experience declines in family size. The fewer children a family has, the more valuable each one becomes, and the less likely a family is to be willing to offer up a child for war. If this viewpoint spreads throughout the world—currently it's spreading everywhere except the Arab nations, with Chinese families especially getting smaller and thereby individual Chinese children becoming more valuable—war might enter a long-term downturn. It is well to remember that the notion of open public opposition to war is relatively recent; when, just nine decades ago, many British citizens openly resisted service in World War I, this was viewed as shocking.[79] Today, in democracies, it is standard to assume that voters oppose war. There is at least a reasonable chance this view will become global.

Now consider a wonderful statistic. Stated in current dollars, annual global military spending peaked in the year 1985, at $1.3 trillion, and has been declining since, to $840 billion in 2002.[80] That's a decline of nearly half a trillion dollars in the amount the world spends each year on arms. Similarly, the world trade in arms peaked in the year 1994, at $39 billion in current dollars, and has mainly been in decline since, falling to $26.4 billion in 2001.[81] These sharp drops in both total global arms spending and arms trading come during a period of population growth, when, other things being equal, military spending might be expected to rise.

The fight against terrorism is a highly negative development that, for good reason, monopolizes attention today. But the larger trends in international affairs—expansion of democracy, less warfare, fewer nuclear bombs, less military spending, less arms trade—are about as encouraging as could be.

Why has so much gotten better? No single thread runs through the many subject areas where life is improving. The crime reduction is sufficiently complex that experts have written dozens of monographs and books on this question—see, for example, the scholarly 2000 volume *The Crime Drop in America*[82]—without reaching consensus.

The aging of the population seems to have been a factor, as was the big increase in the number of people jailed owing to get-tough laws and the end of federal parole. In 1972, there were about 200,000 people in U.S. state and federal prisons; by 2000, the figure had risen to 1.3 million, which took many career criminals off the streets. About 450,000 of the jailed are nonviolent drug offenders put away by merciless "mandatory-minimum" sentencing adopted in recent years. Though some who plead guilty to nonviolent offenses and accept mandatory-minimum sentences do so to escape conviction for worse crimes, the number of nonviolent offenders in U.S. incarceration currently is so huge that many must be the poor, the foolish, or the down-on-their-luck who are locked away to improve prosecutors' conviction numbers: "mandatory-minimum" sentences cry out for reform.[83] The career-criminals population also decreased because many killed one another during the 1980s homicide wave; a significant percentage of homicide victims are people with prior involvement in crime. Don't want to be murdered? Don't commit any form of crime or hang around with those who do. Squares are the hands-down winners of life's longevity contest: Leading a straight-arrow lifestyle is your best defense against becoming a crime victim.

The strong economy of the 1990s must have helped reduce lawbreaking, proving the point that people are less likely to turn to crime when legitimate employment is available. Declining use of crack cocaine is a factor in less crime, as crack led both to lawbreaking for drug transactions and to a huge increase in shoot-outs. As Alfred Blumstein, a criminologist at Carnegie Mellon University, describes it, crack crews carrying wads of cash themselves became the targets of robbery, and since drug dealers couldn't exactly dial 911 to get help, they armed themselves; the result was thousands of teenagers toting guns in tense situations. Now that crack commerce is down, the toting of guns is down. Crack popularity has declined partly through the "little brother effect." The generation that grew up disgusted by the older brothers who had turned themselves into crackheads became determined not to ruin its lives, too.

New policing tactics have helped. Most police departments now endorse some version of the "broken windows" theory, arresting people who break windows or violate other minor laws in order to create an environment of respect for the laws that really matter. Everywhere, police have placed more emphasis on seizing illegal concealed handguns, to prevent thugs from carrying firearms that would escalate street arguments into murders. Putting more officers on the street has helped, as has the upgunning of law enforcement. During the 1980s, when most police carried single-action revolvers, drugrunners with machine pistols or assault rifles had a weapons advantage. Now that most law enforcement officers carry high-rate-of-fire semiautomatic sidearms such as the fearsome Glock, only a fool would try to shoot his way out of an arrest.

The puzzle of police tactics is that crime has fallen by about the same amount everywhere in the United States, regardless of changes in local tactics. New York City has emphasized a statistics-based police philosophy that shifts personnel to whatever city blocks are reporting the most crime; Boston has emphasized breaking up gangs; Baltimore has focused on getting guns off the streets; San Diego hasn't adopted any special theory. Yet all these cities have experienced about the same rate of crime decline—and San Diego did it with only one-third as many police officers per capita as New York City.

Beyond why crime declined—the ultimate murder mystery— no single thread runs through other areas of improvement. Some seem a case for more regulation: Environmental protection is arguably the most impressive achievement of progressive government since the establishment of the Social Security system. But "outside of pollution control, it's hard to see where federal regulations have been the driving factor in recent social improvements," says Gary Becker, a Nobel Prize–winning economist at the University of Chicago. Some seem a case for less regulation: The economy clearly benefited from the deregulation wave that is attributed to Ronald Reagan but actually began under Jimmy Carter, who deregulated the telephone, trucking, and airline industries while lifting price controls on oil and gas.

In the betterment of public health, advancing medical knowledge is the primary factor. Welfare reform and the inner-city comeback have been spurred mainly by state and local initiatives. Betterment of personal behavior, such as the reduction in drunken driving and in teen pregnancy, has been inspired mainly through private efforts and moral and religious argument.

It's possible that the upswing in good news tells us that the many reform initiatives of the 1960s and 1970s finally took effect. Pollution-control regulations, affirmative-action programs, crime crackdowns—all started off clunky and problem-plagued, but as the snafus were ironed out, results began to flow.

It's possible that the surge of national good news tells us that as pragmatism supplants ideology, society will get better at fixing things. "We're living in an age with few romantics and revolutionaries," says political scientist John Mueller of Ohio State University, a rising star in the study of what makes societies work well. "People with vast, sweeping visions caused most of the problems of the 20th century. Most of the time you don't want leaders with visions, you want society run by cautious pragmatists. At the moment, the pragmatists are in control of most nations, and it's making things better." And it's possible that what the late-twentieth-century trends of the United States and European Union convey is what these societies might have looked like sooner if so much of their brainpower and resources had not been diverted to the Cold War.

Diverse explanations aside, there is one bright thread laced through all the examples of favorable trends: an indication that it's never too late to change the world. Intractable or "impossible" dilemmas can be improved. As John Gardner, an official of the Lyndon Johnson administration, said in 1965 of the social issues facing the United States, "What we have before us are some breathtaking opportunities disguised as insoluble problems."[84] Gardner would be pleased if he could see the nation of today: Virtually every issue viewed as insoluble when his statement was made—pollution, race relations, welfare dependency, the Cold War—has improved markedly if not disappeared altogether.

....

THE FALLACY OF THE GOLDEN AGE. Which leaves us with the Fallacy of the Golden Age. Americans speak of the 1950s as a Golden Age, a time of affordable life and a simpler, unsullied ethos. Yet in real dollars almost everything costs less today than it did then, health care is light-years better, three times as many people now make it to college, and the simpler, more innocent ethos of the 1950s denied the vote to blacks and job opportunities to women.

The British speak of prewar London as a Golden Age of quieter life and higher culture. Yet pollution in prewar London was hellish and the class system then operated on unstinting prejudice, while today far fewer Londoners live in tenements, street crime is way down, and the theater district is busier than ever. Numerous similar examples could be offered of past eras spoken of as magnificence lost, when by any objective standard the present is preferable.

Nostalgia plays a role in the glorification of the past, as does the progression from childhood to adulthood. As Christopher Jencks, a professor of government at Harvard University, says, "When we think about the past, we focus on our childhoods, to a time when our parents protected us from the world. As adults, even if society's gotten better, the sense of being sheltered is gone. Nobody's taking care of you anymore, so it feels like everything is getting more worrisome, even if objectively everything is getting better."

Today, many Americans and Europeans speak of previous

generations as having lived in superior circumstances, then grit their teeth when the topic turns to the present day. The Fallacy of the Golden Age holds that good times could only have happened in the past. Yet if the Western world has known a Golden Age, it is right here, right now.

Chapter 3

WHY THE GOOD NEWS SCARES PEOPLE

If most things are getting better for most people, why don't Americans behave as though they believe this? Why do so many walk around scowling, rather than smiling at their good fortune in being born into the present generation? Indeed, at their very good fortune. In his extraordinary book *Mapping Human History,* the science writer Steve Olson estimates that 80 billion "modern" humans—from the first beings recognizable as our forebears to the advent of *Homo sapiens sapiens*, our official name—have walked the earth down through the millennia.[1] Supposing this number is correct, the men and women at middle-class standards or above in the United States and the European Union now live better than 99.4 percent of the human beings who have ever existed.

Average Americans and Europeans not only live better than more than 99 percent of the human beings who have ever existed, they live better than most of the royalty of history, if only owing to antibiotics. As Robert Frank, a professor of economics at Cornell University, has noted, gas-station minimarts now sell cabernets and chardonnays "far superior in quality to the wines once drunk by the kings of France." Today supermarkets offer at low cost dozens of items almost everyone who has ever lived considered unattainable delicacies and died without tasting.[2] But we don't seem particularly pleased about our lot. In 1997, 66 percent of Americans told pollsters they believed "the lot of the average person is getting worse."[3]

People once had it better, back in the good old days. That's what many would now protest. Perhaps not in the days of flint arrowheads and wooly-mammoth-skinning, but surely things were better and people were happier in the recent past.

Consider a thought experiment. If the means existed, would you exchange places with a typical person living in any year before your birth? Exchange places permanently—not, say, observe the Battle of Hastings and then rematerialize in the present. You could pick the year and place in the past, but could not specify trading places with someone specific like Catherine the Great or Leonardo da Vinci, and you could not specify that you would be a lord or lady or hold some similar advantage. In this deal you'd be transported back to the year and society of your choosing to live out the rest of your life as an ordinary person.

A good guess is that hardly anyone in the United States or the European Union today would accept a one-way ticket to the everyday life of the past. The physical beauty of the world would be greater then, before the mixed blessing of development. And most moments in the past would be quieter than ours, though not necessarily less stressful—the lives of pioneer farmers for whom a crop loss meant destitution, or of seamstresses working fourteen-hour days in early industrial-era sweatshops and unable to afford more than tea and bread, were hardly serene. Nor was the quiet, small-town atmosphere of the past, which many today idealize, necessarily ideal. Everyone knew your name, but everyone also knew your secrets; men and especially women enjoyed much less personal freedom in small-town life of the past than is typical today.

For essentially all of human history until the last few generations, the typical person's lot has been unceasing toil, meager living circumstances, uncertainty about food, rudimentary health care, limited education, little travel or entertainment; all followed by early death. (Keep in mind these remain the conditions under which more than a billion people live in the developing world today.) Even if you could somehow carry the benefits of modern medicine with you into the past—health care alone would make almost everyone decline the one-way ticket backward— the toil, low living standards, and isolated lives of past generations would seem awful to us compared to the sorts of things we complain about today.

Even the near past might not seem, on reflection, terribly attractive as a destination. The first decade of the twentieth century? City air in the United States and Europe was thick with choking smoke from unrestricted coal burning; pigs roamed the streets of New York City and Philadelphia, eating garbage that was thrown out windows; there were three million horses drawing carts within city limits of American cities, meaning horse manure everywhere; in Chicago, elevated trains pulled by steam engines rained sparks and cinders on pedestrians; in pleasantly pastoral small towns, only 2 percent of dwellings had running water, causing many women to be little more than serfs to the carrying of water and doing of laundry, to say nothing of child-rearing; most people expired before age forty-five.[4] The second decade of the twentieth century? The Great War, in which millions died in pointless conflict, followed by twenty-five million more dead in a global flu epidemic that accompanied the conflict, while in the United States, one person in a hundred owned a car, and, adjusted for population and miles traveled, railway deaths were five times as common as automobile deaths today. The third decade? The Great Depression; one person in twenty-five was a college graduate; most homes and apartments still lacked a telephone or electricity. The fourth decade? Another global war, this time a just war but mandating years of sacrifice for those at home as well as those who fought. The fifth decade? Children still dying of measles (the first vaccine did not appear till 1966) and polio (3,300 killed by polio in the United States in 1952; the first field test of the Salk vaccine did not occur till 1954), strong prejudice against gays and repressive sexual atmosphere for everybody else, typical house less than half the size of today's, air conditioning still rare in the South. The sixth decade? Voting rights for blacks not secure till 1965, workplace rights for women still rare, U.S. poverty still above 20 percent, Medicare for senior citizens not available till 1966, air and water pollution still unregulated, birth control pills still outlawed in many states. Only by the 1970s did living standards, life expectancy, health care, education, and personal freedom begin to approximate today's.[5] And no one would choose to time-travel to the 1970s because you'd have to wear the clothes.

As far back as 1918, in his autobiography *The Education of Henry Adams,* the descendant of president John Adams declared that America enjoyed "prosperity never before imagined." Today the average person's real income is sevenfold greater than when Henry Adams wrote, and yet Americans feel dissatisfied and tell pollsters they believe life is getting worse. Back in the year 1958, one of the top-selling books in the United States was *The Affluent Society* by John Kenneth Galbraith. One thesis of *The Affluent Society* was that Americans already had so much they were becoming spoiled; another contention of the book was that standards of living had risen so high that they couldn't be expected to rise much farther.

The materialistic summit, Galbraith thought in 1958, had been reached because the typical family possessed a home, a car, and a television, and included one person who had graduated from college.[6] One generation after *The Affluent Society* declared that America would not get much richer, average real income in the United States has more than doubled, huge houses with three cars and a wide-screen television have become common, the majority of children attend college: What were once luxuries are now necessities, and polls show most people think they do not have enough. Typically, regardless of how much money an American today earns, he or she estimates that twice as much is required to "live well."[7]

The fundamental reason so many Western citizens don't seem pleased with their lot, or even to believe their lives are mainly favored, is the discontinuity between prosperity and happiness. That—and what we can do about it—will be the subject of the second section of this book. For now, let's look at factors at work in the collective refusal to believe that life is getting better.

First is the unsettled character of progress. We'd like to think progress causes problems to be solved in a final sense, and sometimes that happens. Polio, for example, is a solved problem, thanks to the Salk and then Sabin vaccines. The supply of coal, an issue that once kept Winston Churchill awake at night, is a solved problem; so much more coal than anyone needs is on the international market that prices keep falling and miners in many nations worry about future employment. The small portable communication device is a solved problem, as even children now carry cell phones. Some problems can be solved, and they go away.

But often as not, problems exist in a chain of cause and effect: For each problem solved, a new one crops up. Polio is solved, but did the vaccines that eradicated this disease play a role in the rise of autism? Wireless communication is everywhere, but that means you can't escape office calls and must exist in dread of the lunatics who speed in SUVs while yakking into cell phones. Use of coal, plentiful and cheap, may trigger an artificial greenhouse effect. The sense that new problems always arise to replace the old is one reason people are reluctant to believe life is getting better, and there is a certain logic to this position.

Let's think a moment about a few subjects in which the main thread is improvement, but the character of progress is sufficiently unsettled so as to cause most people to focus on negatives.

Agriculture represents one such example. Modern high-yield farming is a marvel, filling the granaries of the Western nations with an annual abundance of fruits, vegetables, and cereals at prices generally lower, in inflation-adjusted terms, than in the 1950s. Modern ranching provides equally impressive quantities of excellent high-protein beef, pork, and poultry, at affordable prices, plus affordable aqua-farmed salmon and other fish. Genetic engineering of crop plants promises foods grown with fewer chemicals, containing less fat and more protein, the elimination of allergens—that is, peanuts to which no one is allergic—

as well as a second round of Green Revolution crops specialized to feed the developing world. Global commerce moves fruits from South America to North America by air, so that nothing is ever out of season; flowers come in the same air freight, high-quality fresh-cut flowers for the table now costing much less in inflation-adjusted terms than they once did.[8] Crop failures have become unheard-of, while erosion and soil loss to wind have declined—the Dust Bowl, it is important to recall, occurred before the widespread adoption of high-yield farming, which has since prevented any dust-bowl effects, even during drought years. Most Americans and Western Europeans alive today have scant idea what it means not to be able to obtain any amount of any kind of desired food. This is as it should be. Ideally, all forms of farm products would be in oversupply for everyone in the world.

Yet many aspects of contemporary agriculture are unsettled. Farm subsidies and price supports cost huge amounts; combined, the United States and the European Union spend almost $1 billion a day to subsidize agriculture. Unsettling, too, is the fact that today's super-efficient high-yield farming could not happen without pesticides and fertilizers. The amount of farm chemicals applied per bushel produced has been in decline in recent years[9]—farmers have a financial incentive to cut pesticide use, since chemicals are expensive. But driving up developing-world food production to meet population growth will inevitably mean more chemicals. Chemicals, in turn, mean contaminated runoff. Though industrial pollution to waterways has declined sharply throughout the Western world, runoff of fertilizer continues as a problem, rendering water bodies such as Chesapeake Bay "eutrophic," or too nutrient-rich, which encourages algae at the expense of other marine life. (That industrial pollution to waterways is now tightly regulated, while farm-caused pollution of water is not, oddly means that in the contest of political arm-wrestling, the farm lobby has shown more muscle than the factory lobby.) Today's agriculture is generally "monocultural," meaning that, in any particular year, huge swaths of Western farmland are planted with exactly the same thing.[10] And the same economic forces that keep food plentiful and costs low can be bad for small farmers, shifting the balance of power toward agribusiness.

Then there is genetic engineering. So far genetic engineering of crops appears safe, with many studies, including by the National Research Council, an affiliate of the National Academy of Sciences, having found no dangers in genetically modified plants.[11] Genetic engineering of the plant kingdom is a much less dicey proposition than engineering of animals or people, since all major crop plants grown today have already been significantly diverged from their natural cousins by centuries of selective breeding.

The "dwarf" wheats that lead the world's grain crop have been selectively bred, beginning hundreds of years ago, to render them shorter than their natural ancestors of Middle Eastern antiquity, much fuller in kernels, and sturdier at the base so that they do not bend under their own weight, allowing for mechanical harvesting. The dwarf indica rice that feeds most of the Asian world is so lush as to appear unrecognizable next to the natural grasses from which it was artificially diverged in antiquity by Chinese plant breeders. The tall, full maize on which beef and poultry production is anchored bears only passing resemblance to teosinte, a wispy wild Mexican plant that indigenous North Americans began to crossbreed thousands of years ago. A century ago, soy barely existed as an agricultural product; the bean as found in nature was close to inedible, and cooks preferred lard. Selective breeding transformed soybeans into the keystone of the world's edible-oil supply. None of these deliberate alterations of crop genetics caused any harm, except in the sense that maize and soybeans are now so cheap and plentiful that Americans consume too much soy-derived fat and too much corn-based sweetener.

Nevertheless there's no doubt that the idea of popping "genetically engineered" food into your mouth is disquieting. And though genetically engineered crops, so far as is known, have never hurt anyone, the system for regulating their use is muddled, because Congress has never passed a regulatory act concerning biotechnology; all biotech businesses are regulated via a patchwork of laws originally designed for other things entirely.[12] The whole situation is unsettling. On the farm, are things getting better or not?

The automobile is another example of arguable progress. Today's cars are far more comfortable than models of a generation ago, and loaded with gadgets, yet in inflation-adjusted terms car costs have risen only somewhat. A generation ago, the whole family crammed into a sedan and please watch those elbows, whereas in today's minivan, every kid expects his or her captain's chair with armrests and cupholder. Almost all new cars sold in the United States are air conditioned; in 1970, only about 20 percent were. Leather, lumbar massagers, audio, and even DVD systems abound. Highway deaths per mile traveled have fallen steadily because cars are much safer than they once were, with airbags and antilock brakes and other, less visible improvements in safety engineering, mainly the switch to automotive frames designed in such a way that, during a crash, the passenger compartment is not crushed. Average acceleration has increased 40 percent since 1970—the glory days of the "muscle car" are right now, not in the 1960s of *American Graffiti*—yet roadholding has also increased, another factor in fewer deaths.[13] Any make or model of new car emits less than 2 percent as much pollution per mile as a car of 1970, and the figure for new-car pollution continues to fall. Cars are far more reliable than they once were; the car that won't start, once common, becomes ever more rare. Autos also now reliably last; you can buy any make or model of contemporary car and plan to own it indefinitely without the vehicle falling apart, once normal for cars by the third year. And despite better acceleration, more room, and ubiquitous air conditioning, cars today on average use less gasoline per mile than in 1970.

Cars are the primary reason for the ever increasing "personal area" of Western life. As Jesse Ausubel of Rockefeller University has shown,[14] "personal area"—the volume of territory through which someone moves in a typical day—has risen tenfold in the West since 1950, mainly because "personal speed" has tripled. Before general ownership of cars, most people were limited on most days to destinations to which they could walk, or that were close to bus or streetcar lines. Now most people head to whatever destination they wish, so long as traffic jams don't intervene. Ausubel has found that the "personal speed" of typical Americans has been rising at about 2.7 percent per annum for a generation; at that rate, the "personal area" the typical individual covers per day doubles every twenty-five years. Racing around from one destination to the next—job, school, stores, gym, restaurant, church—may be stressful. But the fact that people are increasingly able to choose where they want to be, and choose when they want to be there, is an addition to personal freedom. Cars are what make "personal speed" and "personal area" possible, and we wouldn't love them so much were they not so damn convenient in this regard.

Aspects of car culture are unsettling, however. Speed and convenience in transit, for example, don't necessarily translate into a more pleasing life. "The mobility of the private car has the paradoxical effect of lengthening how far people go rather than saving them time," Alan Durning has written.[15] Between the desirability of cars and rising prosperity, every year the roads are clogged by more of these mechanical trolls. The one-car family gave way to the two-car family, and now gives way to the multicar family. Once it was rare, practically scandalous, for a teenager to own a car. Now it's commonplace, with high schools experiencing parking problems as so many students drive themselves to school, alone, in their own cars. We're all in such a hurry to exploit our "personal speed" that road rage gets worse annually, creating an uncivil driving atmosphere and turning driving, which used to be mildly relaxing and even fun, into a nerve-racking aggravation.

Parking hassles have become nearly ubiquitous. Now in many downtown areas, it's not only impossible to find street parking, it can be hard to find a place to pay to park. In recent years it has become difficult to find parking spaces at many suburban malls, places that were originally devised with easy parking in mind. It has even become hard to park at many national parks. Grand Canyon National Park is vast, larger than all of sprawling Los Angeles, but five million cars per year now flood into this preserve, and parking spaces are often gone by eight in the morning. Visitors become outraged when they discover they have driven hundreds of miles to the great outdoors and, once there, can't find a place to get out of their cars.

The ever thicker traffic caused by cars is not in your mind. In the last thirty years, John Seabrook has written, "the population of the United States has grown by 40 percent, while the number of registered vehicles has increased by nearly 100 percent—cars have proliferated more than twice as fast as people."[16] Through the same period, vehicle-miles traveled have increased by 143 percent, but road capacity has risen only 6 percent.[17] You can't enjoy the speed, handling, power, and safety of your handsome high-tech car if every street and highway is blocked by traffic. The scene so avidly promoted in car commercials, of a smiling driver roaring down the open road, simply never occurs in present-day life because there are no more open roads.

Equally, it's hard to enjoy your suburban lifestyle if you spend significant time each day stuck in infuriating traffic jams: the car's air conditioner, power lumbar massager, and other gizmos running, of course. Studies by the Federal Highway Administration show that daily time stuck in traffic in the thirty worst U.S. cities has quintupled since 1980, while traffic congestion has begun to arrive even in exurban areas and one-stoplight towns. Nationally, Americans spend 17 percent more time stuck in traffic today than they did in 1980.[18]

Since the number of cars continues to rise, while new road-building has almost stopped owing to environmental and NIMBY opposition, traffic headaches are only going to get worse. Opponents of road construction sometimes claim the effort is pointless because roads "only cause more traffic." But this is like saying it's pointless to feed a child because tomorrow she'll only be hungry again. Traffic does rise when new roads are built, but traffic also rises when new roads are not built. That traffic has become far more congested in the United States in the last twenty years, during the very period when the preferred NIMBY response—no new road-building—was in force, gives the lie to claims that "roads just cause more traffic." Cars, not roads, are the root cause of traffic, and cars will continue to proliferate whether road mileage is increased or not. If Western society is to remain oriented around cars, more roads must be built in response.

America is a car culture and has been for almost a century, the phrase "traffic jam" dating to 1910, meaning we're stuck with car culture for the time being. In the United States, the number of trips taken on public transportation has since 1998 been rising more rapidly than trips taken in cars. But public transportation nevertheless cannot be a cure-all for traffic congestion, since only a total of 1 percent of all U.S. trips occur on public transit.[19] Double the share, which would require notable effort and capital expense, and it's still only 2 percent. A car culture with a rising population and rising prosperity has little choice but to keep investing in roads and parking.

Another unsettling aspect of the car is that the period in which cars have become safer, more comfortable, and more reliable has coincided with the fad for SUVs and "light" pickup trucks, which at this writing constituted slightly more than 50 percent of U.S. new-auto sales. These Godzilla-sized vehicles create their own rolling self-propelled traffic congestion as they physically crowd the road, taking up more space than conventional cars. Owing to the fad for SUVs and pickup trucks, the average fuel economy of U.S. vehicles has been declining since 1988, increasing American dependence on Persian Gulf oil and also contributing to global warming. (Since greenhouse gases are proportional to fuel consumed, the lower the MPG, the higher the greenhouse contribution.) SUVs and light trucks are not bound by the same fuel economy and antipollution standards as regular cars, and Congress has repeatedly refused to impose higher standards on these vehicles.[20] The favorable statistics you just read regarding low pollution emissions refer to new regular cars, not the new SUVs and pickup trucks, many of which spew four times as much smog-forming contaminants per mile. Also, new SUVs average 40 percent lower fuel efficiency than new regular cars; were it not for the fad for SUVs and pickup trucks, U.S. dependency of Persian Gulf oil would be much less of a problem.[21]

To top it off, the common assumption that SUVs are safer than conventional cars is not true. Studies by the Insurance Institute for Highway Safety show that SUVs have higher collision-loss rates than regular cars,[22] while the National Research Council has found that, overall, drivers and passengers in SUVs are slightly more likely to die than drivers and passengers in regular cars.[23] In most cases, SUV passengers are safer in front-to-front and front-to-side collisions, but mortality for SUV rollover crashes is so much higher—and rollovers cause one-third of highway fatalities—that the death rate for travelers in SUVs is worse than the rate for travelers in standard or midsize cars. "Women love their SUVs . . . because of their safety," Senator Barbara Mikulski of Maryland said in 2002, casting her vote against fuel economy standards for SUVs.[24] Women—and men as well—may *feel* safer in SUVs, but they're not. Instead these leviathans make the road more deadly, because many studies have shown that a heavy SUV is more likely to harm the passengers in a car it collides with.[25] "When a regular car strikes another car in the side," writes Keith Bradsher in *High and Mighty*,[26] a history of the SUV, "the driver of the struck car is 6.6 times as likely to die as the driver of the striking car. But when an SUV hits a car in the side, the death ratio rises to 30 to 1."

In addition to making roads dangerous, the SUV has made respectable the underside of driving, which is using the road as a means to express hostility to neighbors. Buyers like SUVs and pickup trucks partly because they feel that in these huge, intimidating masses of metal they can cut into traffic and others will have to jump out of the way; that they can speed willy-nilly, shouting into the phone, and frightened fellow motorists will clear a path. As Bradsher details in *High and Mighty*, many SUVs and pickup trucks are designed and marketed to present an antagonistic impression, visually raising the middle finger to fellow citizens. Probably some Americans tell themselves they need the scary, antisocial look of the SUV because of road rage. But the mid-1990s rise of road rage coincided with the onset of SUV mania. Arguably, it is the advent of SUVs that caused road rage, rather than the other way around—filling streets and highways with oversized, dangerous, hostile-looking vehicles whose sales psychology strives to make buyers think their purchase renders them invincible, to say nothing of conferring permission to cut others off at will. Perhaps this whole class of vehicles should be renamed FUVs.

Finally there is the vilifying complication that the car is a metaphor. Somehow Americans and Europeans have come to believe that a listless activity—sitting in a seat and pressing a pedal—represents virility. What could make a stupider metaphor for human self-expression than a car? Nothing is more demeaning than the idea that our cars say something about us.

All told, cars get safer, more comfortable, and more reliable, while the driving environment simultaneously becomes more unpleasant and SUVs are marketed to emphasize belligerence— the archetypical unsettling development.

A third example of the ambivalence of progress is medical care. Americans are the healthiest they have ever been: living longer, suffering less from almost every disease, and suffering less from health care itself as arthroscopic procedures and noninvasive therapies replace traditionally painful and debilitating surgeries. Even the paperwork has gotten simpler for most people, as medical insurers have replaced complex reimbursement-filing systems with plans in which the patient does little more than flash a card. With most health trends auspicious, you'd think people would look favorably on the medical system. Yet Americans mainly grumble about health care. Prescription drugs cost too much, insurers are too bureaucratic, physicians are too money-hungry, HMOs give patients the runaround—complaints about the health care system are ubiquitous throughout the news media and in popular entertainment.

It's true that the health-maintenance organization, originally created as a force for patient advocacy, was transformed into a creature of heartless corporate red tape. But the idea that HMOs routinely deny necessary care to patients does not stand logical scrutiny. Considering that more than half of the American public now belongs to an HMO or similar "managed-care" plan, if these organizations really were denying medical treatment on a widespread basis, longevity would not be rising nor illness declining. Supposedly, HMOs are killing patients. Where are the bodies? As a group, the patients of managed-care plans continue to grow healthier.

Of course, there are instances of HMOs botching the treatment of patients, but there are instances of traditional fee-for-service, Marcus Welby–style sole practitioners botching treatments, too. The idea that managed-care institutions are systematically denying therapy to patients has become something of an urban legend, widely believed but more real in the universe of prime-time television than in medical offices. During the 1980s, when managed-care plans underwent a rapid national expansion and exhibited many management flaws, there were cases of patients refused care, among them the widely reported experience of Nelene Fox, a California woman who died in 1992 after her HMO denied coverage for a bone-marrow transplant. When Fox's survivors won an $89 million judgment against her insurer, most managed-care plans changed policies and began rarely to deny care, if only for fear of tort liability.[27] Today most HMOs and similar plans cover almost any treatment and don't restrict access to specialists, yet Americans continue to speak as though denials remained widespread practices.

Complaints about the cost of medical care are constant, though since an aging population requires more health care, and advanced therapies and drugs allow people to live longer with less pain, other things being equal, costs would be expected to rise. Health spending was $3,858 per capita in the United States in 2001, the highest figure in the world, which works out to $15,432 per year for a family of four. Yet the typical family of four spent about $4,000 on medical insurance, deductibles, and co-pays in 2001, meaning most Americans did not bear most of the medical expense they complain so lustily about: Employers, the government, and insurance firms did.[28] Sometimes individuals or families without insurance—and lack of universal coverage is the true fault of the American system—are clobbered by medical expenses. For the majority of Americans, health care is an excellent buy.

America's expensive medical system provides the very best in drugs and technology, and what constitutes the baseline constantly rises. When the heart-bypass operation was initially devised, in the 1960s, it was considered absurd to suggest the operation for those over about sixty-five years, since the surgery was debilitating and a patient of that age, with heart problems, wouldn't be expected to live much longer anyway. Even today, the nationalized health systems of Canada and Europe, often praised for spending less than the American system, generally will not pay for bypass operations for senior citizens. But in the United States, Medicare provides this very expensive therapy at almost any age. Considerable research has gone into refining the bypass technique so that it is less traumatic in the surgical sense, allowing senior citizens to survive the operation, recover, and live many more years. While bypass operations for the over-sixty-five were once exceptionally rare, now many thousands occur every year. Americans live longer and in better health as a result, though like most types of medical progress, ever higher cost is ensured.[29]

Less noticed but just as important, the American medical system spends generously on capacity—doctors, nurses, and hospitals standing by to treat you instantly. Empty hospital beds or five MRI machines in the same small city may seem like "waste" when you're healthy; when you're sick or injured, having these items at the ready seems like enlightened social policy. Consider that Canada spends only $1,899 per capita (in U.S. dollars) on health care, and waits there for elective treatment may run into the weeks or months. Waits of more than a few days are rare in the American system. Having loads of medical capacity is a good idea, but also runs up the bill.

In July 2002, I watched a segment on the excellent PBS show *Newshour* in which numerous Californians were interviewed complaining vehemently that HMOs in their state were beginning to charge co-pays for office visits, rather than assessing a single annual premium and then providing all services free. One mother described having to fork over a total of $165 to various physicians and hospitals for the treatment of a daughter's broken leg; she was furious at this expense. And if well-trained doctors and nurses, a top-notch emergency room, and an operating theater with the very best of equipment and supplies had not been standing by at the moment her daughter's leg broke? One reason Californian medical costs are rising is that the state recently enacted a law requiring all hospitals to be earthquake-proof. This is a sensible precaution, but somebody's got to pay for it. To be outraged over a relatively small charge for the healing of a child is a strange reaction, but in keeping with the current American propensity to gripe about medicine even as medicine gets ever better at keeping Americans alive to continue griping.

Similarly, Americans object to the rising costs of pharmaceuticals—drug prices are escalating faster than other aspects of medicine—but not to the countervailing benefits. Recurrent conditions such as arthritis plague people steadily less as advanced drugs, designed with the profit motive in mind, come into use. People with insomnia get a night's sleep because of Ambien; sufferers from allergies, anxiety, and depression have normal days owing to a range of new pills. Would we really be better off if pharmaceutical companies did not have a profit incentive to discover medical compounds that improve quality of life in such ways? In recent years *The New York Times*, especially, has crusaded on the point that drug patents should be curtailed so that any manufacturer could produce lower-cost generics. By that logic, why should *The New York Times* be allowed to charge one dollar per edition when it's only reporting the same news as everybody else? Plus, its stories are manufactured using the same words as less expensive newspapers! Perhaps Congress should order *The New York Times* to become a twenty-five-cent generic newspaper; bylines could say, BY A REPORTER. Or Congress could curtail the paper's copyrights, decreeing that anyone could run *New York Times* articles without fee. Such steps would cut costs. They would also, of course, lead to reduced product quality, and the same logic applies to drugs.

Many dilemmas in contemporary Western health care can be observed at the United States–Canada border. There, a steady flow of Americans crosses into Canada to purchase the low-cost prescription drugs of the country's state-controlled system. They pass a steady flow of Canadians crossing into America to get access to superior medical technology and to the elective procedures that can be treated immediately under a free-enterprise system. This sort of situation is unsettling. Who's right, America or Canada? Who's better off?

THE TYRANNY OF THE SMALL PICTURE. Ever safer cars, yet everyone menaced by Godzilla SUVs; ever more food, yet now it's stamped "genetically engineered"; ever better health care, yet unhappy patients stream back and forth between nations to exploit quirks of each other's systems. Solving one problem often creates another; the new problem is noted and fretted about while the original, being solved, is forgotten. Call this the "tyranny of the small picture." Instead of the big picture we often see the small picture, aware only of the lesser negative within the greater positive.

Other factors color our aversion to believing that most things are getting better. One is an active preference for bad news.

Some of this preference stems from the dictates of fundraising. A clear lesson of modern life is that money awaits on the extremes of an issue, but not at the consensus center. Right-wing fund-raisers ceaselessly depict the United States as sliding into the Slough of Despond, if not becoming the modern Sodom; this view is entirely unhinged from reality but resonates with certain right-wing marks and separates them from their money. Left-wing fund-raisers ceaselessly depict the United States as a quasi-police state based on oppression and exploitation, another view lacking any ballast of reality, but that can be relied on to separate certain left-wing marks from their money. Most contemporary fund-raising turns on high-decibel assertions that everything's going to hell. It is not, but because fund-raisers have grown so adept at targeted marketing, their contaminated messages surround us nonetheless. Versions of these make-believe views dominate politics as well, as Republicans utter gloomy exaggerations of the right and Democrats gloomy exaggerations of the left, again mainly with fund-raising in mind.

Environmental fund-raising is telling as an example of the money being at the extremes. The steady environmental improvement of the United States should be a subject of national pride—there ought to be crowing about how activists, government officials, business managers, and average citizens worked together to overcome an "insoluble" problem without penalty to national prosperity. This especially ought to be true for political liberals, who could say, with justification, that environmental recovery is the most important accomplishment of American government since the creation of the Social Security system. If liberals want voters to believe in government, they must present examples of government success; for the postwar generations, the first example should be environmental optimism.

But there's no money to be made in harmony. Environmentalists and Democratic candidates can raise funds by crying environmental doomsday, so it is doomsday they cry. On the flip side, right-wing think tanks and Republicans can raise money, and industrial lobbyists can score hefty contracts, by falsely claiming that environmental regulations are destroying the economy. Each side's financial incentive is to be relentlessly negative. The positive analysis may be what matters to the typical person—but no actor in the system has a financial incentive to be positive. This dynamic can be observed in many contemporary issues. Alarmism and anger are good to the pocketbooks of advocates of all ideological stripes; consensus and optimism are bad for business.

Next is a preference for bad news on the part of elites. Some of this might be explained as a conditioned yearning felt by the privileged to look down on the societies that create the favored lives they enjoy. To much of the elite ethos, if things are bad then the privileged may float above events feeling superior and asserting that they knew it all along. In Ivy League universities or similar places, depressing or pessimistic news is received with a welcoming sigh, as if the preferred outcome, while favorable news or optimistic trends are viewed as at best some sort of deception.

Many elites love writers such as Jean-Paul Sartre, who viewed all human action as meaningless, or Thomas Pynchon, whose novels, such as *Gravity's Rainbow,* purport to present hard-science arguments that ours is a pointless universe doomed to meaningless demise. Pynchon's grasp of physics is debatable;[30] what matters is that when he claimed to have found scientific proof the universe is pointless, many of a certain ilk were eager to believe him. Eighty years ago, elites of the United States and Europe gushed in praise over the social historian Oswald Spengler's work *The Decline of the West,* which argued not only that American and European civilization "one day will lie in fragments, forgotten" but that the downfall of Western civilization was imminently at hand. Similarly, William Butler Yeats in the early twentieth century was praised by Western intellectuals for predicting pending social disintegration through his famed phrase, "Things fall apart; the centre cannot hold."[31] Spengler even maintained that the collapse of Western civilization would be a beneficial development, because America and Europe were contemptible. Eight decades later, the West is far stronger, richer, more secure, more diverse, and more free than when Spengler declared it a decaying relic about to vanish. Nevertheless, his work and similar predictions of impending Western collapse are still spoken of reverentially among intellectual elites, a portion of whom delight to hear anything American and European called bad.

If elites like bad news, then the eagerness of intellectuals, artists, and tastemakers to embrace claims of ecological doomsday, population crash, coming global plagues, economic downfall, cultural wars, or the end of this or that become, at least, comprehensible. The riposte here might be that for every one tastemaker programmed for pessimism, there are a hundred middle-class suburbanites who could not care less what intellectuals say at the sherry hour. But the fact that elites prefer bad news has disproportionate impact, as elite views are disproportionately represented in the media.

An example: In 1994 there appeared a book titled *The Coming Plague,* by Laurie Garrett,[32] which declared that vast numbers of people, perhaps hundreds of millions, would soon die in unstoppable pandemics of mutant diseases, especially Ebola. The book was lavishly praised and inspired many television dramas and one movie, *Outbreak*, depicting unstoppable Ebola-based pandemics. Not addressed in the book was the fact that when Ebola was accidentally released from a laboratory near Washington, D.C., in 1989, it killed a shocking total of—no one. Garrett followed up with a 2000 volume called *Betrayal of Trust: The Collapse of Global Public Health*,[33] which declared that illnesses of all types were just about to skyrocket everywhere—skipping the inconvenient complication that life expectancy is rising in nearly all nations and that nearly all diseases other than AIDS are in global decline. This work was also lavishly praised, winning the National Book Critics Circle Award, and causing middle-class television news shows of the *Today* type to tell viewers that global illnesses of all sorts were about to break out everywhere. Lesson: Claims of disastrous decline will be praised in the elite parts of society. Since many crave recognition or rewards from elites, people oblige by producing claims of disastrous decline.

More generally, when things really are bad we naturally turn to eminent or powerful people for their advice and succor; when things are fine, the elite classes are of diminished importance to society. Important people like to feel important, and thus are biased toward viewing events in bleak terms. Consider that, during the 1990s, when nearly everything in the United States was trending positive, left-wing leaders as exemplified by the Manhattan chardonnay circuit, and right-wing leaders as exemplified by the Heritage Foundation circuit, slugged it out as though the world was ending: the left claiming religious fanatics were taking over the country, the right claiming the left was destroying the family and opposed to reading of the classics, to name a few totally cooked-up charges of that period. As Orlando Patterson, a Harvard University sociologist, noted in 1998, "It's astonishing how the Washington and New York elites, who benefit so much from the improvement of the United States, are so out of sync with it, endlessly talking about how things are getting worse when the country is clearly improving."[34]

To those who benefit from bad news, either by fund-raising or increased self-importance, problems are not just problems but crises—the health care crisis, the farm-bill crisis, the tax crisis, the welfare crisis, the litigation crisis, the postage-rate crisis. Surely we will awaken some morning to read about a presidential commission declaiming the bridge-abutment peeling-paint crisis. Problems are inflated into crises in part because, during a crisis, elites gain stature. World War II was a crisis; the current Middle East situation is a crisis; 99 percent of the issues facing the Western world are not crises. But in contemporary public discourse, everything is a crisis—a notion talk shows and media outlets have an interest in promoting. The other day, I heard a foundation president being interviewed on CNN proclaim a "serious crisis." What the "serious crisis" was doesn't matter here; what mattered is that the word "crisis" has so been devalued by overuse that now we must speak of the "serious crisis."

Like elites and intellectuals, most politicians prefer bad news to good. In contemporary Western politics, the party out of power drastically exaggerates all negative trends while denying all positive developments, in hopes of creating voter anger and getting back into power. Early in the 1990s, when Democrats were the party out of power and most things were getting better, Democrats spoke as if the nation were going down for the third time, Al Gore for example saying in 1992 that the United States faced "the greatest calamity in the history of man." A few years later, when the Republicans were the party out of power and practically everything was getting better, Republicans spoke as if the nation were in deep catastrophe, Speaker of the House Newt Gingrich in 1995 calling the United States "a civilization in danger of simply falling apart." During the 2000 presidential campaign, out-of-power Republicans declared that the United States military had been "hollowed out" and ruined by Democrats; the same military performed phenomenally well just a few months later in Afghanistan, and a year after that in Iraq. Democrats handed power over to Republicans in January 2001, and the very Democrats who weeks before had been saying the country was well-managed began declaring the country in horrible shape. The point of self-parody for politicians talking as pessimistically as possible for self-serving reasons came during the 2000 presidential nomination campaign, when one of the Republican hopefuls, Alan Keyes, gave a speech in which he declared that the United States was riven by awful, awful calamities, but, "Unfortunately these crises are not evident in the country today, and they are unlikely to appear before November." How unfortunate the country isn't collapsing! That would be good for my political career!

Because Democratic and Republican political charges and countercharges dominate newspapers and television talk shows, we hear constant exaggeration of the faults of the country, coupled to little discussion of what's going well. Often, pessimistic messages fall on receptive ears. Many Christian Americans, particularly, may be inclined to believe declarations of national decline, since some fundamentalist interpretations hold that not only is an ideal society impossible to achieve, social decay is actually welcome because it will hasten the Lord's return. Dwight Moody, the leading fundamentalist evangelist of the late nineteenth century, phrased it this way in 1888: "I don't find any place where God says the world is going to grow better and better. I find that the Earth is to grow worse and worse."[35] The contemporary expression of the view is the popular *Left Behind* series; fundamentalist readers eagerly have snapped up a serial of books depicting the United States as a shattered wreckage in which small groups of tormented survivors must fight off the very forces of Satan. Because many Christians expect the worst in each day's news, they tend to believe claims of Western or American breakdown, then reinforce the claims by repeating them.

Spurious crisis-talk not only backfires in the sense of being misleading: It means that genuine troubles, such as the millions of Americans without health insurance, fail to receive sufficient attention because they cannot penetrate the static field around the news. Constant talk of crisis and decline also can make individuals feel their efforts are pointless, another backfire effect since the record shows that when people lower their shoulders to a problem, they almost always accomplish good.

The desires of fund-raisers, politicians, elites, and scaremongers of all stripes to cry woe regardless of the actual state of the nation might be called the "gloom interest groups factor."

News organizations adore the word "crisis" and use it as often as possible. News-organization internal incentives toward negativism are the next reason many are convinced life is getting worse rather than better. To cite one of almost countless examples, in 2002 promotional spots for the CBS broadcast *Sixty Minutes* declared, "Add to America's health care crisis a nursing shortage. It's a recipe for disaster! A report you don't want to miss tonight!"[36] There are all kinds of problems in the American medical system. But a health care crisis in a nation where longevity is rising and nearly all forms of disease declining? Nevertheless, invoking crisis makes it "A report you don't want to miss tonight!"

The news-organization incentive to emphasize the negative can be defended up to a point, since negative news usually is what the public most urgently needs to know. It's one thing, though, to highlight when the bad happens—as the media should—and another to pretend that the good does not happen, as the media also do.

Highly speculative bad news is often given considerable play by the United States media, while confirmed good news is barely reported. In the winter of 2001, for example, a *New York Times* page-one lead story declared in breathless phrasing that the White House had just "canceled" regulations limiting arsenic in drinking water; taking their leads from the *Times,* all national newscasts that night declared that arsenic protection had been "canceled." The *Times* went on to editorialize that government actually wanted Americans to "drink poisoned water" because this would serve the sinister interests of corporations, though how the conspiracy would serve sinister corporate interests was not explained, since the arsenic in drinking water occurs naturally.[37] Government poisoning your water—a report you don't want to miss tonight!

Except that nothing had been canceled. The White House had held up a pending rule to make arsenic protection more strict; while the pending rule was reviewed, prior rules remained in effect. The Environmental Protection Agency continued regulating arsenic in drinking water during the entire period when such protection was supposedly "canceled." Then, in November 2001, the White House ended its review and put the much stricter rule into force. *The New York Times* did not play this as a headline lead, where the original scare story had been; enactment of the strict rule was buried in a small box on page A18.[38] Network newscasts that had presented a shocking scandal of "canceled arsenic protection" as their big story also said little or nothing when instead stronger rules went into effect. This sort of puffing up of a phony scare, followed by studious ignoring of subsequent events that deflate the scare, is not rare. It is standard operating procedure in many quarters of journalism, including at the top.

Lately, with most actual events mainly positive, the media have become obsessed with bad things that *might* happen. This shows most colorfully in weather coverage. As data reporting services such as Weather Channel have grown in popularity, networks have begun to send their anchors to areas where hurricanes *might* strike, while local stations devote more and more air time to weather extremes that *might* happen. About a decade ago, the local NBC affiliate in Washington, D.C., during a week of snowstorms changed its weather-report segment logo from "WeatherCenter" to "StormCenter." Now the logo always says "StormCenter." It can be a bright sunny day and the weatherman will stand in front of an ominous insignia that reads "StormCenter."

Western life is methodically made to sound perilous or precarious by media spin, which emphasizes the negative aspects of developments while downplaying the positive. For instance, the initial effect of the advent of genetically engineered crops is a decline in the use of farm chemicals. (Fertilizer use is declining relative to increased production, and pesticide use is declining in absolute terms.) The first generation of "transgene" crops was designed to incorporate into corn, cotton, and other staples the DNA code for a naturally occurring soil bacterium called *Bacil-*

lus thuringiensis, which kills some insects that attack plants. Crops that contain the *Bt* gene require far less spraying than regular crops. Use of pesticide on cotton in the United States has declined by about 400,000 pounds per year since *Bt* cotton strains were introduced, though cotton production has risen during the period. Genetically engineered crops are also better suited for "no-till" farming in which there is less plowing than other forms of agriculture, which reduces erosion dramatically. Media stories about transgene crops could fairly be spun as BREAKTHROUGH REDUCES PESTICIDE USE. They are spun as OH MY GOD!

Here's a related example of distorted coverage. Ever higher farm yields per acre allow fewer acres of land to be tilled each year in the Western world; that is good news, because the steady withdrawal of acres from farm production means more acreage returned to forest or nature preserve. As the forest analyst Roger Sedjo of the nonpartisan think tank Resources for the Future has noted, Connecticut is today 59 percent forest, versus 35 percent in the nineteenth century, though the state's population has tripled and its agricultural production quintupled.[39] Figures for most of the country show comparable simultaneous population growth and forest expansion, made possible by more farm production from fewer acres. Indeed, as Norman Borlaug—America's unknown Nobel Peace Prize winner—has noted, if it were not for ever higher agricultural yields, across the world an area the size of India would have had to be leveled for farmland in the past fifty years, with devastating effects on the global environment.[40] But how is the reduction of agricultural acreage spun in the press? SHOCKING CRISIS OF VANISHING FARMS.

At other times, the media leave out key words to create the impression of an outrage. Staying with our agricultural theme, in August 1999 *The Washington Post* ran an apparently shocking page-one story saying that Pioneer Hi-Bred, the seed conglomerate, had spliced protein DNA from a Brazil nut into soybeans, creating a bean that triggered reactions in children with peanut allergies. "In trying to build a better soybean," the *Post* intoned, "the company had made a potentially deadly one." Yet the story skimmed past the reason Pioneer Hi-Bred had spliced a Brazil-nut protein gene into its product—to improve the nutritional value of soybeans, so that soy-based vegetable oil would cease being empty calories. Equally important, the story skimmed past the fact that it was the company's own researchers who discovered the error, and they promptly destroyed the experimental seeds. Nothing containing the suspect material was ever shipped to farmers, much less made available in stores; the "potentially deadly" product had harmed no one.[41]

The media further create an impression of a country getting worse by obsessive focus on smaller and smaller risks. Brain damage from cell phones, extremely rare allergies, claims of all-new psychological complexes, strange turns of events that affect only tiny numbers of people—increasingly newspaper, television, and news-magazine reports dwell on one-in-a-million risks. Journalists often display little ability to place small risks into perspective. The arsenic-in-drinking-water controversy, for example, involved, according to estimates of the National Research Council, at worst a one-in-three-million cancer risk for the typical American.[42] In recent years, press reports have focused extensively on whether vaccinations in rare cases cause permanent harm to children, but even the worst-case estimate of vaccination-caused harm shows that it is far more dangerous to let child go outside in dark-colored clothing than to have him or her receive an inoculation.[43] And when was the last time you saw a newspaper story about the dangers of dark-colored children's clothing?

AMPLIFIED ANXIETY. Small risks may be perfectly real, and there is no reason society should not try to eliminate them or care about conditions that affect only small numbers of people. Obsession with small risks may itself be a positive sign, telling us that the number of substantial risks is declining, freeing up resources to focus on lesser worries. Obsession with smaller risks may also be seen as a propitious phenomenon of prosperity: Today we have the knowledge necessary to detect small risks, the leisure in which to notice them, and the wherewithal to act against them. But everyone misses the larger-picture point about the press trend toward reporting smaller and smaller risks: that big risks are in decline. Instead of realizing this, we feel under siege from ever rising tides of very small dangers. Overall, the pessimism-promoting effect of the modern media might be called "headline-amplified anxiety."

The journalistic media combine with the entertainment media in one especially pernicious misrepresentation of social trends: exaggerating the amount of crime.

Many local news shows now devote more air time to crime than all other news combined, suggesting that crime is rampant. Some of this power of suggestion arises from the post-CNN reality that word of any crime anywhere is instantly flashed to the entire country, if not the entire world. Studies show, for example, that kidnapping of children by strangers is extremely rare, and such crimes have been in decline for decades.[44] But when a child kidnapping occurs, word is broadcast everywhere and the crime takes over cable and talk television, owing to its heartbreaking nature. This gives viewers the impression that child kidnappings are happening all the time, though they are not. Other awful-but-rare crimes, such as sex murders, are also given so much television play that viewers come away convinced such crimes are common.

Christopher Jencks of Harvard University notes: "When I was growing up there was violence on TV, but it was cowboys having imaginary shootouts. I never worried that rustlers would come over the hill into my neighborhood. Now the violence on television is presented as if it's about to get you personally. No wonder people think the country is out of control." Presenting violence as if it's about to get you personally makes for compelling television, keeping people glued to the tube. But this also engenders a false portrait of society, making us think things are worse than they are.

Studies by George Gerbner, former dean of the Annenberg School for Communication at the University of Pennsylvania, have shown that the more television a person watches, the more likely he or she is to overestimate the prevalence of crime, or to believe that crime is rising even if it is actually in decline.[45] Senior citizens, who watch the most hours of television, are most likely to overestimate crime prevalence, Gerbner's research shows. As Western society both ages and becomes more prosperous, an ever larger group of retirees has the leisure time in which to watch hour after hour of CNN or MSNBC or Fox News, beholding endless images of fires and explosions and yellow police tape and sobbing survivors, until the impression is given that life consists entirely of peril and tragedy. For residents of the United States and the European Union, at least, daily danger is in steady decline. But in a world of six billion people there will always be something burning, blowing up, or surrounded by officers with guns drawn. Now we see each such place on television in unbroken succession, and take away the impression that life has spiraled out of control.

Overestimation of crime is amplified by the fact that 45 percent of crimes reported in the media involve sex or violence, though only 3 percent of all crimes involve sex or violence. Television's sex-and-violence–obsessed approach causes viewers to have highly unrealistic impressions of the risks in their own lives, Jason Ditton, a researcher at the University of Sheffield, in the United Kingdom, has found.[46] American women, for example, as a group believe they are highly likely to be victims of violent crime, though the typical American woman is never involved in a crime, and men are far more likely than women to be violent-crime victims.

The entertainment media—television drama, the movies, songs, video games—further the distortion by their glamorization of crime and violence. Bad enough that, in contemporary culture, movie depictions of helpless people being stalked, tortured, and murdered are classified as "entertainment." Bad enough that the big conglomerates, even Disney's film divisions, eagerly promote cinematic scenes of torture and murder, especially the torture and murder of women.[47] Bad enough that big entertainment corporations titivate violence when numerous studies have shown that the more violent acts a child observes on television or in the movies, the more likely is the child to commit violence after growing up. (Except in rare cases, adults are not made violent by watching video violence, studies show; it is children who are affected, because their minds are malleable.) Leonard Eron, a psychologist at the University of Michigan, has documented the link between television-watching in childhood and crime-commission in adulthood.[48] In 2002 the American Medical Association, the American Psychological Association, the American Academy of Pediatrics, the American Academy of Child and Adolescent Psychiatry, the American Academy of Family Physicians, and the American Psychiatric Association issued a joint study declaring, "Data point overwhelmingly to a causal connection between media violence and aggressive behavior in some children."[49]

Set aside, though, the harm done to children by excessive violence in cinema and on television. From the perspective of understanding whether life is getting better, what matters is that video and cinema violence presents crime as far more common and far more sadistic than it actually is.

Movies depict serial killings and "thrill" murders as everyday events that reveal the horrid truth about a warped society. But actual examples of such homicides are exceptionally rare. Peter Smerick, a retired agent from the FBI's Behavioral Sciences Division, which hunts people who kill for thrill reasons (that is, not during robberies, domestic disputes, or for revenge; almost all murders occur during robberies, domestic disputes, or with a revenge motive), estimates that, in the last quarter-century, the United States has averaged about thirty murders per year that could be characterized as thrill killings.[50] That's plenty awful enough, but represents just 0.2 percent of total murders, and leaves the odds that an American will be the victim of a serial killer at less than the odds of being struck by lightning.

Tote up the death count in each year's Hollywood movies, though, and annually the film industry depicts far more than thirty people as serial or thrill-kill victims. That is to say, thrill-killing happens more in the movies than in real life. We'll skip here what it reveals about the psyches of movie industry executives that they consider it fine to profit from forcing on viewers—often children—scenes of screaming people being slaughtered as a form of fun. The point here is that Hollywood tries to rationalize the glamorization of thrill killing as "realism." It is not in any sense realism; rather, it is vulgarianism in pursuit of money. But the constant presentation in movies and on television of serial killings as everyday events, as if this were realism, is another factor causing people to think that life is getting worse.

Movies and television also vastly exaggerate the killing of police officers. According to the National Law Enforcement Officers Memorial Fund, an average of 154 law-enforcement personnel of all agencies were killed in the line of duty per year in the 1990s. (More die in car crashes than shoot-outs.) The real figure is plenty awful enough, but, if you tote it up, each year many more police officers are depicted as slain in movies and on cop shows than die in real life. Each of the three *Die Hard* movies, box-office hits, depicted dozens of police officers being gunned down; the series finale of the CBS show *Walker, Texas Ranger,* a mainstream program whose target audience was senior citizens, depicted more than twenty police officers murdered. Movies and shows like this suggest that everyday life is a deadly Wild West of shoot-outs, a view that bears no relationship to reality, but may be mistaken for reality by the media-addled.

By a similar token, the tube and the movies misrepresent how often police officers kill in turn. Each of the three *Lethal Weapon* movies, also box-office hits, depicted their protagonist officers as shooting and killing dozens of people, while showing cops casually blazing away left and right. Yet it is exceptionally infrequent for a law-enforcement officer to discharge a weapon. Some 95 percent of New York City police officers, for example, retire without ever firing their guns except on the training range.[51]

This figure is believed to be common for all law-enforcement agencies. In part because it's so rare for police officers to fire their sidearms, the killing of suspects or bystanders by police happens far more in "entertainment" than in real life. New York City's 41,000-person police force shot and killed eleven suspects in 1999, for example.[52] In the movies and on television crime shows, people are gunned down by New York City police willy-nilly.

Beyond their impact in making people think there is more crime, and more sadism, than society actually contains—cautioning, again, that society's actual violence is plenty bad enough—movies and television present a distortedly pessimistic view of Western life in other ways. Disasters lurk around every corner, and not just ridiculous environmental calamities (Kevin Costner's *Waterworld*) or preposterous mega-epidemics (Dustin Hoffman's *Outbreak*). In movies and television, government officials are invariably corrupt megalomaniacs bent on destruction; they possess astonishing, unstoppable power, and to top it off travel exclusively by limousine.[53] Hundreds of movies and television dramas advance this cliché of government—to save space I'll cite just one, the 1998 Will Smith vehicle *Enemy of the State,* in which the CIA director nonchalantly murders a United States senator and then, using astonishingly advanced techno-gizmos that tell him anything about anyone's life, murders anyone who might know about the first murder. Unrealism is evident here both in the plot and the ridiculous exaggeration about how much the CIA, or any government agency, could know. As we learned in the aftermath of September 11, the United States government assuredly does not possess advanced techno-gizmos that can tell anything about anyone's life in seconds.

Nearly all institutions—especially business and religion—are depicted in the movies and on television shows as under the control of sinister, corrupt forces whose secret plan is to mistreat average people. Just how it is that things can be getting better in the real world when, in the video universe, government and industry are run exclusively by evil conspirators, is never explained.

Of course viewers know most movies and television shows are fundamentally preposterous. But by bombarding audiences with exaggerated representations of violence and disaster, by advancing the view that all institutions are crooked and venal, the entertainment industry generates negative propaganda on a colossal scale. Preposterous negative propaganda, to be sure. But negative propaganda nonetheless; and another reason so many think life is getting worse when it is mostly getting better.

Beyond these are factors of human nature itself. One is the possibility that evolution has conditioned us to believe the worst.

The new field of evolutionary psychology has produced evidence not that genes dictate behavior—we are always free to choose—but that certain patterns and attitudes were more likely to be passed down from prehistory than others. Evolutionary psychologists believe, for example, that in prehistory males were likely to want many sex partners because this behavior spread their genes widely at little cost, whereas females were likely to want one committed partner to help raise the offspring who bore the genes. How these sexual proclivities play out today is fairly obvious. What other attitudes might come down to us from prehistory? Perhaps our uneasy and anxious progenitors, the ones who never really relaxed or felt comfortable, were more likely to survive, while our smiling, flower-sniffing forebears got eaten by something. More on this theory in a later chapter; here we need only note that *Homo sapiens* might be predisposed by evolution to focus on the negative.

COMPLAINT PROFICIENCY. In the modern-day context, an evolutionary predisposition toward the negative might translate into always being edgy, stressed, and unsatisfied, even if, objectively, most things in your life are going reasonably well; or always thinking the country was just about to veer over the cliff, even if, objectively, social indicators were propitious. The constant anxiety our ancestors must have felt about predators in the distance may now be transferred to aspects of life that aren't dangerous. Complaining may be a defensive mechanism to prevent complacency, but one whose side effect is making it hard to appreciate the moment.

Similarly, it might be said that the human condition is characterized by "complaint proficiency." Whether through natural selection, God's touch, or simply practice, human beings as a group are really good at complaining. We complain to our parents for bringing us into the world; complain to our teachers for educating us; complain to our bosses for employing us; complain to the merchants who feed and clothe us; complain to the lovers and spouses who embrace us; complain to the children we summon to join us; complain to the Maker for starting the world in which all this happens. About many things, especially injustice, we should complain. But we practice complaining so much, and on such minor issues, that we become too proficient: And then complain more, if only because we are confident we are good at it. Expressing gratitude or appreciation does not come easily to us because we practice it so little.

ABUNDANCE DENIAL. Next, it seems almost a matter of human nature that most people reject the idea they are prosperous. Surveys show that the majority of Americans think only the rich are "well-off," despite the fact that most Americans live quite well compared to more than 99 percent of the human beings who have ever existed. One reason Americans and Europeans deny they are well-off is that this connotes being the beneficiary of favoritism, since through history most of those who were affluent obtained their prosperity via inheritance, a rigged class system, or various forms of larceny, much of the latter disguised as business. We don't want to think of ourselves as in any of these categories—"I got where I am the hard way, no one did me any favors" is a common sentiment—so we reject the idea of being called "well-off."

And until the postwar era, the majority of Americans and Europeans were not prosperous. This means most of us today are descended from men and women who truly were not well-off and who ingrained both in our ways of thinking, and in the culture's way of speaking about itself, the notion that the rich get everything while the average get nothing. Once this was true; it is no longer. Yet we remain conditioned to think this true, a phenomenon that might be called "abundance denial." Our forebears, who worked and sacrificed tirelessly in the hopes their descendants would someday be free, comfortable, healthy, and educated, might be dismayed to observe how acidly we deny we now are these things.

Finally, there is in many people's behavior an element of what might be called "complaint yearning." In some ways we may want a situation to be perceived as bad, because this takes certain kinds of pressure off us. If times are tough, or others are being unfair or unkind, or you've just had some unpleasant news, or you wanted something and didn't get it, or you loved someone and were not loved in turn, or some other source of complaint is in evidence, clearance is given to feel sorry for yourself. When you're feeling sorry for yourself, you don't expect to help others or show them kindness, or to do important things, or even just to stop and smell the flowers. When you've got a grievance against the world, all the pressure is off.

These factors may add up to a social circumstance in which most of life is getting better for most people, and yet hardly anyone acts as if this were so. That is the social circumstance we are in today.

Chapter 4

....

PORTABLE CARPETED

DOG STEPS

In the year 2002 in the United States, it became fashionable for women to show their navels. Midriff-baring outfits were standard throughout the country for teen girls, and even some executive women wore to the office ensembles in which the top didn't quite connect with the skirt or pants. As the midriff became a public matter, some women felt their belly buttons didn't look right; certainly not flawless, like that of pop singer Britney Spears, who started the fad and who seemed to go bare-naveled even during snowstorms. The response? Plastic surgeons began offering a procedure that would make any belly button cute and symmetrical like Britney's. The goal was not health (some navel conditions do require correction for medical reasons) but looks. The cost ran about $5,000, paid by the patient, not insurance.[1] Cosmetic surgeons reported that navel touch-ups were a hot business,[2] partly because the procedure is painless and does not involve two weeks in seclusion waiting for the bruising to subside, often required by face-lifts and rhinoplasties.

While women were pushing the envelope on cosmetic surgical intervention—in addition to standard face-lifts, tucks, and breast augmentations, "Botox" injection for wrinkle-reduction became popular—men were hardly inactive. Procedures for men have been the biggest growth area in plastic surgery for about a decade, with male face-lifts and beer-belly reductions popular. Paralleling breast implantation, men have begun to purchase pectoral implants: silicon embedded along the chest muscles to give a man barrel pecs without hours spent in the gym. The ostensible point of most male cosmetic surgery is to make the patient look younger, though on many men a face-lift is so easily detected the true purpose must be to proclaim that the man can afford it. As a status marker, perhaps either one—either the simulacrum of youth or the broadcasting of possession of sufficient money to buy same—will do.

Perhaps your wants are not self-focused; let's say, focused instead on flora. So many Americans and Europeans love flowers, and have the leisure time and discretionary income in which to breed them, that the number of varieties is beginning to exceed the available supply of names. As Cynthia Crossen has written,[3] there are now in the world at least 100,000 named lily varieties and 14,000 named dahlias, most coming into existence recently.

Week's Roses of Upland, California, a flower-breeding firm, will let you name a new rose variety for $10,000. Most people choose to name the rose after themselves, and the buyers are not necessarily dilettantes but often typical middle-class people who save or even take out loans for the thrill of having a rose in their name, even if their flower must compete with thousands of other signature roses. For $75,000, Jackson & Perkins of Somis, California, another producer of hybrid flowers, will give a new rose variety the name of your choosing, fly you and a companion to

Los Angeles for a weekend that includes a fine dinner with the company's plant-breeders and, once the new hybrid blooms, ship three hundred of them FedEx around the country to anyone you select, so that friends and family will smell the rose that bears your name. More than a hundred Jackson & Perkins rose varieties, named in this way and funded by rose-lovers at the cost of more than $7.5 million, now exist.[4]

Augmented Britney-class navels, simulated barrel chests, $75,000 personal roses—it would be easy to make fun of such things as runaway materialism. But if what you want in life is a perfect midriff or a flower that bears your name, and a physician's office or hybrid-plant laboratory can make your wish come true, why not? You only live once.

To think that in the West today not just a landed elite, but millions of people have the resources to choose to have their bodies surgically altered to seek visual perfection, while the medical profession possesses the knowledge to do such things safely, is stunning when we ponder that it is only necessary to step back three generations to reach the time when for most people anything beyond a routine doctor's visit was a prohibitive expense, and in any event physicians could do nothing about most basic conditions. By the same token, for many centuries only the wealthy possessed the time, resources, and leisure in which to breed and contemplate flowers; today, specialized flowers and bulbs are a multibillion-dollar industry, as millions of people in the United States and Europe produce private gardens with flowers more exquisite than any a king might have strolled past in previous centuries. But to think that we live in a world where millions of people, tens or even hundreds of millions, can indulge themselves so immoderately.

Indeed, though the contemporary acquisition-oriented mode

of Western life exhibits many forms of immoderation that could be ridiculed, in a sense the only unimpeachable objection to materialism is that everyone can't join the merrymaking. In the United States one person in eight lives in poverty, while most of the population suffers some form of money uncertainty. Globally, more than a billion are destitute while another two billion, though reasonably fed and clothed, will never know circumstances like Western suburban life. That everyone cannot have too much is a strong indictment of the Western system. Most other complaints about modern materialism reduce, by comparison, to various forms of covetousness and shouting against the wind.

The catch is that there is no relationship between having a perfect navel or named rose, or grand home or expensive car or any such item, and happiness. A perfect navel makes you look better; a large home allows daily life in comfort; a fine car means you get where you are going; you might look good, live grandly, travel in style, and still feel forlorn. We would be foolish to expect possessions to make us happy, or an economic system to care about our emotional state. All any economic system will ever "care" about is the manufacture and distribution of the maximum volume of goods and services. Western economics attains that goal, but the manufacture and distribution of the maximum volume of goods and services turns out to have comparatively little to do with whether men and women are happy.

As ever more material things become available and fail to make us happy, material abundance may even have the perverse effect of instilling unhappiness—because it will never be possible to have everything that economics can create. Each year the world offers more alluring items to buy and acquire, yet many find being deprived of material items "more cruel than possessing them was sweet, and people were unhappy to lose them without being happy to possess them." A summation of consumer dilemmas from Dr. Phil? Jean-Jacques Rousseau said this in 1754.[5] If you don't have the things of the world you are unhappy, but having the things of the world may do no service to your well-being.

THE REVENGE OF THE PLASTIC. That perhaps as many as five hundred million middle-class or above men and women of the Western world get more all the time and expect the stuff to make them happy may, in itself, explain much of contemporary discontent. If you expect the stuff to make you happy, you are sure to be unhappy. Your American Express card cannot buy you happiness but, paradoxically, it can buy you unhappiness: Call this "the revenge of the plastic." But let's set that aside for a moment to consider the stuff and the way we obtain it.

In case you're thinking of purchasing a wristwatch, the Patek Philippe Calibre 89 costs $2.7 million, as it is not only formed of gold and jewels but contains an internal gyroscope to compensate for tiny distortions in the earth's gravity, producing time readings accurate to the microsecond—which would be useful in case you're thinking of launching a space probe. Sales of the Calibre 89 are infrequent, but there is a waiting list for Patek Philippe models costing $45,000. Rolex watches that sell for around $6,000 are actually mass-marketed, offered in malls, advertised in *Time* and *Newsweek*. Most high-end watches are self-winding, so what to do if you own more than one? More than one means you can't wear each timepiece daily, providing the wrist motion on which a self-winding watch depends. What you do in that event is go to the Asprey & Garrard store on Fifth Avenue in New York City and put down $5,700 for a calfskin box in which six electrically powered wrists slowly rotate, winding your self-winding high-end watches.

Wild spending by the very rich, always a factor or else the world would not contain beautiful old manors and chateaus, in the contemporary era has taken on an almost comic air. In the 1970s, there were believed to be about 200 privately owned yachts longer than 100 feet in the world; today there are at least 5,000. A yacht of this length costs at least $10 million to purchase, plus at least $1 million annually for crew and upkeep. In 2000, one of the founders of the Blockbuster video-rental chain paid $56 million for an entire small island near the Bahamas. Its amenities included a manor home, four houses for guests or staff, powerplant, on-beach fitness center, and desalinization facility. Pop singer Barbara Mandrell in contrast was looking to sell her 27,000-square-foot residence; the property included a helicopter landing pad and handy indoor shooting range. Bill Gates has finally moved into his $53 million, 66,000-square-foot megahome, with three underground parking garages and a reception hallway itself larger than the entire typical American house. In this price-no-object ego indulgence, Gates probably feels lonely.

As spending by the rich is supposed to trickle down to others, the desire for wild spending has trickled down to the huge Western population that is not rich but is well off. At this writing there was a two-year waiting list for the Hermès "Kelly" handbag, which costs $10,000 and is barely distinguishable from far less expensive handbags. Barneys, a New York City department store, was at this writing selling crocodile-skin eyeglass holders for $255 and a $930 designer teapot. Sharper Image was selling a $1,590 robotic dog toy that "produces amazingly realistic movement." Mercedes and Volkswagen were offering cars list-priced at more than $200,000. Several auto manufacturers had begun to offer not just heated seats but chilled seats—air conditioning pipes run through them, so that the seat is cool to the touch in summertime. Ford's Expedition, a luxury SUV, was offering "power running boards." Press a button and servomotors make the running boards descend and swivel outward to form steps, helping passengers ascend into the huge vehicle. That's all well and good, but it's so inconvenient to have to push the button! When will they offer automatic power running boards?

CATALOG-INDUCED ANXIETY. High-end products can sell in numbers because 205,000 American households had incomes exceeding $1 million in 1999, according to the Internal Revenue Service. In the Gilded Era, the number of millionaires (by the income standards of the time) was perhaps a few hundred. Today's society produces so many very-well-off people that millionaires could populate the entire city of Rochester, New York, a remarkable thought.[6] And though, in the past, the typical person could only wonder what it might be like to be an Astor, today anyone can peruse the specifics of millionairehood. Television obsessively documents the lavish lives of the wealthy and glamorous; glossy-stock magazines such as *Architectural Digest* let you into their homes; catalogs for the most expensive things imaginable are readily available to anyone; the floor plan and elevations of Gates's megahome can be downloaded from the Web.

Ready viewing of lifestyle information about the rich creates, for some, a condition that might be called "catalog-induced anxiety." People can see, in agonizing detail, all the things they will never possess. Catalog-induced anxiety, whether from catalogs themselves or from other forms of public exposure of the lives of the rich or celebrated, may make what a typical person possesses seem paltry, even if the person is one of the many tens of millions of Americans and Europeans living well by objective standards and extremely well by the standards of human history.

....

As the desire for wild spending trickles down, ostentation about money becomes ever more common, and not just among surgeons and celebrities. In recent years, suburban communities have begun to suffer not only from the McMansion craze but from "house bloat," the building of huge homes on a block of average-sized houses. "Bloated" homes may come right up to the property setback line to achieve maximum mass; in addition to being a way to burn money, visually they scream "my house is bigger than yours!" Certain buyers find a bloated home on a block of average-sized houses more satisfying than a McMansion on a McMansion block, since the bloated home appears so much bigger than what's around it. Bloated homes often have pillared entrances and similar ostentatious touches. In 2001, Mamaroneck, New York, a bedroom community for Manhattan, enacted a statute limiting to seven thousand square feet the residences that could be built on the half-acre lots beneath the town's housing stock. Seven thousand square feet is three times the interior volume of the typical new American home, which itself is double the volume of the typical home just a generation ago. Builders protested that the Mamaroneck statute was unfair because there was already a backlog of buyers who wanted homes larger than seven thousand square feet. In 2000, *The Wall Street Journal* quoted an official of Toll Brothers, a leading builder of bloated homes, as saying, "We sell what nobody needs."[7]

In 2000, around the peak of the stock-market bubble, builders in the Hamptons, a favorite beach destination of Manhattanites, were offering not some but hundreds of new summer homes priced between $5 million and $8 million.[8] So many homes coming onto the market had maxed out on luxury features that driving the price up farther had become a sort of challenge, with one builder putting $25,000 worth of imported faucets into a single bathroom. Another challenge had arisen to see how much customers could drive up the price of add-ons. As recently as a decade ago, $200,000 was top dollar for a built-in swimming pool with all possible extras. By 2000, *The New York Times* reported, a Hamptons firm called Tortorella Swimming Pools was charging $1.5 million per pool and its order book was so full that the company was turning away business. One and a half million dollars buys a "themed pool"—Atlantis and Stonehenge were popular—with bridges, spa grottos, and theatrical lighting effects. The buyers are not movie stars or Hugh Hefner, rather doctors and lawyers and investment bankers desperate to find a way to burn money.

Though the supply of oversized homes may be increasing, especially in the United States, to object to this is different from objecting to the fact that the supply of all real properties—all homes, stores, offices, schools, and parking lots—must also increase. The former may or may not be good; the latter is simply a necessity, owing to population growth. Ever more homes, stores, offices, schools, and parking lots is widely denounced as sprawl. But sprawl is caused by affluence and population growth, and which of these, precisely, should we ban? The Census Bureau projects that the United States population will increase by nearly another 50 percent, from the current 286 million to about 400 million, before stabilizing beginning around the year 2050.[9] If 50 percent more Americans are on the way, that means there must be 50 percent more suburban subdivisions, 50 percent more malls, 50 percent more of everything—unless anyone thinks it is fair to deny to newcomers the physical space and comfort that current Americans enjoy.

Sprawl may be managed well or poorly, and "smart growth" is better than dumb growth. But when people object to development per se, what they almost always mean is that they have achieved a nice lifestyle and now wish to pull up the ladders against others—and, not coincidentally, to make their own properties more valuable by artificially limiting supply. California real estate prices in particular have shot up in the last decade because slow-growth ordinances and no-growth judicial rulings have artificially restricted housing supply. Opposing sprawl can be a financial boon to anyone who's already entrenched.

Anything that runs up housing prices is of particular concern to educational equality, since today, in many parts of the United States, the housing market in effect regulates access to the best public schools. Buyers pay significant premiums for homes in the districts of high-quality public schools; in the Washington, D.C., suburbs, a home in the excellent Fairfax County or Montgomery County school systems may sell for $200,000 more than an identical dwelling from which children would attend the troubled schools of Prince George's County or Arlington County. In turn, SAT scores rise in tandem with family income—each $10,000 increment of increase in family income adds twenty to thirty points to a child's total SAT scores, studies show.[10] Why does family income raise SAT scores? Partly because a high income enables parents to give children extra advantages, partly because low-income parents or parents in broken families may shirk their responsibility for helping children succeed in school, but mostly because the higher a family's income the better a school district it can buy into, via the housing market. Since education is closely linked to success in later life, the nation has an interest in preventing exclusionary housing prices. That means there must be more sprawl and more growth to increase the housing supply and thereby reduce prices.

<hr />

Returning to the topic of excess, someone who can afford a $1.5-million themed swimming pool or a $25,000 faucet had better be giving money away to those in need. Many who indulge in excess do also give money away. Rates of charitable giving are much higher in the United States than in other Western nations, the average American giving $953 to charity in 2002, versus $15 on average in Japan. An average American annual charitable gift of $953 means that many at the top give away significant amounts, since many at the bottom cannot afford to make donations.[11] But judged by buying habits, Americans could give away much more still, since the desire to possess money-burning products has trickled down from the very rich to the merely well-off to practically everyone.

Recently, for example, the Whirlpool appliance company began to offer a washer-dryer set called Duet with a high-fashion stainless-steel appearance and the ability to handle twenty-two bath towels in a single load. Priced at $2,200, Duet was expected by the company to be a niche product for high-end homes, since excellent washer-dryer combinations are available for $1,000. Yet Duet became one of Whirlpool's best sellers, moving in large numbers to typical, middle-class buyers. The machines had the visual appeal of Sub-Zero refrigerators, which are also furnished in stainless steel and have been a middle-class hit despite costing

$5,000, versus $1,500 for top-quality conventional refrigerators.

The Weyerhaeuser lumber company has begun to offer, for home buyers, a joist-and-beam system that promises a "silent floor"—those on the ground level of a house won't hear anyone walking around on the second level. Weyerhaeuser said it had developed the silent joist, which it hoped new-home buyers would specify from builders, "after nearly a decade of researching how people feel about floor performance." Not just whether the floor looks okay and holds together; how people feel about their floors. The product's advertising, targeted to architectural and women's magazines, asserted that if you were the sort of person who cared about having a Sub-Zero refrigerator, isn't it time you cared about the brand of your floor? This may seem archetypical creation-of-demand, though for all anyone can guess today, at some future point it may be considered incredibly gauche to be able to hear footsteps through the floor in someone's home.

For all that can be guessed today, at some future point there may be multiple brands of floor-hushing products, each with slightly different properties, driving buyers to distraction. Barry Schwartz, a professor of psychology at Swarthmore College, has argued that Western consumers "are overwhelmed with relatively trivial choices," such as, when purchasing blue jeans, whether to select slim fit or regular fit or baggy fit or regular fly or button fly or acid washed or stone washed or unwashed or low-rise.

Economic theory says the marketplace benefits from increased choice: If consumers can decide from among a hundred breakfast cereals, or dozens of types of cell phones, they can find the optimal product. But the modern tyranny of choice, Schwartz contends, causes in consumers an unending sense of regret.[12] No matter how carefully one compares products, a buyer can never be sure that he or she chose the right thing, and so buyers experience anxiety before purchases, disappointment after. We'd actually be better off, Schwartz thinks, if the array of possible purchases were smaller. We would spend less time agonizing about what to buy.

Modern stores and catalogs offer aisle after aisle and page after page of stuff we don't need. It is true there are times when a consumer item initially seems profligate but later, after the price drops, seems sensible. Initially miniature portable phones were a pricey frill, and today society is better off because so many people carry phones in their pockets. There were about eleven million mobile phones in the world in 1990, and the total rose to a billion in just a dozen years, by 2003; by the time this book is published, it is expected there will be more cell phones in the world than conventional "land-line" telephone lines. Yet much as the occasional luxury ends up becoming an essential, a huge proportion of what's for sale today truly is a monument to that which is unnecessary.

One Christmas catalog that arrived in my mailbox in 2001 included such necessities as:

> Heated bubble-bath massager, $129.95
> Electric cigar-tip cutter, $49.95
> Radio-controlled "factory authorized"
>   VW Beetle toy car, $139.95
> Microwave flower press, $29.95
> "High-performance" earmuffs, $24.95
> Insect vacuum, $59.95
> "Personal" shredder, $39.95
> Travel shredder, $29.95

Perhaps the microwave flower press was a dud item, but a better guess is that it was advertised because consumers are buying. "Personal" shredders, for example, have sold well at Kmart and other mass-retail outlets. The advent of the personal shredder—don't leave home without your travel model—may reflect rising paranoia about government and neighbors, or a desire to feel important by inference: "I've got to shred my papers to keep them from falling into the wrong hands!" Perhaps the sale of these devices means Americans and Europeans are writing far more first drafts of love poems, or coded messages to foreign intelligence services, than anyone would have guessed. Whatever the reason, ever more homes have not just TVs, ACs, PCs, PDAs, VCRs, and DVDs, but also shredders.

What has come to be called "wealth porn"—teenagers riding limousines to a catered sweet-sixteen party at an expensive hotel, for example—is based on the having, and exhibiting, of that which is not needed. The whole point of "wealth porn" is to make known that you've got so much money you can spend it heedlessly or even wastefully. Wealth-porn thinking has always existed among the rich, but through the postwar era in the West had trickled down toward the middle class.

That which is unneeded comes in both expensive and affordable forms. Tuna is now available in vacuum-packed pouches, advertised as saving the time required to drain off the water. Which takes, what, thirty seconds? "Individually sliced" peanut butter is now sold in American supermarkets; it saves the time required to spread the product on bread, then wipe the knife. The freezer case offers premade macaroni and cheese, so you don't have to do the three steps required to make one of the simplest dishes ever, along with ready-made microwavable p-b-and-j sandwiches, presumably so you don't have to exhaust yourself unwrapping an individual slice of peanut butter.

In tandem, products offer more features than anyone really needs. Recently, I bought a Kenmore dishwasher; it works well but has sixteen switch settings and fourteen monitor lights. Electronic devices related to music, movies, or entertainment have become so phenomenally complex as to cause an attenuated stress in anyone inspecting the owner's manuals, though nearly all the utility of such products is derived from the two buttons "play" and "stop." New BMWs have a bizarre joystick controller and video-screen system that is said to allow drivers to select among seven hundred possible settings of car controls. To use the device, you must pull off the road and park, as merely setting a preferred radio station can require several minutes of intense study of menus and options.

Then there are the products that represent answers to questions no one asked. One catalog that landed at my doorstep this year offered, for $89.99, a gizmo that lets you know if you have an incoming voice call on a line being used to browse the Web. "How many important calls do you miss while you're surfing the Internet?" the blurb asked. None, probably, but since the device exists and can be acquired, some people will want it. Call-waiting features have proven popular, though their principal effect is to allow you to be rude to two callers simultaneously— rude to the person you put on hold to check the waiting call, implying you care more about an anonymous caller than about the person you are already speaking to, and rude to the person whose call you pick up only to say, "I'm on another call." But millions of people have signed up for call-waiting services, because they are possible to buy.

Another catalog offered me, for $99.95, a set of portable dog steps—small risers to be put next to the couch so that Fido can walk up onto the cushions, rather than exert himself by jumping. For $139.95, carpeted portable dog steps were available.

There may be cases in which senior citizens or the lonely can be excused for lavishing money on pets. But the thought that a dog needs not just special steps but carpeted portable steps to get up on the couch, and that people in the United States actually buy such things when the funds expended could in the literal sense save human lives in the developing world, ought to stun us today just as much as we consider it stunning in retrospect that the royalty of medieval Europe lavished unlimited amounts on gilt tables or silk drapes while even a small diversion of monies could in the literal sense have saved human life among the huge class of the destitute.

THE BLURRING OF NEEDS AND WANTS. Because there will always be something you don't have, the ever greater profusion of goods for sale in the Western world tends to place many people in a blurred state of perpetual restlessness regarding possessions. Stuff becomes desired for the brief pleasurable moment of the acquisition; being handed some glistening object in a shopping bag has become to the modern ethos a short sumptuous thrill akin to the kiss at the end of a date, but more reliably attained. The distinction between needs and wants is lost. Financial planners who help people struggling with credit card debts, as many millions of Americans must, report that clients frequently say, "I need a new suit" or "I need this necklace" or "I need a satellite dish." What they really mean is that they want these things. But as George Will has written, a need "is defined, in contemporary America, as a 48-hour-old want." The result is a "blurring of needs and wants," which leads to a "tyranny of the unnecessary."

Almost every man and woman of history ordered life around needs, and usually this meant hard, meager existence. Today there are hundreds of millions of people in the West who rarely lack for anything in the urgent food-and-medicine sense. Their thoughts turn to wants.

Once focused on wants our thoughts can never be at peace, because wants can never be satisfied; not even a billionaire will ever have everything. Wants, by definition, are impossible to satisfy, though you may placate them now and then. Seeking to placate the pang of want through acquisition can become like habituation to a drug—you need to keep buying more and more to get the same high, and the high wears off faster all the time.

Want tends to fixate not on the improbable—alone on a desert island with a beautiful woman or handsome man—but on more, or slightly better, of what is already possessed. Consider the television set. At this point even purists should give in and accept that every household ought to have a television. But it doesn't; in the United States today, the typical household has three televisions, while five is hardly uncommon.[13] A generation ago, for a child to have a television in his or her bedroom was viewed as almost risqué; 6 percent of American children had televisions in their bedrooms in 1970. Today, according to a survey by the Henry Kaiser Foundation, 65 percent of Americans under the age of eighteen have sets in their bedrooms,[14] meaning the typical American child has his or her own television. Not only does this profusion of televisions ensure children will spend too much of their precious childhoods having their minds turned to oatmeal by the tube; it represents the assumption that if one of something is good, as it often is, then many of the same thing must be better.

THE TYRANNY OF THE UNNECESSARY. On this assumption, Americans purchase not one VCR or CD player but several, falling victim to the latest-model syndrome, that each year the latest model of a consumer good must be obtained in order to have the latest feature. Buying another of what you already possess is considered a routine act, resulting among other things in "ten-hammer syndrome." You know you've got a hammer somewhere amidst all the piles of stuff, but rather than search for it you run out and buy another; pretty soon, you own ten hammers. A presumption arises that it isn't enough for a household to possess a car or DVD player; each individual must own at least one of every item that consumer culture considers important. So each child in the family has his or her own boom box, say, rather than the family owning one and working out reasonable sharing. Most of the time, all the boom boxes or DVD players are idle; they are never all running at once.

Builders report that even with the average square footage of new American homes having doubled from a generation ago, while the average number of people in the household has fallen, a leading complaint of home buyers is that there is not enough space for their possessions. Wardrobes, attics, basements, and garages become crammed with stuff so quickly that boxes end up stacked in the halls. The vans used by airport rent-a-car agencies have been redesigned in recent years to leave as much space for stuff as people, since it is now common to drag three or four enormous suitcases even on short trips. The clean, safe, efficient Metro subway system of the Washington, D.C., area, aboard which I commute to my downtown office, has in recent years begun to suffer a crowded-doors problem because an ever higher percentage of riders drag behind them suitcases on wheels—not because they are leaving from the office for a trip, I suspect, but in most cases because people have come to feel they just can't go anywhere without various forms of stuff, so the solution is to drag a valise. Automobile "aftermarket" companies now sell storage capsules designed for the tops of station wagons and SUVs—the capsules are those aerodynamically sleek roof-top boxes that resemble the photon torpedoes in *Star Trek* movies. Americans have such cargo shells mounted atop cars not for summer vacations but permanent use, because even a three-ton SUV doesn't have enough room for their stuff.

At some level it's nice that Western society creates so much prosperity that everyone can own his or her own computer and a dozen similar items. But selfishness or at least self-centeredness almost inevitably arises once it is assumed that it is not enough for everyone to have access to a car or a DVD deck; everyone must own their own example of each. Status anxieties go hand-in-hand with the assumption that everyone must have at least one of everything, or obtain whatever is in fashion.

Writing in the eighteenth century, at a time when linen had just become generally available and linen clothes were the rage, Adam Smith noted that while no one needs a linen shirt in order to be protected from the elements—many fabrics will suffice for that—people do need linen shirts if they would feel ashamed walking in public dressed in a manner that caused others to look down on them. The equivalent, today, is that while no teenager actually needs a shirt from Old Navy—or whatever clothing chain is in fashion on the day this book is published—teenagers do in fact need such items if they would feel self-conscious or be teased for failing to wear what is approved by their peer group. Writ small, this problem can make the poor and working-class, especially poor and working-class children, feel bad about themselves in a society where it seems everyone has unlimited everything. Writ large, a person's sense that he or she *must* have ever more possessions, because others expect him or her to have ever more possessions, can make Americans and Europeans feel discontent even as they become more materially comfortable.

CALL-AND-RAISE-THE-JONESES. This goes beyond the traditional keeping-up-with-the-Joneses to a new phenomenon that might be dubbed "call and raise the Joneses." In call-and-raise-the-Joneses, Americans feel compelled not just to match the material possessions of others, but to stay ahead. Bloated houses, for one, arise from a desire to call-and-raise-the-Joneses—surely not from a belief that a seven-thousand-square-foot house that comes right up against the property setback line would be an ideal place in which to dwell.

To call-and-raise-the-Joneses, Americans increasingly take on foolish levels of debt. In addition to mortgages, auto loans, general bank notes, and loans for appliance purchases, American households today average $5,800 in outstanding credit-card debt. (Americans also have the lowest savings rate in the Western world.) Credit-card debt is the easiest sort of loan to obtain, but also the costliest. At a 2001 average of 18.3 percent interest, the typical credit-card debtor that year paid nearly $1,000 in carrying charges, a significant fraction of the typical American's after-tax income.[15] There is no way to determine this scientifically, but a reasonable guess would be that perhaps half of the typical credit-card debtor's arrears is for purchases he or she could have lived without.

Easy debt is not without benefits. Borrowing allows people to live in the future by having now that which they would otherwise not be able to acquire till later in life; a young family should have its washer-dryer now, not years in the future. Surely the

American philosophy of relatively easy access to home mortgages, pursued by federal policy for three generations, has been a boon both to the average standard of living and to social stability. Easy debt also helps sustain consumers during an economic downturn. And for the responsible poor or working-class person, credit can be one of the doors to a decent life.

But the pitfalls are obvious. Many people can't resist the temptation to sign a piece of paper and immediately possess whatever shiny bauble they have just glimpsed; to bring home the new car or jewelry or stereo they really can't afford, to stay at the hotel or eat at the restaurant they should instead drive past. The impulse lasts but a moment while the debt lingers for years, gradually becoming crushing as other impulse liabilities are added. Finance companies mail unsolicited credit offers to people who may not fully understand the terms, or issue cards to those with poor credit histories or with incomes that cannot support their spending habits. (In economic terms, the high finance charges on cards designed for people with poor credit histories compensate the issuing companies for their risk; but this too readily becomes a business based on giving whisky to alcoholics and then selling them recovery services.) At this writing, with home equity levels rising for many Americans owing to a strong real estate market, the latest wrinkle in pushing easy debt is home-equity lines of credit that can be accessed in seconds using ATM cards. That tennis bracelet, that jet ski—just swipe the home-equity card through the ATM and it's yours! Much long-term unhappiness is likely to come from this short-term convenience.

Perhaps the most telling point about the snare of debt is found in the work of the Boston College economics professor Juliet Schor. Overspending, she notes, leads not only to harassing calls from collection agencies but to constant low-grade nervousness. If Americans and Europeans saved more and spent less, Schor supposes,[16] our material circumstances might diminish somewhat, but our psychological and emotional circumstances would improve to an equal degree. Stress about debt would decline, as would fears of getting through the week financially; having a little savings to fall back on would make people feel more secure and less vulnerable. Many people who have trouble resisting excess spending are spending because they believe it will make them happy. What might really make you happy, Schor thinks, is spending less—you would be buying a reduction of financial worry.

The logical end result of a consumer culture addicted to acquiring ever more merchandise is the emergence of products designed to store other products. This very thing began to happen in the United States around 1990, when shelving, "shelf systems," storage products, storage centers, and what economic data calls "closets and containers" became growth industries.

Ikea, Home Depot, and similar retailers now present entire departments of storage supplies. An entire chain, The Container Store, is now dedicated to helping consumers manage the excess of their purchasing. Under-bed storage drawers have become popular; why waste that space beneath the mattress when it could be crammed with stuff? Storage gimmicks sell. A recent catalog of Improvements, a company that markets handy around-the-home paraphernalia, offered an $89.95 rack that mounts atop televisions; the banner proclaimed, "Now you can store things on top of the TV, too!" Presumably that way you could simultaneously look at television commercials and the available rack space atop the television and think how nice it would be to buy whatever was being promoted in the ad and place the item onto the rack.

California Closets, an upscale chain, sells both prefab and custom-installed possession-maximizing closets that cost up to $30,000—that's just for the closet, not what you put in it. The average contract at California Closets is for a $2,000 purchase. The chain's Web site, done in tasteful earth tones with fashion photography of young professional men and women, tastefully asks, "Where do you put the stuff that you're about?" In this worldview, your stuff does not exist to serve you; rather, you are "about" your stuff. A company called Poliform specializes in closets for those for whom California Closet would seem too downscale, having built specialty closets, a company press release asserts, to hold "300 ties" or "several dozen golf shoes."[17]

Owing to profusion of that which is unneeded, how-to books such as *Let Go of Clutter* and the best-seller *Clear Your Clutter with Feng Shui* promise better sleep and even better sex to people who screw up the courage to toss excess into the trash. A profession of assistants has come into being for this purpose, giving "organizer" new meaning as a career path. An organizer is no longer someone who ventures to a mine or factory to urge workers to form a union, but someone hired by the hour to enter a home and assault the stuff. The National Association of Professional Organizers, based in Norcross, Georgia, boasts 1,500 members; it offers a certification program and says that its member professionals can "create a newfound freedom and sense of being in control" for clients by bringing their possessions to heel.

The new profession even has a media star, Julia Morgenstern, who bills herself as "America's number-one organizing expert" and often appears on *Oprah*. Usually, Oprah dispatches Morgenstern to the cluttered home of a viewer, where America's number-one organizing expert is filmed revealing her incredible insider secret—she marches through the halls throwing stuff into green garbage bags, which she then takes to the curb and leaves for the trash collector. And it's not necessarily a well-to-do person's home to which she is sent. Morgenstern marches through dwellings of typical middle-class people, even of homes of the working class, and finds the halls impassable from the accumulation of boxes of products and clothes: Often, she finds there's no place to sit because stuff is stacked on every chair, couch, and other surface area.

Perhaps people who own eight sets of golf clubs or fifty housecoats do need someone's services to help them dispatch encumbrances. Many contemporary men and women in the United States and European Union have fallen into the trap of emotionally driven consumerism, in which shopping bags from the right department stores and other stacks of merchandise take on the roles that connections to fellow human beings should play; some people become more emotional on seeing their excess possessions thrown out than they do regarding friends or family. But as Caitlin Flanagan has written, often "the real purpose of cleaning the closets is to make room for more stuff."[18] Midmorning television shows and popular magazines such as *Real Simple* preach that "simplifying" one's life by discarding excess leads to psychological balance, and this certainly sounds appealing. But, Flanagan notes, the same shows and magazines describe in euphoric terms the shopping spree a person goes on the week after emptying years of detritus from the closets and garage. *Real Simple* bulges with advertising for expensive extravagances that visually suggest a temperate life and a less-stressful age but are either totally unneeded—antique wrought-iron doorstoppers, to cite one—or beyond the means of most of the world's population. One article advised readers to "simplify" their wine racks by purchasing only expensive vintages.

Of course, it is standard to denounce materialism in others while lusting for it ourselves. At the end of the 1990s, Hillary Rodham Clinton decried "a consumer-driven culture that promotes values that undermine democracy" and blasted "materialism that undermines our spiritual centers." Shortly thereafter, she bought a $1.7 million home and signed an $8 million book contract. As the novelist Daniel Akst has noted, Rodham Clinton thus joined the long line of commentators "bent on saving the rest of us from the horrors of consumption" while taking care to make themselves rich and comfy.

The line Clinton joined is long. In 1897, the great writer Edith Wharton published a book, *The Decoration of Houses,* arguing that people should live modestly, without pretense or shows of money. At the time, Wharton, one of America's first literary celebrities, herself lived in a thirty-five-room mansion called The Mount, where she was attended by ten full-time servants. Many figures in philosophy, religion, politics, and other fields have recommended that others pay no heed to material concerns, while being obsessed with the same things themselves. For example, the nineteenth-century philosopher Arthur Schopenhauer, who advised people to renounce their desires for popularity or status, nevertheless suffered intense, almost debilitating fits of depression over the fact that Hegel's public lectures drew larger crowds than his.[19]

In a way, denouncing the material desires of others while avidly pursuing acquisition for yourself is a rational strategy: If others actually do seek less, then by the rules of supply and demand, prices of the material things for which you are grasping will decline. Denouncing materialism by others while being desirous of worldly goods yourself may also, simply, be the public face versus the private thirst.[20] As James Twitchell, a professor at the University of Florida, has written, "No one ever rises to the defense of materialism" because to say that you covet worldly things is considered poor taste.[21] Yet almost everyone practices acquisitiveness in his or her own life. A small percentage of people genuinely do not care about what they accumulate, emphasizing the spiritual. But in the United States and European Union, this faction is a clear minority, while often those who call themselves spiritual or religious are the most voracious, insatiable acquirers.

Though the only indisputable objection to the acquisitive Western lifestyle is that everyone cannot sample it, there are nevertheless many reasons to dislike contemporary free-market materialism.

One is that the Western lifestyle backfires on its practitioners physically, mainly through overconsumption of food. This subject is worth considering briefly because although too much food is low on the list of worries that a person ought to have in life, and minor indeed compared to the problems of half the earth's population, overeating may be indicative of excessive material focus in general.

Though public-health outcomes have improved steadily throughout the postwar era, Americans would be healthier still

were it not for intemperance regarding calories. Today an estimated 280,000 Americans die prematurely of obesity and its
complications each year: the second-worst preventable cause of
death after lung cancer from smoking, and dozens of times more
than the worst-case fatalities toll from environmental exposure
to toxins and similar issues over which Americans obsess.[22]
Today the *typical* American is overweight, according to the Centers for Disease Control, with two-thirds of Americans exceeding the recommended "body-mass index" for their height. A
third of Americans are now obese, versus 12 percent in 1960,
and the figure continues to rise each year.[23] The greatest rate of
increase in being overweight, according to a study published in
the *Journal of the American Medical Association*,[24] is among the
young, signaling more obese adults on the way. And there's no
herald of change in this trend—both genders, all age groups, and
all ethnic groups are getting heavier at a bracing clip.

The relationship between weight and premature mortality is
not clear-cut. Some research indicates that absence of exertion,
rather than presence of pounds, is the real malefactor. In this
view, if a person is heavy owing to a sedentary lifestyle, the lack
of exercise, not the weight itself, causes harm, by failing to keep
the cardiovascular system fit. Regular brisk walking has been
shown to be almost as good as jogging or other strenuous exercise when it comes to reducing long-term risk of heart attacks.[25]
If a person is heavy but regularly participates in vigorous
activity—equal to brisk walking of at least half an hour each
day—weight becomes less of a concern.[26]

But weight and lack of exertion go hand-in-hand. Today citizens of the United States live in a society that lionizes the one
person in a thousand who can run a marathon but otherwise
seems devoted to eliminating physical activity altogether. People

will drive a few blocks—even a single block—rather than walk. Neighbors drive to each other's houses on the same street. When shopping, people drive from one part of a mall parking lot to another. Schools don't hold recess but do allow candy machines in the cafeteria. People prefer elevators to escalators because escalators involve minimal effort. Whole suburban subdivisions are designed without sidewalks, rendering it unsafe to walk; and visually suggesting that anyone who actually wants to walk is out of his or her mind.

Ninety-nine percent of the human beings of history walked everywhere and engaged in constant exertion; they would have wished for their descendants a world of riding and watching rather than walking and doing. Now Americans and Europeans exist in that world, and at some psychological level, may feel they are obligated to live as a class of those who sit comfortably while some machine performs all exertions: to show that our lineage has won history's contest against physical effort. But restructuring society so that the typical person participates in moderate activity each day would be in everyone's medical interest.

Otherwise the abundance of affordable, delicious food is the obvious root cause of the Western weight problem, and you can hardly recommend that food be made scarce or overpriced as a palliative. Nor can you campaign against food, both a necessity and one of life's pleasures. It is fair and wise to say to the young, "Don't smoke and don't do drugs." One can hardly tell teenagers, "Don't eat."

The manner in which Americans—and, increasingly, others around the world—eat is disturbing, as the focus is ever larger portions of high-fat, high-sugared foods. Per-capita American sugar consumption is today 2.5 times what it was in 1961, with

Americans consuming an average 686 calories of sugar per day, according to the nonpartisan Worldwatch Institute.[27] That equals three candy bars per American daily, and a third of the recommended 2,200-calorie daily intake for the typical person snarfed as sugar alone. A "supersized" serving of McDonald's fries now contains about six hundred calories, mostly from fat. As the science writer Shannon Brownlee has pointed out, today's "medium" McDonald's fries contains more fries and more calories than the chain's "large" serving of thirty years ago.[28] A supersized McDonald's meal of a double Quarter Pounder, mammoth fries, and enormous sugared drink can contain as many calories as the entire recommended daily intake for the typical person.

Supersizing, a dubious McDonald's idea, has spread to many aspects of food marketing. The hard-to-lift sixty-four-ounce Double Gulp fountain soda now sold by the 7-Eleven chain—and having many imitators—contains about six hundred calories, like slurping several candy bars through a straw. Since a Double Gulp costs just thirty-five cents more than the sixteen-ounce Gulp, who can resist four times as much for so little extra? Soda, being sugared water, is sufficiently inexpensive to produce that 7-Eleven can come out ahead by selling customers four times as much for thirty-five cents more; the added 450 calories are another matter. McDonald's supersizing and similar instances of relatively low prices for big increases in portion size make financial sense for food companies because what is being added to the portion is just more fat and sugar, two of the cheapest commodities in existence. McDonald's must make a significant investment to build and staff a restaurant. But the marginal cost of doubling the size of your fries is only a penny or two; if you're willing to pay thirty cents to have the portion doubled,

McDonald's comes out ahead. The added hundreds of empty calories are another matter.

Restaurants now commonly advertise "huge" portions, and often serve high-fat, high-sugared fare. Most restaurant food is higher in fat than home-cooked meals, as cooks liberally add oils and butter to ensure that patrons depart with a feeling of satisfaction. At this writing, a popular new restaurant chain, Chipotle, was running an advertising campaign based on touting its outsized portions. One ad showed a Chipotle lunch and declared, "If we charged by the ounce you'd be broke." Another showed an enormous Chipotle burrito and cautioned, "So big it has to beep when it backs up."

But while abundant, tasty, low-cost, who-could-resist-it food is at the root of the growing heft of the West, and of Asian and other nations adopting the Western diet, some of the problem stems from flaws in our life structures and economy. The sense of always being rushed makes us want fast food, with its bottom-of-the-scale nutritional quality. (McDonald's says in its defense that what customers want is junk, and the company is right; buyers, not sellers, ultimately are to blame for most bad eating habits.) Prosperity allows us to eat out more, where the food is likely to be higher in fat than a home-cooked meal. An automobile-based lifestyle means we do ever less of the most basic and reliable form of exercise, walking, thus sending calories straight to storage. Driving to a restaurant for a high-fat fast-food meal and then driving home without an after-meal stroll—the worst of both worlds!

A milestone of the consumer-excess lifestyle was first recorded in France, where, during the 1920s, riding passed walking as the most common mode of travel. A century ago, Americans averaged three walking miles per day, and today average about a quarter-mile.[29]

Kids walk and bicycle less and less, thereby accumulating more and more girth, because modern car-focused suburban design makes it impractical or even dangerous to walk or bike to friends' houses or playgrounds. In Bethesda, Maryland, the pleasant car-focused suburb where I live, the local swimming pool is a mere half-mile away, but I won't let the kids walk or bike because they must cross a street where SUVs barrel at fifty MPH in a thirty-five-MPH zone, drivers clutching cell phones; even entering a pedestrian crosswalk on this road can be terrifying, as drivers make right-on-red turns without glancing or slowing down.[30] Between speeding SUVs and the lack of sidewalks, parents feel they can't tell children, "Just go out and play." Either parents arrange elaborately booked "play dates," at which a parent must drive each way, or they give up and let the kids park in front of the television or video games, resulting in the dreary facts that from an early age about one-third of modern American children engage in no regular physical activity,[31] while American children between the ages of six and eleven watch an average of four hours of television daily.

Going everywhere in cars not only detracts from normal maintenance of health, it detracts from human interaction with others, from awareness of nature and of the seasons. Consider that people move to California in part because of the state's beauty and spectacular climate. Yet Californians on average spend only 5 percent of their time outdoors, versus 7 percent in "enclosed transit" and 88 percent indoors.[32] More time inside the car than outdoors—and surely most of that time with the windows rolled up—in California!

....

Americans, and increasingly Europeans and the Japanese, eat too much, shop too much, own too much, covet too much, watch too much television, spend too much of their precious lives in too-large cars. These are failings of the Western system, but shortcomings rather than fatal flaws. Better people have too much rather than too little; better they be spoiled than deprived. Though the Western system falls far short of ideal, no rational individual would choose the lot of the average person in the developing world, the Arab nations, China, or the former Soviet republics over the average person's circumstances in the West.

If too much of everything is not necessarily a fatal flaw of the Western system, is top-heavy wealth the inexcusable fault?

Existence of extreme wealth in the egalitarian, democratic societies of the United States and European Union might well give pause. The *Forbes 400,* the register of America's richest individuals, now is nearly two-thirds billionaires; the top three people on that list have greater net worth than the forty-eight poorest nations of the world combined.[33] Those 205,000 American millionaires may be a testament to an open, vibrant system that rewards hard work and creativity, but at least some of this group are rich not through any effort of their own but rather inheritance (about a third of the *Forbes 400* are rolling in dough only because they chose their parents wisely) and some of the rich have not created anything or contributed to society,[34] merely dedicated themselves single-mindedly to taking money away from others.

The 250 or so billionaires and 205,000 millionaires means America hosts a huge cohort of people who have more money than anyone needs, indeed more money than even may be good for the people holding it, when every night large numbers of Americans go to bed crying from desperation over lack of small sums of money.

There is no need to fear unequal money outcomes in and of themselves: Within reason, society is served by unequal outcomes. Physicians should earn more than cab drivers; managers of businesses should earn more than mail clerks. You would not want to live in a society where physicians and cab drivers earned the same—particularly, you would not want to get sick in such a society. Those societies in which physicians and cab drivers did make the same, such as the Soviet Union or Maoist China, were horrible places for typical people. That having everyone earn the same has been tried in the postwar era, and caused a spectacular fiasco, is hardly just a small drawback of pure-equality theory.

Perhaps pure equality will work in some future order; surely it is imaginable that there will be a future reconceptualizing of society in which democratic equality can be achieved at a high income level, as opposed to the communist goal of making everyone equally miserable. We'd be foolish indeed to think capitalism, with all its avarice, materialism, insecurity, and lonely striving, is the best possible ordering of society. Capitalism is merely the best ordering of society possible today; to paraphrase Churchill, the worst economic system except for all other systems. Today market democracy passes the utilitarian test of producing the greatest good for the greatest number. But that's today.

Some superior future system may await, especially if technology makes possible unlimited production, and in a future light, contemporary economics may seem little more than a transitional system. The 1990s notion, advanced first by Francis Fukuyama, that history had "ended" with market democracy both the winner and the best possible social system[35] seems short-sighted in this regard. Market democracy was the winner of the twentieth century, and what a relief it won. But you've got a restricted view of the human prospect if you think market economics, with all its anxiety and callous treatment of the untalented or unlucky, is really the best men and women can ever do.

Any free-market system inevitably will have unequal results because individuals have unequal talents, exert unequal effort, and experience unequal luck. "Some degree of inequality will arise even in perfectly fair economic systems," the psychologist Stephen Pinker, of the Massachusetts Institute of Technology, has written.[36] As the social commentator Jackson Lears has shown, luck is often more of a factor in unequal outcomes than economic textbooks care to admit.[37] We shouldn't fear this because luck is simply part of life, but should acknowledge this means that those who experience good luck acquire significant obligations to those who do not.

Today's market system to an extent even depends on unequal results. Unequal pay for physicians attracts talented, hardworking people to medical school; this is in the interest of the sick. And if going to work didn't pay better than going to the beach, society's labor would not get done. That one product is worth more than another, or one use of time pays better than another, is the "signal" market systems rely on to allocate resources. Though this signal is far from perfect, it has proven superior to any other resource-allocation system; especially, vastly superior for the average person.

On the point of whether unequal outcomes can serve typical

people, it is important to recognize a concept that economists call "Pareto Efficiency," named for a nineteenth-century Italian theorist, Vilfredo Pareto.[38] Pareto's main contention was that social welfare is improved by any transaction that makes at least one person better off and no one worse off. (When economists say "welfare," they mean the condition of society overall, not public-assistance programs.) Pareto Efficiency holds that if a buyer and seller, or an employer and employee, enter into an agreement voluntarily, then at least one must be better off or they would not have agreed, and the transaction increases welfare so long as no one is rendered worse off. If a voluntary transaction between two parties benefited them but made someone else worse off—causing pollution is the standard example—then it's a different matter. The competing view is called "Kaldor-Hicks Efficiency," named mainly for the early-twentieth-century British economist John Richard Hicks. The Kaldor-Hicks approach focuses on total welfare rather than individual welfare. It would say, for example, that if a buyer and seller enter into an agreement that causes pollution but brings more gain than the loss suffered by the victim of the pollution, that's okay.

Though Pareto might sound left-wing because his view forbids transactions that harm others, and the Kaldor-Hicks approach might sound right-wing because in this example it justifies pollution, in actual application the lineup is the reverse. Pareto was a market purist and his views are beloved by market purists, who tend to think that any voluntary transaction that causes no harm to others is kosher. The Kaldor-Hicks coefficient, in contrast, is used to justify market intervention because a third party is required to determine whether one actor's gain outweighs another's loss, and under Kaldor-Hicks that third party is government. Kaldor-Hicks theory for example can say that deliberate harm to someone is okay—for instance, by seizure of property—so long as the gain to others exceeds the harm.

This short diversion into economic philosophy is necessary because it seems that by the standards of Pareto Efficiency, having the rich get richer does not harm those who fail to get rich, so long as whatever makes the rich become rich causes no loss of income to everybody else. In times of feudal economics, the rich became richer by expropriating property and forcing average people into servitude. Today, in most cases the rich become richer without causing anyone else loss of income (with an important exception to be discussed in a moment), and therefore their wealth is unobjectionable.

In a Pareto world, unequal outcomes are not a concern; what matters is preventing the rich from harming others in their quest for excess. By many standards, Western society through the past century has grown steadily better at preventing the rich from harming others—through the rule of law, through antitrust enforcement, through consumer-protection rules and truth-in-lending practices, and so on. This makes a Pareto analysis of Western income difference attractive, at least to a point, because Pareto transactions are voluntary, and all except hardcore ideologues acknowledge voluntary outcomes as superior to imposed-from-above orderings of society.

That most Americans believe income differences are not necessarily bad helps explain "American exceptionalism," or the fact that there is relatively little class hostility in American life. Academics for years have been obsessed with "American exceptionalism," bewildered about why the United States doesn't have violent labor rioting or open public hostility to wealth or prominent politicians running on platforms that call for soaking the wealthy with confiscatory taxation—all standbys in European politics, and all forces that Marx thought would eventually engulf capitalism. Some academics seem positively disappointed that class warfare refuses to impinge on American life.

The United States did once have class warfare, labor rioting, open public hostility to wealth, and prominent politicians running on platforms that called for soaking the rich with confiscatory taxation. The period in which these were elements of American life ran roughly from the 1880s through the beginning of World War II—and then things began to get so much better for almost everyone that such feelings fell out of favor. Average Americans abandoned class resentments commencing roughly at the beginning of the postwar era because they found it was in their interest to surrender such resentments; with the average person's lot improving, why denounce the social order? When Al Gore ran for president in 2000 using as his slogan "The People Versus the Powerful," this pitch was a century out of date. American politics of the year 1900 did pit the people versus the powerful. By the year 2000, most although not everyone was benefiting from the American system. Class resentments are relatively minor in the United States because today the typical American falls into the "have" category, while have-nots are a minority, reversing the historical pattern in which have-nots formed the bulk of the population.

There are fair questions about whether the current people-powerful mix is a truly voluntary result. Those with no marketable job skills, or who have a family to support or a money emergency, may "voluntarily" agree to work for the minimum wage of $5.15, but only because they don't want to starve. Is this true free will? And does it make the minimum wage fair? A white-collar worker may "voluntarily" agree to a job without health insurance, but only because no employer is offering this benefit to new hires. Is it truly the worker's free-will wish to lack health coverage?

Beyond that, truly free, truly voluntary transactions may lead to outcomes that consign people to the status of life's losers, usually based on IQ. As the social commentator Mickey Kaus documented in his book *The End of Equality*, through universal education and equal-opportunity laws the American system grows steadily more free, open, and based on merit—but if you compete in a free, fair, open merit-based system and lose, what does that make you?[39] The losers of the current free-and-fair competitions for places in American society not only end up materially deprived but feeling that they *ought* to be losers—that janitors aren't good for anything but sweeping. In a survey taken in 1924, 47 percent of Americans said it was your own fault if you did not succeed; by 1979, 65 percent of Americans answered yes to that question.[40] Growing steadily more open and fair, Western societies suggest to the losers that they ought to have lost, an outcome that may in some sense be coldly correct but surely is too harsh for a good-hearted community to accept.

That it is reasonable to pay doctors more than cab drivers does not necessarily mean doctors need to earn *far* more than cab drivers; that it's reasonable to pay business managers more than mail clerks does not necessarily mean *Fortune 500* CEOs should earn 419 times as much as typical workers in their firms, the multiple at this writing. Such disparities—not necessarily pure results of impersonal market mechanisms, since many CEO-pay outcomes were rigged—cause some to wallow in excess, cackling as they count their gold, while others lead nervous, insecure lives on the edge of money catastrophe.

Unequal wealth outcomes may be fine, even desirable; extreme wealth outcomes are not, for they violate the sense of justice—to say nothing of the dreams of Pareto—by harming those who are effectively compelled to work at $5.15 an hour so that the purchases of the wealthy will cost slightly less. This is something about the Western, and especially the American, system that must change, and will be discussed in greater detail in a coming chapter.

For now let's make the self-interest argument, and say that extreme disparities of wealth neither necessarily serve, nor reflect well on, the recipient.

As Steven Weinberg, a Nobel Prize–winning physicist, has written,[41] the person of achievement in any field, whether business or academics or art or sports, will always receive the special reward of respect and admiration. Weinberg asks, Why isn't a comfortable income and the admiration of society enough to motivate exceptional people to achieve? People with healing gifts should have special incentives to do the hard work necessary to become physicians; this is in society's interest. But why isn't a comfortable life, respect, and the admiration of the community reward enough? Why must the reward be two vacation homes and two Mercedeses? The reverse of this question is to ask why millions of people who were not blessed by chance with the genetic gifts that make possible a life of high achievement are expected to exist in relative privation so that the achievers can know luxury. "Whatever purposes may be served by rewarding the talented," Weinberg notes, "I have never understood why untalented people deserve less of the world's good things than other people."[42]

Economists call celebrity, respect, personal power, or social admiration "psychic income," an odd phrase that reflects an important point. Successful people are compensated in ways other than with money—sometimes with what money cannot buy, such as respect. Earlier it was said that unequal outcomes are not necessarily bad; also, that we can hope for a future, superior ordering of society in which wealth is more evenly distributed. How could both be true at once? If unequal outcomes were mainly in respect, admiration, or celebrity—"psychic income"— rather than money. In a better-ordered society than ours, successful people might still enjoy unequal status, but might view respect and admiration as their great reward while regarding material possessions as mere stuff to which all persons ought to have roughly equal access.

That's enough for now on two maddening faults of the Western system: too much buying and consuming by everybody, too-high extremes of wealth at the top. The faults of the Western system, and especially the American system—principally inaction against remaining poverty, lack of universal health care, and greed at the top—are topics that will be picked up again in a later chapter. Even though most trends in the United States and the European Union are positive for most people, no one should mistake this for an argument that significant problems do not remain, and cry out for significant reform.

....

For now let's put aside these meta-problems of sweeping theory and concentrate on the foremost fault of the Western system in everyday life. That fault is that the incredible rise in living standards for the majority of Americans and Western Europeans has made them more affluent, healthier, more comfortable, more free, and sovereign over ever taller piles of stuff—but has not made them any happier.

The United States and European Union have spent the last fifty years conducting an enormous social-engineering experiment in whether prosperity causes happiness, and the answer, unequivocally, is no. The comedian Henny Youngman once quipped, "What good is happiness? It can't buy money." In case there was any doubt, we can now feel utterly certain the equation does not work in the other direction, either.

Of course, today's citizens are much better off being well-housed, well-supplied, overfed, and free—yet never satisfied—than in any of the many less agreeable possible outcomes. Researching this book, and thinking about the alternatives, has caused me to begin whispering a regular prayer of thanks: Thank you that I and five hundred million others are well-housed, well-supplied, overfed, free, and not content; because we might be starving, wretched, locked under tyranny, and equally not content.

Using utilitarian calculus, surely many philosophers would say that a Western world populated by huge numbers of flourishing, well-supplied, but insistently grumpy people represents a magnificent leap for progress. Our failure to exhibit gratitude to those who came before, and sacrificed so that we could know prosperity and liberty, would to a utilitarian philosopher be rather beside the point.

And in a sort of ultimate utilitarian calculus, it might be said that the world's ever larger population and ever higher longevity creates a favorable "happiness math."

Suppose that men and women experience, on average, one unit of happiness per year of life. Today the typical person lives twice as long as a century ago, and there are six times as many people in the world as a century ago: This means a twelve-fold increase in global units of happiness. We may be losing perspective person-by-person, but we are making it up on volume!

The fact remains that men and women in the West have ever more health, possessions, and freedom, but these advances do not make them joyful. Why not? And what can be done about it?

Chapter 5

MORE OF EVERYTHING

EXCEPT HAPPINESS

If you sat down with a pencil and graph paper to chart the trends of American and European life since the end of World War II, you'd do a lot of drawing that was pointed up. Per-capita income, "real" income, longevity, home size, cars per driver, phone calls made annually, trips taken annually, highest degree earned, IQ scores, just about every objective indicator of social welfare has trended upward on a pretty much uninterrupted basis for two generations. Many subjective graphs would also show steady upward trends: personal freedom, women's freedom, reduction of bias against minority groups.

But your graphs would lose their skyward direction when the topics turned to the inner self. The trend line for happiness has been flat for fifty years. The trend line is negative for the number of people who consider themselves "very happy," that percentage gradually declining since the 1940s. And the trend line would cascade downward like water over a falls on the topic of avoiding depression. Adjusting for population growth, ten times as many people in the Western nations today suffer from "unipolar" depression, or unremitting bad feelings without a specific cause, than did half a century ago. Americans and Europeans have ever more of everything except happiness.

Drawn to this paradox of progress, in recent years a number of researchers have begun to study happiness or "subjective well-being," in the ten-dollar term that researchers prefer. They join the National Opinion Research Center at the University of Chicago, which has been conducting polls on the topic since just after the end of World War II. So far the findings of such research have been published mainly in academic treatises, such as *Loss of Happiness in Market Democracies* by Robert Lane, a political scientist at Yale University.[1] Roughly 60 percent of Americans described themselves as "happy" in the year 1950, Lane found, and the figure has not changed since, except for tiny ticks up and down. Through the same period, the portion of Americans who call themselves "very happy" has declined from about 7.5 percent in 1950 to about 6 percent today. The decline of the "very happy" class continues, while the big action is the increase in the depressed class.

About 25 percent of Americans and Europeans now experience at least one bout of depression in their lives—clinical in the sense of sustained or debilitating, not just a few days of being in a bad mood. A study by Ronald Kessler of Harvard Medical School recently estimated that 6.6 percent of Americans now experience at least one episode per year of "major" depression, not just bad feelings, but the kind of depression that makes you not want to get out of bed.[2]

Incidence of bipolar or "manic" depression, the condition in which a person alternates between bouts of animated glee and immobilizing gloom, has not increased during the postwar era;

this illness is now thought to be mainly chemical in origin, and is treated with drugs. Unipolar depression, on the other hand, just keeps rising in incidence, with no end in sight. Unipolar depression is thought not to be a physical disease; something within our society, or within our own minds, causes it. And though the rising rate of Western depression may relate to some extent to better diagnosis and the loss of taboo associated with this topic—often the depressed of previous centuries were quietly kept in darkened rooms and not discussed—a tenfold increase in two generations is far too great to be an artifact of improved diagnosis alone.

From the standpoint of happiness math, it should be reiterated that it is far better there be millions of free, prosperous people who have the time and leisure in which to become depressed—many undergoing their depressions in nice houses and attempting to distract themselves with nice vacations or nice dinners out—than numerous possible alternatives. Unipolar depression has not risen in the developing world, probably because so many people there are focused on simply staying alive that they have no time or leisure in which to experience depressed frames of mind. Many of our ancestors might also have been so engaged in constant exertion, and so dependent on each day's work outcome for sustenance, as to have had no time for depressing moods. Our ancestors might also have had few expectations beyond daily exertion, and thus been less prone to suffering depression in response to setbacks. The United States and European Union generate enough wealth to spoil their citizens with depression; huge numbers of people in these places can, in terms of money or time, afford to feel badly.

Yet unhappiness is a genuine concern. Unhappy people are not merely feeling sorry for themselves or guilty of descent into solipsism, although of course there are examples of both. (We all know people who trudge around acting theatrically disconsolate, to the point at which there is temptation to shove the person against the wall and holler, "You idiot, snap out of it!") Most men and women who suffer depression are experiencing a condition they would like to escape, one that detracts from the quality of their lives. Millions of others are not clinically depressed but feel the sort of unfocused unease that prevents their one chance at life from conferring the satisfaction it should. This, too, is a genuine concern. Sadness should not be the default human condition.

Happiness, in turn, is a worthwhile and important goal. To be happy is not an exercise in self-indulgence, rather, one of the primary objectives of life. Aristotle called happiness "the highest good" and said that an enlightened society would be ordered with the goal of helping its citizens become happy. The framers of American democracy did not laud "the pursuit of happiness" because they considered this self-indulgence. Rather, they knew that happiness both ought to be a goal of life, and makes for better citizens. Dennis Prager has devoted an entertaining, quirky book, *Happiness Is a Serious Problem,*[3] to the notion that people have a duty to become happy, because happiness is the wellspring of altruism. Higher up the scale of literature, a century ago the poet Robert Browning wrote, "Make us happy and you make us good"; twenty-three centuries before that, Aristotle said, "Living well and doing well are the same as being happy." In Aristotelian usage, "doing well" meant exercising virtue. Aristotle and Browning both anticipated current research, by sociologist David Myers of Hope College and others,[4] showing that happy people commit fewer crimes, donate more to charity, perform more volunteer work, are more likely to aid strangers, and exhibit other traits of virtuous citizenship.

It's impossible to be certain, of course, precisely what happiness is. Men and women may go back and forth on whether they feel happy; there is no hard metric, like an SAT score or a forty-yard dash time. Much of what is known on this subject from a data standpoint is "self-reported happiness"—what people tell researchers or pollsters. People talking to pollsters or psychological researchers may feel they ought to describe themselves as happy, because unhappiness implicitly suggests rejection by others, or some private failing. Many people genuinely can't make up their minds whether they are happy. They might describe themselves as happy if the phone rings with a pollster's call at 7 P.M., and unhappy if the same pollster calls with the same questions at 8 P.M.

Psychologist Daniel Kahneman of Princeton University, who won the 2002 Nobel Prize for Economics, and a colleague named Amos Tversky spent the better part of two decades trying to devise a reliable, impartial scale of "subjective well-being," and eventually gave up. Kahneman tested various sets of questions on groups of volunteers, and never came up with anything conclusive.

Kahneman found, for example, that if he asked college students whether they considered themselves happy, most said yes. But if he first asked college students how long it had been since they went on a date, and then asked whether they considered themselves happy, most said no. Other small tricks skewed results, or generated information that was amusing but inconclusive. For instance, "There's absolutely no difference I could detect in overall happiness in California versus Kansas," Kahneman says, "but people in both places believed that people in California should be more happy." At one time, Kahneman asked subjects if they presented a smiling face to the world but were privately unhappy. He stopped asking this question because it caused many people to burst into tears.

....

Even if research data on "self-reported" happiness must come with an asterisk, it is illuminating nonetheless. Edward Diener, a psychologist at the University of Illinois, has spent his career studying this topic. He views it as a research field of rising import, as societies everywhere "are starting to assume that not just the affluent, but every individual should achieve some kind of satisfaction in life," Diener says. His studies have led him to the following conclusions.

- Lacking money causes unhappiness, but having money does not cause happiness.
- As a group, the old are happier than the young; for most people the sense of well-being increases with age.
- Millionaires as a group are no more happy than people of average income.
- The disabled and chronically ill report a slightly higher sense of well-being than the population at large, perhaps because they have a heightened appreciation of the value of their own lives.
- The psychological norm for the United States is positive, but only by a tiny bit. On a test of life satisfaction that Diener has designed, the average score is "slightly satisfied."

Since popular culture worships youth, many might profess disbelief at Diener's contention that aging increases happiness. But nearly all researchers find a higher sense of well-being among the old than the young, defying the standard assumption that youth is the acme of life. "The minds of the young are full of all the things they want to achieve and have not, whereas most of the elderly have either achieved what they wanted or made peace with the fact that they never will," Diener explains. There is, Diener reports, also no evidence that the approach of death causes panic or dread among senior citizens. As a group, even those facing the age of death "experience more satisfaction with their overall life than young adults," Diener says.

Diener's discovery that the impoverished are unhappy is hardly surprising. In a classic confirm-the-obvious exercise, Diener traveled to Calcutta, interviewed its street-dwellers, and came home with irrefutable evidence that people who are very poor experience "a low level of life satisfaction." Studies by Diener, a Dutch researcher named Ruut Veenhoven, and others show that in all nations and cultures, the poor are unhappy, and for the obvious reasons. Some philosophy and art romanticize the idea of the person who has nothing and cheerfully lives from hand to mouth, rewarded by finding tranquility in the lack of material grasping. The Roman philosopher Seneca, for example, declared, "No one can be poor who has enough, nor rich who covets more." But a good guess is that hardly any person without resources has ever achieved a serene life, not even saints and bodhisattvas. Seneca, bear in mind, himself occupied a suite on the emperor's palace grounds.

As income begins to rise, Diener's research shows, the sense of well-being rises with it—but only up to a point. The ascent from poverty to a middle-class existence with a home and reasonable financial security markedly improves happiness. But once the middle-class level is reached, money decouples from happiness and the two cease having anything to do with each other. Diener has tested a fair proportion of the multimillionaires (now, often, the billionaires) on the *Forbes 400* list of the world's richest men and women, and found they have only a tad bit more life satisfaction than people living at the median income. Money has made them rich, but there are things money cannot buy; the data on this point are now in.

Nearly all well-being research supports the basic conclusion that money and material things are only weakly associated with leading a good life. Kahneman sums up his research in the simple phrase, "Life circumstances don't seem to have much effect on happiness." Veenhoven's work suggests that the magic number at which money decouples from happiness is about $10,000 per capita per annum. "In the relationship between national happiness and national income," he says, "we see a very clear pattern of diminishing returns, with the bend-off point at about $10,000 annual income." Per-capita income in the United States in 2000 was $29,499.[5] Both the United States and Western Europe are long past the statistical point where, on average, money can still buy happiness.

As to why money stops buying happiness once people become middle-class, there are several theories. One is that the goalposts constantly move. Diener notes that although inflation-adjusted income has risen spectacularly for almost all Americans and Europeans since World War II, "What people want in terms of material things and life experiences has increased almost exactly in lockstep with the postwar earnings curve."

A generation ago, to own a home, a car, and to take one annual vacation using the car was viewed as material success. Now the goalposts of the good life have moved. Huge numbers of Americans aspire to a large home, at least two cars, regular dining out, and jet vacations to alluring destinations. Fancy watches, expensive SUVs, free-spending parties, and other extravagances can start to look like necessities, as part of the blurring of needs and wants. Abundance itself may prevent ever higher incomes from having any relationship with happiness by creating a never-ending progression of new things to want, so many new things entering the market each year that no one could keep up with it even if money were no object.

The blurring of needs and wants is important here because needs can be satisfied. A person needs food, clothing, shelter, medical care, education, and transportation; once attained, these needs are fulfilled. Wants, by contrast, can never be satisfied. The more you want, the more likely you are to feel disgruntled; the more you acquire, the more likely you are to feel controlled by your own possessions. "The victor belongs to the spoils," as David Myers has memorably phrased this quandary of affluence.

The transition from modest community to affluent suburb or other desirable address—a graduation ceremony that many millions of Americans and Europeans have attended in recent decades—may only serve to instill an insidious new form of dissatisfaction. In a small town or a modest community, a person might not be able to afford all that he or she wants, yet most of what is available is reasonably close in money terms—the stores are Target, the restaurants TGI Friday's, the housing three-bedroom. Land in an affluent community and you are immediately confronted by all kinds of pricey stuff that even the well-off have trouble affording. Tiffany, four-star French restaurants, new BMWs, and gated McMansions with circular drives now surround you, making what you have attained seem insufficient.

In 2001, the writer David Brooks spent several months comparing median-income towns such as York, Pennsylvania, with affluent suburbs such as Montgomery County, Maryland. Entering stores and restaurants in median towns, Brooks realized that businesses had sized up their market and priced accordingly. People he interviewed in the median-income towns did not envy the better-off residents of New York City or San Francisco, and had few resentments about money "because where they lived they can afford just about everything that is for sale," Brooks wrote.[6] In York, Pennsylvania, the top of the local market was Red Lobster restaurants, Laura Ashley clothes, and above-ground swimming pools—within the reach of the typical resident. On the other hand, residents of Montgomery County, Brooks found, often were upset and unhappy about money, even though their average income was three times as high. Higher-income residents of the fancy suburbs constantly drove past huge homes of people much better-off than they, and exclusive stores selling items only the rich could afford. This rendered them discontent even though, objectively, they were well-off. For them, money had utterly decoupled from happiness.

If there were some way to create a society in which everyone had a three-bedroom house and a Honda Accord, with no mansions or Ferraris but also no housing projects or homelessness, the sense of happiness might be served, as people would not see around them extremes to covet. But there is no known way to create such a society while maintaining freedom and economic vibrancy; the primary experiment along these lines, the old Soviet Union, resulted only in housing projects.

In a kind of nature's-revenge law, the fact that there will always be something you desire but cannot possess ensures that even the rich will never be materially satisfied, since no matter how loaded you become, some estate, some company, some work of art, some prize or honor will always be denied to you.

The richest individual in world history, Bill Gates, cannot have what others possess and will not sell, while Gates has consistently been frustrated in his attempts to acquire what he seems to desire most, public respect.

....

Sociologists have long assumed that rising income does not necessarily confer rising happiness owing to "reference anxiety," a fancy term for keeping up with the Joneses. As incomes rise, people stop thinking, "Does my house meet my needs?" and instead, "Is my house nicer than the neighbor's?" Contemporary psychology tends to view this traditional assumption as not quite right; Veenhoven, for example, believes many people have become aware of the keeping-up-with-the-Joneses pitfall. Instead, current research suggests that it is the trends in a person's own life, not in the neighbors' lives, that induce dissatisfaction even when times are good.

Here, research suggests, the essential element is an expectation of more. A person with a middling but rising income may be happier than a person with a high but stagnant income. A person with a small house who expects to move into a medium-sized house may be happier than a person with a large house who knows it is the largest he will ever own.

Suppose you could have either an income of $50,000 with a promise of a $5,000 raise annually, or an income of $250,000 that would never rise. The latter deal would bring you far more money over any working lifetime; studies by Diener and by others suggest that the former would be more likely to confer a sense of well-being. A moderate but rising income would make every year better, materially, than the one before, whereas a higher but stagnant income makes each year seem like a repeat of the last. The sense that things are not still improving—even if you've reached a high level—brings discontent because, as David Myers likes to say, "the second helping never tastes as good as the first."

This factor would appear to shed much light on why citizens of the highly prosperous United States often seem so unexcited about their circumstances. Starting from the comparatively low point of the 1950s—an era of smaller houses, far more poverty, far less education, and far more intolerance than today— everything seemed to be headed up. Most Americans believed their nation, and their own material circumstances, were sure to get steadily better. For most people, the expected improvements did in fact come, and today the better-off condition that so many dreamed of has been attained by huge numbers of Western citizens. But if for no other reason than that life improved so much so fast, it's hard to imagine that the decades to come will be even better still. Children who grew up in two-bedroom houses now own four-bedroom houses; their children, in their turn, might also own four-bedroom houses, but the odds are that most will not own six-bedroom houses. The expectation that each new year should be notably better than the last, once deeply ingrained in the American psyche, now fades. We are constantly eating the second helping and it does not taste as good as the first.

ANTICIPATION-INDUCED ANXIETY. Thus belief about whether the future will be better may prevent us from appreciating that the present is good, an effect that might be called "anticipation-induced anxiety." Despite the clichéd complaint that men and women are shallow and live for the moment, psychology shows that if anything, tens of millions of Americans and Europeans live too much for the future and ignore the moment. Kahneman's work suggests that many people are obsessed with whether the years to come will be better or worse, to the point of overlooking that things are nice right now. Parents and schools teach the concept of delayed gratification, of always looking ahead while keeping the nose to the grindstone. Many people learn this lesson so well that they can *only* look ahead, growing excessively concerned about future improvement. "We are much better at preparing to live than at living," the Buddhist philosopher Thich Nhat Hanh has written.[7]

Carol Graham and Stefano Pettinato, two researchers at the Brookings Institution, have found anticipation-induced anxiety at work in many nations.[8] "Individuals' subjective assessments of their economic progress, as well as their expectations about the future, are as important as objective trends," Graham and Pettinato have written in the voice of social science. Their research shows, for example, that although average income, health, and living standards have improved steadily in most of Latin America in the last two generations, Latin Americans as a group are unhappy, because their expectations for the future are not positive.

Nations, not just regions, have differing levels of well-being. Veenhoven has studied the relative levels of happiness among nations. His top five are the Netherlands (his home!), Iceland, Ireland, Denmark, and Sweden while his bottom five are Russia, Latvia, Lithuania, Belarus, and Bulgaria. The United States finishes number eight for national well-being on Veenhoven's scale.

Scandinavian countries have such high well-being, many have speculated, because their socialism-lite governments have gotten almost everyone to the level of middle class, creating something vaguely like a society in which everyone has a three-bedroom house and a Honda Accord. Also, dishonesty is severely sanctioned by Scandinavian culture, and an atmosphere of trust seems to promote general well-being.[9] This does not necessarily mean the Scandinavian model would work elsewhere. The Scandinavian states have until recently accepted almost no immigrants, have stagnant economies owing to excess regulation, and have such perilously low birthrates that the relationship of rising pension costs to falling taxes may wreck these nations' national budgets. The former Soviet states may be places of stark unhappiness in part owing to dashed expectations—citizens thought the end of communist tyranny would rapidly improve standards of living, and instead that goal now seems a generation distant. This makes former Soviet citizens unhappier than those of the ravaged nations of central Africa, where many people have minimal expectations.

Note how high Ireland finishes on Veenhoven's scale. This nation's per-capita income is less than half that of the United States or Switzerland, but Ireland has a "count your blessings" culture and things have gotten so much better so fast in Ireland in the past decade that national optimism is rampant. In contrast, Japan finishes almost at the bottom of well-being surveys, despite one of the world's highest per-capita incomes. To researchers, the Japanese describe themselves as abjectly miserable. Perhaps this is because Japan's four decades of ever better economy has now been replaced by economic contraction, causing an anticipation-induced anxiety that life is no longer trending up. Or perhaps this is because Japan is even more money-obsessed than the United States. Much of the Japanese national sense of well-being is premised on money, and money emphatically cannot make anyone happy.

A fundamental reason that acquiring money does not sync with acquiring happiness might be stated in cool economic terms: Most of what people really want in life—love, friendship, respect, family, standing, fun—is not priced and does not pass through the market. If something isn't priced you can't buy it, so possessing money may not help much.

True, many have used money in attempts to buy respect, love, or friendship, and you can certainly use money to buy sex. But the kind of sex you get for money isn't likely to be as good as the unpriced kind—and the same obtains for the kind of respect, love, or friendship you can buy with money. There are ways to make an economic purchase of fun: vacations, amusement parks, movies, sports events. But when it comes to fun, there's little relationship between price and value, as a simple inexpensive picnic might turn out to be a wonderful time while a cost-is-no-object resort stay might turn out unsatisfying. Even this intangible of life, which the market does attempt to price, doesn't relate to money in any way that reliably produces the desired result. We've all spent money on things that were supposed to be fun, and later wished we hadn't.

Surely most people would say that the most important commodity that lacks price and thus cannot be bought is love. The human need for love may not just be a matter of sentiment: In their groundbreaking 2000 book *A General Theory of Love*,[10] three academic psychologists, Thomas Lewis, Fari Amini, and Richard Lannon, proposed that love is actually a physical necessity. "Love is simultaneous mutual regulation, where each person meets the needs of the other because neither can provide for his own," the authors wrote.

In the clunky theorist's phrase "simultaneous mutual regulation," the authors were referring to studies showing that the limbic portion of the brain, from which emotions arise and where dreaming takes place, only functions properly among those with love, family ties, or close friendships in their lives. People who lack for love or close friendship often develop limbic abnormalities; the limbic part of the brain doesn't keep watch over regulatory chemicals properly. The chance discovery, in the 1950s, that certain drugs intended to treat tuberculosis also palliate depression is considered evidence of this concept, because this demonstrates that the emotional self is at least partly biological in origin. At first glance, the fact that drugs improve mood can sound like depressing determinism—"chemicals make us happy." But if emotions are biologically seated within the brain, then they are real and central to human life, not just some weepy distraction, and they must have evolved, just as our physical forms evolved.

Enlightenment thinking revered abstract thought, which arises from the neocortex portion of the brain, over all other mental functions; Enlightenment theorists viewed emotional needs as handicaps people must rise above, and many in the West have embraced this view, perhaps to their detriment. *A General Theory of Love* counters with the contention that the human yearning for love and intimacy is part of our evolution—even that, chemically, the brain evolved a need for closeness as part of the stimuli that make it function correctly. "Isolation, sorrow, bitterness, anxiety, loneliness and despair," the three psychologists supposed, "are in today's United States and European Union greater concerns than supply of any material item."

There's no need to dwell on the modern lament that trends in Western life tend to break up friendships (constant job-switching and travel), scatter families (moving for schools and career), encourage people to give up on relationships (in some European Union nations, such as Sweden and Belgium, two-thirds of marriages end in divorce),[11] and persuade people to view themselves as disconnected individuals rather than as parts of communities. America has always been a nation of "joiners," and a plethora of religious, community, sports, fraternal, academic, artistic, professional, leisure, and similar organizations continues to thrive in the United States: Given population growth, most likely more Americans today belong to more organizations than ever before. But it's hard to argue that we are not steadily less connected to each other.

Research by Lewis, Amini, and Lannon, and by others, has shown that human beings are happiest around other people. The Harvard University researcher Edward O. Wilson has called this the "biophilia" hypothesis—that living things yearn for proximity to other living things, which in the case of *Homo sapiens* means people need close connections to other people.[12] There are of course men and women who genuinely wish to be left alone, but, on the whole, married people are happier than singles, people in large families are happier than those in small families, those who are busy and attend lots of events where they interact with other people are happier than those who hang around the house. Research finds that a person is more likely to feel happy in a friends-or-family social setting than when alone. This stands to reason; in a social setting or in the household you are interacting with others, your mind stimulated or diverted, while when sitting alone, nothing distracts you from thinking about your disappointments. One of the haunting points Lewis, Amini, and Lannon have made is that Americans and Europeans live longer and are healthier than ever, yet are also lonelier than ever. In 1957, 3 percent of Americans described themselves as "lonely." Today, 13 percent do.[13] Rising loneliness may be canceling out the other positives.

The same forces that are causing standards of living to rise and longevity to improve also promote loneliness. Steadily smaller households, made possible by prosperity, mean steadily less human interaction. Telecommuting, a personal convenience made possible by technology, means less human interaction. The culture of complaint, in which Americans and Europeans are encouraged to carp about ever smaller matters, drives us to take offense, which may cost friendships; the adulation of the family grievance, a prime topic of daytime television, drives us to find fault with those whom genetic chance made our relatives; the idealized images of romantic partners in entertainment and advertising can make a date, or a life, with an admirable but not-extraordinary person seem a disappointment rather than a privilege.

THE NICE-HOTEL-ROOM FACTOR. Forces of prosperity are likely to continue to render it practical for more and more people to live alone, work alone, be alone. Americans and Western Europeans have ever longer lives in which to enjoy achievements and possessions, while losing the sense of closeness to others that helps make it all worthwhile. This might be called the "nice hotel room factor." For increasing numbers of Americans and Europeans, life is like being in a really nice hotel room, but not having a good time because no one else came along on the trip.

This dynamic alone may constitute half the reason why the Western nations may be steadily better off but no happier. Or perhaps the epidemic of depression sheds a better light. People aren't merely failing to become happier—which, after all, is only the absence of a positive. By the measure of depression, citizens of industrial nations are feeling worse by the year.

The tenfold increase in unipolar depression in the industrial nations during the postwar era surely qualifies as an epidemic, if a silent one. According to the World Health Organization, there are a hundred million people alive today, most of them in the United States, Canada, Australia, Japan, and the European Union, who are clinically depressed. Depression annually costs the United States $50 billion in treatment expense and lost wages,[14] plus an incalculable amount in human heartbreak.

Not every researcher accepts the tenfold-increase estimate, in part because it is based mainly on "cross-sectional" studies, meaning research staged all at once, rather than "longitudinal" studies, in which the same group of people is tracked over several decades. Longitudinal studies are considered the gold standard of social science, but are also the most expensive kind of study; the leading goldmine of U.S. psychological data, something called the National Comorbidity Study, was cross-sectional. Ronald Kessler of Harvard Medical School has estimated that the increase in Western depression may be on the order of two- or threefold, not tenfold.[15] An estimate of tenfold increase is too high, some researchers suppose, because current therapy tends to classify ever milder problems as depression, while an aging population will include a rising share of despondent older people whose multiple bouts of depression raise overall averages. (Senior citizens as a group may be happier than those of other ages, but seniors who do suffer depression often experience frequent episodes; generally, psychological damage is thought to accumulate over a lifetime, growing more acute among the afflicted as they age.)

Nevertheless many prominent researchers have embraced the estimate of a tenfold increase in unipolar depression in the Western nations. One who endorses this number is Martin Seligman, a psychologist at the University of Pennsylvania and a past president of the American Psychological Association. Seligman has developed a four-step theory on why depression is rising so much.

The first cause, Seligman thinks, is individualism. "Unipolar depression is a disorder of the thwarting of the 'I,' and we are increasingly taught to view all through the 'I,' " Seligman believes. Past emphasis on family, faith, patriotism, and community was sometimes suffocating, but also allowed individuals to view their private setbacks as minor elements within a larger context. Today in the United States and Western Europe, where formal adherence to religion is declining, community loyalties are diluted by constant moving, families are smaller and fragile, and, where only a minority now tell pollsters they consider devotion to country important,[16] the "I" is practically the only lens through which to view events. "Rampant individualism causes us to think that our setbacks are of vast importance and thus something to become depressed about," Seligman continues. If your life is centered in family, community, faith, or nation, and things aren't going well for you, surely there will be some person or some part of an institution to whom you are connected for whom or where things are going well, or, at least, where the problems seem more important than yours. If, however, your life is centered on pure individualism and something goes poorly, there is no counterweight. You feel bad and nothing pulls on you in the other direction.

From the beginning of the Enlightenment, through the establishment of Jeffersonian democracy, through the French existentialist movement and up to the present day, writers, thinkers, artists, and huge numbers of typical men and women have fought for the idea that people should be free agents, unhindered by the demands of church, state, or social convention. Now that condition is largely achieved in the West, bringing with it un-precedented liberty. But freedom isn't free, as military theorists like to say. In the case of depression, the cost of freedom is leaving every person to the fate of pure individualism, without consola-tion or context. If all goes well in your life, pure individualism may work out fine. But the setbacks that almost everyone en-dures may, in the unanchored framework of pure individualism, accumulate into a cause of depression—about which, then, you may have no one or no institution to turn to, other than the dis-embodied voice on the 800 number at your HMO.

As his second cause of the depression epidemic, Seligman blames the self-esteem craze. It may seem counterintuitive that focus on raising self-esteem, which is supposed to make people feel good, results in them becoming depressed. But then, many initiatives have unintended consequences. "Self-esteem empha-sis has made millions think there's something fundamentally wrong if you don't feel good, as opposed to just, 'I don't feel good right now, but I will later,' " Seligman says. If you don't feel good now but will later, that's a minor matter. If something is fundamentally *wrong* with your life, that's pretty depressing.

Self-esteem counselors and others in the movement maintain that people ought to feel good about themselves all the time, a notion most psychologists find hopelessly unrealistic. Everyone has setbacks, or bad days, or simply periods of time when things are boring or crummy; don't obsess because you'll have better days, is Seligman's advice. The preaching of self-esteem, now common in public schools and in the midafternoon-television and talk-radio universe, instills the idea that a person ought always to be beaming with satisfaction, and if not, that he or she must have been wronged by someone or some institution and should be angry. Fixation on self-esteem may, in the end, only cause us to go looking for things to become upset about. People who go looking for things to become upset about rarely fail to find them.

Seligman's third cause of depression flows from the second, being the "postwar teaching of victimology and helplessness." Intellectuals, politicians, tort lawyers, and the media have in the last few decades become ever more proficient at discovering victims. So many classes of victimhood have been proclaimed that, in cumulative terms, today every person in the United States may be able to call himself or herself a victim of something or other; leaving aside the question of, if we're all victims, then who did the victimizing?

Surveys, Seligman notes, show that ever higher percentages of Americans describe themselves as victims. A steadily rising percentage of incoming college freshmen, for example, characterize themselves as having been victimized or possessing little control over their fates. For university freshmen, such views may actually be rewarded—those claiming victimhood on admissions essays probably increase their odds of being accepted to college, and the more innovative the victimhood claim, the better. But for contemporary Americans to claim lack of control over their own fates is striking, since, objectively, personal freedom has never been greater. The We're-All-Victims worldview only serves to deter men and women from asserting control over their own psyches.

Seligman finds particularly counterproductive, and depression-inducing, the craze for adults asserting they were victimized by their parents. Only in extreme cases, such as sexual abuse, is there a clear link between parenting behavior and adult person-ality, Seligman thinks the psychological data show. "You are en-titled to blame your parents for the genes they gave you but you are not entitled, by any research that I know of, to blame them for the way they treated you," Seligman says. Yet the blaming of parents has become a minor industry in the contemporary United States, inspiring talk shows and whole categories of junk-science litigation. A relevant note: Depressed patients often blame their parents for their condition, but once recovered from depression, usually stop blaming parents and describe their for-mer claims as a crutch.

Fourth of Seligman's inventory of causes of depression is run-away consumerism. Shopping, sports cars, expensive chocolates, and the like are "shortcuts to well-being," Seligman supposes. Acquiring material things may produce a momentary feeling of gratification, but the feeling rarely lasts. Incessant purchases may be piled atop one another in the quest for the same gratifi-cation that purchases once brought—this is the basic dynamic of shopaholism—while ever higher spending activates the cycle of work-and-spend. Spending as a "shortcut" to well-being is crippling owing to debt, or by locking a person or a head of a household into the soul-draining existence of always chasing maximized income.

That runaway consumerism may be a malady in the clinical sense is suggested by the fact that it sometimes responds to medication. Recent studies have suggested that shopaholism can be treated by the antidepressant Celexa.[17] This may sound like a postmodern practical joke—if your problem is that you spend too much money, what you need is an expensive prescription drug. But it's inarguable that runaway consumerism harms some people's well-being: They spend too much, or waste too much time shopping, or make compulsion-driven purchases of things they don't even necessarily want. Perhaps excessive consumerism is a cause of depression, or perhaps a symptom, with people shopping too much because they are depressed—metaphorically, endlessly seeking that which they do not find. In either case, if an antidepressant relieves the condition, this tells us consumerism and depression are linked. That is not good news for a society grounded in consumerism.

WAKING UP FROM THIS AMERICAN DREAM. To the many research-based theories of why rising Western living standards have not increased happiness, instead being accompanied by a wave of depression, there might be added one more factor: call it "waking up from the American dream."

From the beginning of the American republic, what the majority of citizens sought, and oriented their lives around seeking, was the American dream. Once, that meant you owned the farmland on which you toiled. Then it meant a decent job in industry and an education. By the early postwar era, the American dream meant a home, a car, some spending money, Saturday night out. By roughly the 1970s, as home- and car-ownership became common, the American dream also meant graduating from college, having a professional career, being an individualist. Europeans have been seeking their version of this dream for centuries longer. In all these dreams, material security and personal liberty are the essence.

Until approximately the current generation, the majority of Americans and Europeans failed to achieve most of the American dream. They longed for affluence and personal freedom, failed to attain it at least in some part, urged their children to continue the quest. Implicit in the longing was the assumption that those who did achieve the dream would become happy.

Today, throughout America, the European Union, Canada, Japan, and Australia, the majority achieve the American dream. Reasonable prosperity, personal liberty, high education, and good health are the daily condition of perhaps five hundred million people in the Western nations. The creation of entire regions of the world in which most people are well-off—in which the typical person lives what all previous generations considered a dream—is without precedent in history.

But having achieved general prosperity, we must awaken from the dream and realize that an overall condition of personal freedom and material prosperity does not make us any happier. Don't misunderstand: It is magnificent that five hundred million Westerners are living the American dream. If only every citizen of every nation could! This condition, however, must now be seen in perspective as in the fullest sense a *dream*, for its vital assumption, that the good life would confer happiness, turns out not to be true.

All the many previous generations denied the circumstances of the American dream reasonably supposed that if only they were better off, they would live in joy. Previous generations reasonably taught their children to strive to be better off in the hope of realizing joyfulness. Now most men and women of the Western nations have attained the condition of which previous generations dreamed, and although this is excellent news, the attainment makes it possible for society to verify, beyond doubt, that personal liberty and material security do not in themselves bring contentment. That must come from elsewhere, making it time to awaken from the American dream.

Chapter 6

....

STRESS—IT'S NATURE'S PLAN

"We are built to be effective animals, not happy ones," pronounced Robert Wright in *The Moral Animal,* his magnificent treatise on the new science known as evolutionary psychology.[1]

Natural selection, this new science supposes, might have favored early humans who were uneasy, distrustful, inclined to assume the worst about life and one another. Much romanticized literature today posits that ancient members of genus *Homo* were blissful children wandering through pastures singing, only later to become corrupted by greed, religious lies, and sinister patriarchal social structures. Unfortunately, as Steven LeBlanc, an anthropologist at the Peabody Museum of Archeology and Ethnology at Harvard University, and others have shown, most anthropology suggests that prehistoric humanity was violent and predatory; people killed one another often, and endured regular suffering.[2] Early humans who were generous or merry or experienced awestruck wonder at their dew-kissed world might have been wiped out in the pitiless primordial competition for resources, while those who could never feel content no matter how much they piled up, but always sought to take more, were the ones who endured, reproduced, and passed their genetic sequences down to us. Thus are we born with DNA coded for discontentment, because in our past, discontent was a survival strategy.

This does not mean we are fated to a primordial psychology. Genes only create proclivities, they are not destiny; a coming chapter will focus on the aspects of life that reward goodness, and urge us to walk the gentle path. But if we are descended from men and women who lived a fretful, suffering existence and could never feel at ease no matter how much they acquired, perhaps it is no surprise that, even as living standards, longevity, and liberty keep rising in the modern West, people have trouble feeling good about it. From an evolutionary standpoint, it may be that we are intended to feel unhappy regarding our circumstances. Certainly the prevalence in human bodies of the hormone cortisol suggests this. What is cortisol? The hormone that triggers stress. To nature, stress is a beneficial condition, and stress nature has engineered us to feel.

"Stress is inevitable and not necessarily bad," says Bruce McEwen, a researcher at Rockefeller University in New York and a leading authority on the biology of stress. In reaction to adrenaline, which is often pumping through the human body in tiny amounts, and in reaction to certain mediating proteins, a small area of the human brain called the amygdala signals the body to secrete cortisol and other hormones that engender stress. Noise, sudden movements, anxiety, perceived dangers, or merely the daily circumstances of life can activate the process. Stress hormones heighten awareness of surroundings, slightly improve vision and hearing, and make muscles work slightly better. This is the main reason researchers believe that the stress response evolved in mammals, and the main reason they guess that the forebears of humanity who were favored by natural selection were the ones more likely to be stress-prone. "Stress protects," McEwen says. "Stressed-out people are wary of circumstances and plan obsessively to avoid dangers, whereas happy-go-lucky people may not notice they are walking into a trap."

In ancient days, stress made our forebears more likely to see predatory animals lurking in the distance—lions, perhaps, assuming we are all descended from Africans—or to hear the approach of warring parties of others like ourselves. Thus, presumably, it was the stress-prone *Homo sapiens* who came out ahead in the contest for survival of the fittest. Today, stress helps us cross the street without being hit by cars, or drive seventy-five miles per hour with other cars mere feet away and remain wary enough to avoid them. Try to cross an intersection on any suburban boulevard anywhere in the contemporary United States and you'd better have a stress response; you'll need the heightened awareness to avoid being mowed down by SUVs.

More generally, stress is a coping mechanism for the demands of life. Studies show that successful or high-income people tend to have more cortisol pumping through their system than others. Whether the pressures of their positions cause the stress or the stress response helps them attain their positions is impossible to say. But since less-successful or lower-income people also exist under pressure, especially money pressure, and exhibit fewer stress indicators than the successful, it's fair to speculate that those stressed out men and women who rise to the top are in some fashion aided by stress. (Studies also show that the obsessive-compulsive tend to be more successful than society as a whole, suggesting natural selection may have favored this condition as well.) So stress can be good—but still unpleasant. Research further shows that highly successful Type-A people, the ones most likely to suffer stress symptoms, are twice as likely as the population at large to describe themselves as "very unhappy."[3]

It is a mistake to consider stress maladies an invention of the electronic age. Men and women of the past experienced many stress triggers, and not just lions. It's worth repeating that to have worked fourteen hours a day for pittance wages in an unventilated turn-of-the-century fabric mill in Fall River, Massachusetts, or to have farmed the 1880s Nebraska prairie gazing up into the sky for rain and knowing your family would starve if it did not come, was surely stress-inducing. A thousand other past circumstances of life must have been stressful as well.

Even some past daily annoyances were every bit as annoying for previous generations as daily annoyances of today, such as people sitting next to you screaming into cell phones. In the year 1850, for example, the typical American was twice as likely to be the target of a lawsuit as the typical American today. In the nineteenth century, when local ordinances were fewer and consumer law nonexistent, it was common for neighbors to sue each other over matters that would now be settled by town codes; and if you had a problem with a business, pretty much the sole recourse was to sue. Because of this, as Ralph Nader has noted, it is an urban myth that conniving lawyers are taking over Americans' lives.[4] Although the number of attorneys is ever rising, most occupy themselves in the background with corporate and regulatory matters. Americans of the twenty-first century are less likely to have to deal with lawyers personally than were our nineteenth-century forebears. Imagine how stressful that must have been.

But though the past was full of stresses, there are solid reasons to believe psychological pressure is increasingly prevalent in Western societies. One, suggests Joseph LeDoux, a stress researcher at New York University, is what this book calls headline-amplified anxiety. "People of the past were stressed by things they encountered personally, that were in the limited field of individual vision," LeDoux notes. "Now everybody knows about everything going wrong all over the world, and about every conjectured threat. The inventory of things that sound like you need to be worried about has risen dramatically."

Our 1880s prairie farmer would have known a great deal about agriculture, animal husbandry, and local politics, but hardly anything about crimes in distant cities or natural disasters in other states or angry mobs chanting in other countries, while military affairs in Iraq or social conditions in China would have been, at most, a subject for books on the shelf of the county library. Today a Nebraska farmer, or anyone else in the Western world, gets minute-by-minute readouts of murders, plane crashes, tornados, and ferry sinkings the world over, plus extensive detail on how the weapons, diseases, and greenhouse gases of distant nations might come after him personally. Even as living circumstances rise, there are ever more entries on the list of worries, activating added stress.

Because many fears are learned responses, ever more worries may lead to the generation of unreasonable or irrational fears; that is, phobias. "Some fears are automatic, no one has to teach you to fear a pack of wolves," LeDoux notes. "You do need to learn to fear a car, since we are not born with instincts about cars. There are so many things in modern life that we must learn to fear, our minds may in a sense become too good at learning to fear, and start applying the stress response to situations where it really is not called for, generating a stressed-out condition or even phobia." Researchers disagree on this point, but many think the overall incidence of panic attacks and phobias—irrational anxiety—is increasing in the Western world. This issue is not fuzzy pop-psychology but a hard-science concern, so much so that the National Institutes of Health now has a Center for the Neuroscience of Fear and Anxiety.

Studies of rats show that, once they learn a fear, chemical pathways form in the brain that allow them to learn additional fears more quickly in the future. Essentially, stress and phobias can snowball, gathering up more of themselves and acquiring a momentum of their own. If nothing else, this may explain why most men and women grow more anxious as they age: A lifetime of learning fears has made them proficient at anxiety. More generally, as headline-amplified anxieties swirl around us, all the men and women of the world may be growing really proficient at learning to worry about things. Biologically, this should result in more stress hormones.

As the clamor, competition, and pace of life keep rising, stress is invoked. Modern circumstances encourage us to view every moment of daily life as a source of nervous tension. In 2003, the Orwellian-named ExxonMobil oil company was promoting Speedpass, a small electronic wand that can be waved at a gas pump to enable motorists to fill up the tank without pausing to insert a credit card. It wasn't long ago that the ability to pay for gasoline at the pump with a credit card was itself promoted as a way for motorists to speed the fill-up and get back on the road. Now, this is seen as an excruciating delay. An ExxonMobil television commercial depicts two people in the same model car arriving at the pump simultaneously; one inserts a credit card while the other magically waves a Speedpass. The motorist with the Speedpass is shown smirking as he roars off while the one who used the credit card wears a look of stressed-out dejection on his face because he must stand and wait for the receipt to print—which takes, what, five seconds?

Similarly, the ritual evening meal has been replaced by scattershot food raids at fast-food joints and at the microwave. This does not necessarily mean parents and children no longer eat dinner together, as is commonly claimed. As Karlyn Bowman, an expert in polling at the American Enterprise Institute, a Washington think tank, has shown, the typical number of meals taken together by parents and children in the United States has scarcely changed since the end of the nineteenth century.[5] Today families are more time-stressed, but back then many parents felt it was inappropriate for children to dine with adults, and deliberately avoided family meals; the two factors roughly wash each other out. Overall it's an urban legend that modern time demands prevent children from being with parents. The sociologist Theodore Caplow has found that, in 1924, only 60 percent of fathers spent at least one hour per day with their children, whereas today 83 percent do.[6] But although parents and children share meals and time together as much or more than they once did, they share time and meals in an atmosphere of hectic hurry. The shared time is in the car, rushing to get somewhere; the shared meal, fast food gulped while glancing impatiently at the clock. All this is stressful.

In a society where most things are basically good for most people, stress triggers may be lowered to ever more delicate settings. Americans and Europeans today get upset, and complain bitterly, about slights or setbacks so tiny our forebears would not even have noticed them. In 2001, the telephone company BellSouth ran an amazing series of advertisements promoting some wireless gizmo that was said to reduce the hassle factor of life. In one ad, a woman looking deeply distressed declares that she had a horrible day because there was traffic in the morning, then was interrupted while she was speaking at work, and then, during dinner, the phone rang! Imagine trying to explain to our ancestors that this is what now constitutes suffering. That complaints have become this small is another sign the arrow of progress points forward. But if complaints this minor can be viewed as unbearable, we are likely to experience stress triggers constantly.

Though free time is rising, we don't sleep or relax enough, which leads to further stress. Americans take too little vacation—meaning either somewhere on holiday or simply off the clock, not reporting to work—averaging only two weeks per year versus an average of six weeks in Germany, according to the International Labor Organization. Some Americans work so much because they have no choice, and must keep the wolf from the door; some because they are careerists whose self-identities are wrapped up in the office; some because the cycle of work-and-spend requires them to produce every possible dollar to support their large houses, ponderous SUVs, and long list of possessions. Whatever the reason, lack of vacation or nonworking time elevates tension.

Prevalence of stress may also be increasing owing to the poor diet, exercise, and sleep habits of modern life. Studies show that people who are overweight or eat high-fat diets produce excessive levels of cortisol: and the phrase "people who are overweight or eat high-fat diets" now applies to more than half the American population.

Lack of adequate hours of sleep—or lack of adequate deep, sound sleep—also links to excessive cortisol. Studies show that the typical American sleeps about an hour less per night than a generation ago, two to three hours less per night than was standard in previous centuries. When the philosopher René Descartes left bustling Paris for the Dutch countryside in the 1620s, he wrote enthusiastically to a friend, "Here it is quiet and I sleep 10 hours per night, untroubled by any care." Ten hours per night of sleep has probably been the norm for most of human history; today, in the United States, the norm is seven hours. Cortisol production almost stops during sleep; one thing from which your body is resting is the stress response. Sleep less, and you get less time off from stress.

In one spooky leading indicator of stressed-out life, thousands of Americans have begun taking Modafinil, a drug designed to counteract narcolepsy. People are taking Modafinil not because they suffer from narcolepsy but because the drug counteracts the urge to sleep. By popping Modafinil, one can spend a greater fraction of each twenty-four hours frantically rushing and doing. Long-term side effects are unknown, but let's take a wild guess here and assume they will include more stress.

People slept more in earlier eras in part because there were no televisions to watch and, more important, no electric lights. Once night fell, only candle or oil lighting was available, the dim ambience setting the stage for retiring, whereas today the flip of a switch makes a house bright as noon.

People now watch television before bed, a national habit throughout the West and becoming a habit everywhere on the globe; researchers disapprove. Those who watch television until lights-out tend to have less deep sleep than those who engage in a quiet activity, because television is full of choppy images, flashes, explosions, shouting, crying, gunplay, superficial sexuality, adversity both real and simulated. Viewing such disquieting material before nodding off prevents the mind from calming fully for sleep, and may inspire nightmares. Reading is the ideal before-sleep activity, and it may be no coincidence that our forebears slept longer and better than we do because reading by oil lamp is practical and other activities are not. The sleep researcher William Dement maintains that if Americans and Europeans would simply go to bed an hour earlier each night, and turn off the television no later than an hour before that, Western society would be happier and healthier; consult his valuable book *The Promise of Sleep*.[7] Probably Dement is right. But we seem too stressed out to take his advice.

Because people in the United States and the European Union are growing steadily more overweight, while sleeping fewer hours and less well, their bodies continuously become programmed to produce more cortisol, elevating stress. "Health outcomes keep getting better, but if Americans were not so overweight and so addicted to high-fat diets I think we'd be much healthier still, through improved sleep and reduced manufacture of stress hormones," McEwen says. He notes that type-two or adult-onset diabetes, whose prevalence is increasing in the West, responds to drugs in only 30 percent of cases, whereas exercise—as little as daily brisk walking—alleviates the condition in 60 percent of cases. But sportswear and glamorization of athletes aside, Americans grow ever more sedentary, creating for themselves the very conditions that promote the biology of stress.

In the past fifteen years, pediatricians, parents, and schools have been claiming an epidemic of ADHD—attention-deficit hyperactive disorder—among American boys, particularly primary-school boys. A 2003 study by Julie Zito, a medical researcher at the University of Maryland, found that the number of American children taking Ritalin and similar drugs on a diagnosis of ADHD, or to improve school performance, tripled between 1985 and 1996, to at least 6 percent of U.S. children.[8] The long-term effects of taking psychotropic medications at a young age are unknown. Many of the same triggers involved in stress are involved in the ADHD diagnosis.

Though some children do have real disorders that require psychotropic treatment, it's hard to believe this is true of anything like the number currently being dosed with Ritalin, Prozac, and similar medications. Teachers and school administrators in many cases encourage parents to give young children attention- or mood-enhancing drugs, as this may lead to short-term improvements in the test scores according to which teachers and school administrators are now mercilessly ranked. Insurers also encourage Ritalin and similar compounds for childhood behavioral issues because drugs are cheaper than regular therapy sessions. One reason Americans pop so many pills for all that is psychological is that insurers would rather pay for pills than for counseling.

McEwen believes the majority of ADHD diagnoses do not reflect any underlying disorder but simply result from boys eating too much sugar, not getting enough exercise, and sleeping poorly because they watch television before bed. Earlier chapters noted that United States sugar consumption is rising, while the prevalence of televisions in children's rooms rises as well. Schools keep reducing recess time and phys-ed classes to free more minutes for test preparation, while kids play video games indoors because parents know it is unsafe to let them run around or bike on no-sidewalk streets. For children, this is a stress-manufacturing formula in clinical terms: that is, a formula that leads to cortisol production. And so we should not be surprised that America's children are exhibiting more symptoms of stress.

Less sugar, more exercise, and less television would cure most ADHD, McEwen believes, but since people want to pop a pill rather than change lifestyles, parents lobby for Ritalin and similar pharmaceuticals. Tens of millions of Americans and Europeans would experience less stress and anxiety if they consumed less, did half an hour of something vigorous each day, and read a book rather than watched the television before bed. But this requires change of lifestyle; most people want an Rx instead.

One puzzling trend, as this book is written, is the opening across the United States of clinics to which patients go to have a class of compounds called "inotropes" infused into their veins.[9] Whether inotropes have any efficacy is a matter of debate among specialists—that aside, what are they supposed to treat? Listlessness. Huge numbers of Americans are now said to suffer such lethargy that they don't feel like doing anything beyond eating and watching television. Supposedly, inotropes boost the vigor of the lethargic enough that they will leave the house, if only to obtain more inotropes. That large numbers of Americans with no specific medical problems have become so sedentary they need pharmaceutical intervention just to get out of the recliner in front of the television is, to science, a recipe for generating more stress hormones.

....

CONSERVATION OF ANXIETY. Stress may also be sustained by what LeDoux calls the "conservation of anxiety." Today almost everyone in the Western world lives better and longer, and in less danger, than a few generations ago. But we know more and fret more. And we have more free time, creating more opportunity to sit around obsessing over secondary problems or imagining tertiary ones. The result is conservation of anxiety: Things get better, but the level of bad feelings is unaffected.

In another nature's-revenge outcome, rising freedom may constitute a source of unhappiness. Today almost all Americans have unprecedented liberty and choice—but there are times when it's easier not to have choice. We have complete sexual freedom, but that hardly means the person you are interested in will sleep with you, or that anyone will. We have complete freedom to marry for love, but that does not mean the object of your affection will reciprocate, or that anyone will. When there was little marital or sexual freedom, people ached but did not necessarily hold themselves to blame for rejection; rejection was often caused by indifferent mechanisms of society. Today, in a Western world of total freedom, rejection is inescapably personal. Today, on paper, we're all free to become millionaires or celebrities, but this only actually happens to a small number of people per year and we're all acutely aware that it is not us.

When you lose a lottery drawing you may say, "Rats!" but don't feel personally to blame, since the result is pure chance and the fact that you lost is no reflection on you. In past generations, many social outcomes operated in similar fashion, beyond the average person's control and, thus, no reflection upon him or her. Today freedom and choice in all things create a pressure that previously did not exist, and can make whatever does not work out in your life seem a reflection on you. This problem might be called "the choice penalty."

THE CHOICE PENALTY. The choice penalty may be especially high for women. Once women were highly restricted in their social and economic roles; now women have so many options that choice itself has become a source of anguish. Specialists debate the point, but evidence suggests that the increase in unipolar depression has been greater among women than men. Christine Berg, a physician and a researcher at the National Institutes of Health, has supposed that the rise in women's freedom syncs with the rise in women's depression. "In earlier eras, women had little control over whom to marry, where to live, number of children or career path," Berg says. "Consequently if a woman was unhappy it was easy to affix the blame on society, or God or on one's husband. Now since women can choose, they are responsible for the outcomes." Today, when women choose wrongly they must hold themselves responsible, and being responsible for a wrong choice can become a source of melancholy. Men may choose wrongly, too, of course. But since men from antiquity have possessed more freedom than women, men as a group have already adjusted to the depression-triggering aspects of the choice penalty, Berg conjectures. Women as a group have only in recent decades acquired control over their fates, and now are in the throes of adjustment to the unwelcome psychological ramifications of being responsible for governing their own lives.

In response to stress, Westerners are consuming ever more psychotropic medications, and not just boys who may or may not have ADHD. The first class of calming drugs designed for routine use, benzodiazepines (Valium and its relatives), which became common in the 1960s, were mildly addictive and potentiated alcohol. The new class of serotonin inhibitors (Prozac and its relatives) has been engineered to have few side effects. There's nothing wrong with taking a calming drug, and if indeed the calming drug has few side effects and improves your experience of life, perhaps you are wise to swallow. Once shy of pharmaceuticals with psychotropic properties, Americans certainly have lost that inhibition. A few years ago, at Rockefeller University, I attended an academic seminar on stress science. Perhaps three hundred medical students, professors, and others crowded into a lecture auditorium to hear top researchers summarize their latest findings. One speaker, Rachel Yehuda of Mount Sinai Hospital, paused to ask if there was anyone in the room who had ever taken Valium, Prozac, or similar compounds. I was the sole person over age twenty-five who did not raise a hand.

But though the new limited-side-effect drugs may make sense for stress, what makes more sense is changing the way we live. Some changes can be as minor as doing a few minutes of deep breathing exercises twice a day. Even a short session of slow and deliberate breathing, in a quiet place, can result in a reduction of cortisol levels. "The Buddhists are right about breathing," McEwen notes. Studies by Kirk Brown and Richard Ryan, two psychologists at the University of Rochester, have shown that what they call "mindfulness"—basically, brief daily sessions of quiet meditation and deep breathing—increase the sense of optimism and self-satisfaction, and that the effect holds across broad categories of people, from college students to construction workers to cancer victims.[10] Long-term goals should be more ambitious than adding deep breathing to the daily routine. "Long-term, society must find a way to care less about how much we acquire, to consume less sugar and, simply, to slow down," McEwen says.

....

Are there other chemical connections? Esther Sternberg, director of a neuroendocrinology program at the National Institutes of Health, started on the path of wondering about the relationship between stress hormones and well-being when, as a young researcher, she was assigned a project on arthritis. She and her colleagues were to induce the condition in a strain of arthritis-susceptible lab animals, called Lewis rats, that had been bred to be prone to this disease. Sternberg realized that medical researchers who worked with Lewis rats never seemed to ask themselves why these particular types of mice were more likely than other rodents to get arthritis.

So she designed a test that was, more or less, intended to determine the mental state of rats, at least as far as can be shown by the measure of stress-hormone response. She exposed various types of rats to loud noises and other causes of nervous tension. When rats are under stress they elevate their blood content of costerone, a substance similar to cortisol. What Sternberg found was that the arthritis-resistant rats were the ones with high stress-response levels—costerone pulsed through their blood-streams, triggering metabolic processes that reduced the likelihood of the inflammations that cause arthritis. The blood of Lewis rats, which easily succumbed to arthritis, was low in stress hormones. Stress, in other words, was keeping some rats healthy.

Unfortunately Sternberg's discovery turned out not to have any therapeutic value against human arthritis. Nor did Sternberg attempt to duplicate her findings in people, by treating them like lab rats—your employer already exists to do that! But this set Sternberg to thinking about the extent to which natural selection might have encouraged the stress response, and the extent to which all of us fidgety, scowling, hard-to-please moderns may be descendants of those members of genus *Homo* who survived the evolutionary contest in part because they were stress-prone.

From there, Sternberg went on to study the mind-body connection, about which she is today a prominent authority.[11] Against the prevailing medical view that a detached consciousness floats above a deterministic body mechanism, Sternberg concluded that emotional states help regulate the body. Chemically, different parts of the brain become ascendant depending on emotional state, and send different messages. Positive chemical signals from the brain help the rest of the body organize and boost immune function, cellular health, and fertility; negative chemical signals dampen or interfere with these health cues. Many body functions—especially the immune response, Sternberg believes—are not automatons working in isolation but rather subtly linked to emotional state, in animals and especially in people. So although natural selection may have saddled us with a dependence on our stress hormones, evolutionary mechanisms also offer the promise of making us healthier if we can become happier.

This is what was believed by the ancient Greek physicians, whose *asclepion*s or healing spas were dedicated to the mind-body concept, and who taught that healthy diet, exercise, and what we would now call supportive relationships with friends and family were fundamental not just to life experiences but to physical health. This is also what New Age medicine teaches, which is why Sternberg has an uneasy relationship with the medical establishment. Some traditionalist researchers are offended by Sternberg's insistence that the mind can aid health.

Her research also suggests that someone who believes life has purpose, or that higher powers exist, may achieve an improved emotional state, and thus better health, than someone who feels anxiety brought on from the assumption that life is pointless. Whether men and women would from the standpoint of self-interest be better off believing that a God exists, or that existence has a purpose, is a topic this book will return to later. Suffice to note here that, during the postwar era, a strong majority of Western Europeans, and a significant percentage of Americans, say they have lost their belief in higher powers or a higher purpose. Many intellectuals and universities have during the same period encouraged the notion that life is a meaningless coincidence of amino acids and molecular heat exchange. "Man knows at last that he is alone in the universe's unfeeling immensity, out of which he emerged only by chance," the Nobel Prize–winning biologist Jacques Monod wrote in 1970, in an influential book that, for a generation of Western intellectuals, served as a manifesto of meaninglessness.

Perhaps life has a purpose, maybe it's sheer fluke; this is an argument for another day. From the standpoint of why life could get steadily better without Americans and Europeans seeming to feel any better, simply bear in mind that the rapid increase in living standards has been coincident with a decline in belief that life has meaning—and losing that belief, Sternberg thinks, makes us more likely to feel badly because our emotional centers will regulate our bodies less well.

Sternberg's basic idea, that emotions play a biological regulatory role, hearkens in some way to the three psychologists' "general theory of love" described in the previous chapter. More important, it hearkens to Darwin. Roughly since the Enlightenment, study of the mind had been flavored by the Cartesian contention that abstract thought is the calling of the brain, its high function; emotional states are low functions, base handicaps people should work to overcome. This view was challenged by Darwin who, in the years after publishing *On the Origin of Species,* became haunted by the notion that if physical characteristics evolved, then emotional states may have evolved, too. Darwin spent a decade on this question and the result was his last work, a little-known book called *The Expression of the Emotions in Man and Animals,* published in 1872.

Darwin speculated that moods, feelings, and psychological qualities must possess some benefit or natural selection would have eliminated them. Being afraid of packs of wolves holds an obvious survival benefit. But Darwin assumed the benefits of feelings must have gone further. Loyalty, for instance, could have improved the survival chances of early humans by causing them to care for one another. To Darwin, the idea that psychological states evolved was a hopeful one, helping explain why there was goodness in the world. The admirable emotions, he assumed, had been rewarded by natural selection.

But while Darwin's views on biology conquered the intellectual landscape, his views on emotions were quietly dismissed by tastemakers. Freud was about to propose a much more negative interpretation, that consciousness is steeped in self-delusion and that human emotions are the repellent byproducts of infantile sexual compulsion. This view has not stood the test of time; much of Freud has been discredited by subsequent research. But the sheer pessimism of Freud's thinking—he once memorably said that the most the typical person could hope for was to rise from crippling neuroses into "ordinary unhappiness"— appealed to the negative intellectual Zeitgeist that prevailed

around the beginning of the twentieth century. Darwin's more
affirmative take on emotions was forgotten.

························

To the extent stress links to the pace of contemporary life, especially of big-city and sprawling-suburb life, people might just
drive away. They don't. Millions of men and women in the United
States and the European Union speak wistfully of how pleasant
it would be to decamp to a peaceful, leafy small town where the
children could ride their bikes to the sports field. Every year
Time or *Newsweek* runs a cover extolling America's hundreds of
highly livable small- and medium-sized towns: Burlington, Vermont, or Ames, Iowa, or Lawrence, Kansas, or Cortland, New
York, lovely places where the schools are great, a beautiful home
costs half as much as in the city, and where you never waste a
single minute of your life in traffic jams. These stories always
predict that waves of stressed-out, fed-up people will abandon
the city and suburban rat races for the quiet countryside. Statis-
tically, this simply isn't happening.

Some people could not pack off to Lawrence, Kansas, because
their jobs require them to be in big cities or rat-race suburbs. But
millions of Americans, perhaps tens of millions, have enough career flexibility to make this change, and they don't. Consider
Burlington, Vermont, one of the most-lauded medium-sized
cities—people call it "small Seattle." The 2000 Census showed
the total number of people who moved from outside Vermont
into the Burlington city limits between 1990 and 2000 was less
than a thousand.

Small communities have many kinds of allure, in addition to
lower prices and less traffic. Paul Bruhn, head of the Preservation Trust of Vermont, says cooperation is the leading virtue of

the small-scale community: "In large cities people struggle more and everything is based on competition. In small areas, people know each other's names, and have to cooperate." Yet people don't move away from the big cities or the rat-race suburbs because, while stress-inducing, these places have compensating virtues—cultural institutions, sports teams, top hospitals, a little of anything you might want. Big cities and suburbs also offer release from having everyone recognize you, which is nice at times and stifling at others; in small towns, everyone knows your business. People may decline to move to the quiet countryside because most people like stuff, and cities and suburbs have more of it. People are willing to bear stress in return for acquisitions, a bargain that evolution may encourage.

Commentators keep predicting that our acquisitions will drown us, or destroy us through environmental harm, or turn against us in some kind of science-fiction nightmare; the real danger of pursuit of stuff may be that most stuff is harmless and, therefore, utterly seductive. As Albert Borgmann, a philosopher who fled the big city to live most of his life in a small Montana town, notes, "The Greens are kidding themselves when they maintain the simple life will be revived because technology will collapse or become sinister. Technology grows ever safer and more benign. There will be steadily fewer arguments against technology per se." For example, all cars, even SUVs, emit steadily less pollution, and within a decade or two may be powered by "fuel cell" engines that require no fossil fuels and produce no greenhouse gases. At that point the car will become environmentally innocuous, which means cars will be around forever.

Borgmann believes that Western society is caught up in a "device paradigm" whereby people are pursuing gizmos to perform every task when they might actually be happier performing the tasks themselves, and then not having to work so frantically to be able to afford the gizmos.[12] But if there may someday be a serious movement to slow down the pace of life by stepping away from frantic big-city existence, or away from a "device paradigm" standard, there is no sign of this in Western culture yet. We could vote with our feet against the rat race, and don't.

Two considerations remain in the contemporary outbreak of stress: One we can do nothing about, and one we can.

First, the one we can do nothing about. It may be that people grow steadily better off, yet seemingly no happier, because there is a baseline anxiety in all our hearts, and that anxiety is the fear of death.

Higher living standards and better health care might help you live longer with more vigor, but cannot alter the fact that your life must end. Many philosophers, prominently Martin Heidegger, who wrote mainly in the first half of the twentieth century, have supposed that anxiety about death is always below the surface of the human mind and simply cannot be salved—even if you were fabulously wealthy and lived in a hedonic paradise drinking champagne and being attended by gorgeous courtesans or handsome gigolos, subconscious fear of death would prevent you from ever really feeling content.

Most disturbance in modern society, Heidegger supposed, traces not to class warfare or economic competition or superpower politics but to our awareness of our own temporality.[13] Ever advancing science can't do anything about the fact that we all will die—can't do anything yet, anyway—and thus a baseline anxiety cannot be relieved. If Heidegger, who died in 1976, were alive now, he might say that endlessly rising prosperity and knowledge makes this anxiety worse, by reminding us that no matter how much we discover, create, or acquire, we will still die.

Heidegger used his chain of logic to conclude that men and women ought to exist in a state of ceaseless, wrenching existential despondency regarding the inevitable closing of their eyes. Only a blithe simpleton would enjoy the world rather than be anguished, Heidegger asserted, and this endorsement of hopelessness has come to inform much of contemporary intellectual discourse. Yet even supposing there is an incurable baseline anxiety about death, this need be no reason not to take pleasure in life. There are two basic poles of possibility: that there is an afterlife and that there is not. If the former, we need not despair. If the latter, and life must end in oblivion, then why worry about it? Should it turn out there is nothing after the grave, then in order to enjoy the gift of life you must accept the inevitability of its conclusion, and fretting only erodes the experience of whatever number of days you've been granted. The Dylan Thomas attitude—that one should "rage, rage against the dying of the light"—seems particularly ridiculous in this case, as raging won't change a thing, but will pretty effectively spoil whatever number of days you've been granted.

FROM MATERIAL WANT TO MEANING WANT. Now the stress cause that does lie within our power to change: rejecting the false sense that life lacks meaning.

For generations—centuries—the longings of most people have focused on secure living circumstances, reasonable comfort, and decent health. People were interested in the great questions of meaning, of course, but material wants had to come first.

Today the majority of men and women in the United States and the European Union have acquired the living circumstances, reasonable comfort, and decent health for which previous generations yearned. Now we begin to hunger both for comfort and meaning. A transition from material want to meaning want is in progress on an historically unprecedented scale—involving hundreds of millions of people—and may eventually be recognized as a principal cultural development of our age.

Meaning can be found. The life-is-meaningless intellectual fad is almost over, wafting away of its own insubstantiality, while the rising interest in spiritual questions shows that average people are way ahead of the intellectuals on this one. The notion—advanced by existential thinkers—that if humanity "emerged only by chance" then our lives lack meaning is perhaps the silliest idea ever entertained by serious people. Meaning can exist regardless of whether our being is the gift of a divinity or a natural result.

Here are the poles of possibility: If God exists, then surely life has meaning. And if God does not exist, then surely life has meaning. Meaning may be divinely conferred. If not, we can create meaning by living decent and admirable lives.

As Western society moves from material want to meaning want, we must always be aware that meaning is harder to come by than a car or house. Freud's contention that the most the typical person could aspire to was "ordinary unhappiness" may have been snide, but recognizes a truth. Look for unhappiness and you will surely find it, as unhappiness is a condition anyone can enter. Look for meaning, and you may be tested.

Ultimately, the reason that possessions and their attendant stress are so alluring is that acquiring possessions is a simpler challenge than acquiring a fulfilling philosophy of life. Western society has concentrated intently on producing a vast output of material goods in part because this was an empirical, tangible goal—we knew we could do it. Now we face a task about which we are less confident, the search for meaning.

Chapter 7

....

HOW TO GAIN YOUR MIND

Endless money anxiety, hassles, and hurry; constant noise, crowding, and demands. Newscasts full of scary reports of crimes and threats. Ubiquitous high-decibel claims that families are breaking down, values are eroding, and society has lost its bearings. The pressures of civilization make it a wonder we don't all lose our minds.

And yet, somehow, most people turn out okay. Only a tiny fraction of the populace commits antisocial acts, develops a psychosis, or loses the ability to function in society. People may fail to become happy but few fall to pieces. Considering modern stress, most of our heads are in surprisingly good condition.

This is the fundamental insight of an emerging field called positive psychology, which seeks to change the focus of study of the mind from figuring out what causes psychosis to figuring out what causes sanity. Traditionally, "researchers have tended to study the things that can go wrong in people's minds, but not the things that can go right," says Robert Emmons, a professor of psychology at the University of California at Davis. Yet what can go right within the mind is at least as important. And, in contrast to much psychological research that has generated interesting data but mainly been of use to psychologists themselves in advancing their careers, positive psychology may produce knowledge that improves lives and makes the world a better place.

....

As a science, psychology had its origins in what the Enlightenment called the desire to "elevate" the mind. At least as early as the Greeks, philosophers speculated about what caused some people to be virtuous and others immoral, some merry and others dreary. The nature-versus-nurture debate dates at least this far back. Socrates, for one, endorsed nurture, viewing the personality as formed of a person's conscious efforts and calling uprightness "an acquired judgment which aspires after excellence."[1] The ancients speculated, as well, about what instills madness, from "possession" to maladies little different than those observed today. (Manic depression is believed to be mainly genetic in origin, so this condition is likely to have existed in ancient times.) By the Enlightenment, psychology had become mainly affiliated with the university and with the church, and its calling was to discover how to teach "elevated" thoughts that would improve people's lives.[2]

Arguably, psychology became a topic of general public interest in the West with the 1774 publication of Goethe's *The Sorrows of Young Werther,* a novel that depicted a protagonist suffering what would now be called clinical depression. Werther found life unbearably sad, and eventually committed suicide when the woman he loved married someone else for money.

Publication of the book caused a sensation across Europe and made *Werther* one of the world's first best-sellers, among the initial books to be printed by the crateload and mass-marketed, in this case including from peddlers' pushcarts. The book caused a sensation because it was considered shocking to discuss someone's innermost thoughts, scandalous to suggest someone could be rendered miserable by being alive; and because large numbers of readers who were themselves in private anguish identified with the central character. Unfortunately, they identified too well: *The Sorrows of Young Werther* triggered a wave of suicides across Europe, mostly by university students and rejected suitors, many of whom left notes attributing their decisions to having read the book.

All historical generalizations are inexact, of course, but Goethe's novel can be said to have placed the concept of psychology into general public debate. Roughly by the beginning of the nineteenth century, it had become common to attribute people's actions to private psychological motives; this seems obvious today, but in prior centuries the standard assumption was that God, Satan, law, and natural compulsions dictated nearly all human behavior. When in 1803 the French social commentator known to history as Madame de Staël (her birth name was Anne Necker) said that Napoleon Bonaparte "believes anyone who says he loves liberty, or fears God, or prefers a clear conscience to self-interest, is just a man following the forms of etiquette to conceal his selfish calculations," she was both commenting on Napoleon's Machiavellian worldview and declaring a radical idea—that people engage in behavior for hidden psychological reasons.

By the middle of the nineteenth century, study of psychology was a hot topic, especially in Germany and Spain, and one associated with the democracy advocates: Understanding the real reasons for people's actions, it was thought, would create ways to persuade Europeans to reject royal rule and demand the vote. Much of the most exciting work in literature—by Dostoyevsky, Flaubert, and Stendhal, to name a few of many—concerned explorations of psychological themes.

So far, so good. But it can be said, again using inexact generalization, that psychology took a wrong turn in the late nineteenth century, around the time of Freud. The analyst from Vienna probably acquired fame not so much because of his theories (few of which are believed today, unlike the ideas of Darwin and Einstein, who were right about practically everything) but because he symbolized the emergence of the notion that psychology plays a pivotal role in the human experience. The good or bad of his theories aside, today what seems significant about Freud is that he turned psychology from a hopeful field—one seeking elevated behavior and democratic ideals—to a dismal science. Behavior, Freud cheerfully pronounced, is the robotic byproduct of mindless sexual urges. The consciousness is steeped in self-delusion; happiness is close to unattainable; large numbers of people should be expected to lose their minds; virtue is an illusion, just something we do to impress others; cures of psychological problems are nearly impossible. The best that can be hoped for, Freud concluded, is to understand why our minds are wretched.

As Edward Diener, the professor of psychology at the University of Illinois, has noted, "Freudian theory offered little of value to society, wanting to convince us we were all screwed up and there was nothing we could do beyond getting our misery under control." And according to Freud, the future would become steadily bleaker: The quickening pace, rising stress, and sheer clamor of industrial society would increase the number of people who go crazy. With each passing year, more men and women of the Western nations would grow "neurotic under the pressure of civilizing trends," Freud pronounced.[3]

Set aside that, under this formulation, society would need to divert ever more of its resources to—well, look here, to psychotherapists! In some ways, Freud's opinions about human psychology sound like asking the Army Corps of Engineers if a river needs a dam.

Today we should bear in mind that the Vienna doctor's profoundly negative view of psychology caught on in part because it was expounded at a time when the intellectual world was adopting negative views on many topics, existentialism and the "lost generation" fatalism of World War I prominent among them. With its huge numbers of soldiers engaged in miserable trench warfare, subjected day after day to nerve-shattering artillery barrages and watching comrades sacrificed by senile commanders in futile charges against machine guns, World War I also created the first large cohort of veterans suffering what was then called "shell shock" and would now be called posttraumatic disorder. Psychologists and psychiatrists of the time invested their energies in treating shell-shock victims. Often they did little good. Psychology came to be viewed as a depressing pursuit without utility, eccentric doctors talking to hopeless nut cases and nothing being accomplished.

Later, after World War II, the federal agency then called the Veterans Administration would fund the education of a generation of clinicians whose first concern was treating the psychological problems of those who had seen combat in that war. Results of the treatment of combat survivors began to improve, but to visit a psychologist or psychiatrist continued to be viewed as an act of desperation, suitable only for someone going over the edge. Psychology remained a dismal pursuit, focused on what goes wrong, not what can go right.

·····················

In the period between the world wars, the enthusiasm for Freudian analysis declined. This happened because Freud had based many of his theories on speculation about the conditions of human prehistory, and anthropology, a growth field in the early twentieth century, turned out not to support Freudian assumptions. As Freudianism faded, an equally unpleasant psychological theory called behaviorism arose to supplant it.

Behaviorism held that we're all mice in a meaningless maze, seeking rewards and avoiding punishments. Behaviorist theory viewed human feeling with open contempt, called morality simply a trained response unrelated to any deeper truths of right versus wrong, and even denied the existence of consciousness, asserting everything is just stimulus response. According to the behaviorist consensus of the time, the ideal person would be *Star Trek*'s Mr. Spock, intelligent but completely freed of emotion.

Most behaviorism was based on animal studies, particularly studies of how mice and dogs respond when confronted with problems or zapped with electric shocks; ultimately, behaviorism came to view human beings as no different from any other animals. The period when behaviorism was the regnant idea of academic psychology, roughly from the 1930s to the early 1960s, was a bleak one indeed, behaviorists advocating bizarre theories of social control and responding with barely concealed disgust to concepts like "morality" or "happiness." The low point came when the behaviorist guru John Watson declared that parents should never hug or kiss children because this would only condition them to want affection. Better to let infants sob, Watson asserted, so they learn life is cold and pointless and grow up feeling contempt for emotion. Watson called his concept "detached parenting"; this idea actually enjoyed a phase of popularity with how-to-raise-baby "experts." Some researchers speculate that a portion of the unhappiness that manifested in the Western nations beginning in the postwar era traces to the adulthood of babies whose psyches were harmed by Watson's crazy ideas. (For an excellent history of bringing-up-baby fads, see *Raising America: Experts, Parents and a Century of Advice About Children* by Ann Hulbert.)[4]

By the 1960s, behaviorism had crumpled under its own inherent absurdity and been replaced by "cognitive psychology," whose proponents believe in demystifying psychological issues and treating them with common sense. Cognitive psychology holds that many problems of the mind can be treated by talking them through, especially by trying to understand what caused the problem to arise.

The founding significant school of cognitive psychology, called humanistic psychology, began to draw notice in the late 1950s. Begun by Abraham Maslow, humanistic psychology argued that life is a wonderful gift—Maslow's was the first optimistic theory of psychology in more than a century—and that people could be happier if they understood that human needs unfold in a hierarchy beginning with the physical and ascending to the spiritual. Humanistic psychology ended up being satirized for the phrase "self-actualization," which was prone to goofy sixties-hippy California-sunset associations. But the theory was a solid one and useful to the typical person, in part because humanistic psychology holds that the final decades of life can be more interesting and rewarding than the early decades, because it is the wisdom that comes with age that allows a person to experience spiritual fulfillment.

Humanistic psychology lost steam when Maslow died in 1970, but the theory laid the groundwork for the positive-psychology movement, which began catching on among researchers in the 1990s. Originally, the new idea called itself the "good life" movement, and its first goal was to figure out why some people—Dietrich Bonhoeffer, Eleanor Roosevelt—led lives of conspicuous virtue. Martin Seligman, the psychologist at the University of Pennsylvania mentioned in the previous chapter, and other early "good life" theorists thought psychology was spending too much time analyzing why some people descend into psychosis and nowhere near enough time figuring out why other people become altruistic, honest, loyal, or noble.

....

Psychology, the new thinkers contended, had grown obsessed with the negative. By one count, during the twentieth century there were 8,166 scholarly psychological articles published on the topic "anger," versus 416 on "forgiveness."[5] The presumably encyclopedic *Encyclopedia of Human Emotions,* a reference work for clinicians, listed page after page after page of detrimental emotional states, but contained no entry for "gratitude." The *Diagnostic and Statistical Manual,* another clinicians' reference work, detailed fourteen major psychoses and dozens of neuroses and other psychology maladies, but no comparable manual lists what Seligman called "the sanities"—positive conditions that psychologists should try to encourage.

To a certain extent, psychology's focus on the negative was a reflection of the disease-treatment orientation of modern medicine. In the same way a physician assumes the normal body has

a temperature of 98.6 and views any deviation as a sign of illness, psychologists assumed a normal person would have no
mental problems and that any deviation meant a disease was
present. In this context, conventional postwar psychologists focused almost exclusively on the negative, what specialists called
the "pathological model" of the psyche. People are normal; if
not, they are sick. Theorists for what would become the positive
psychology movement felt that was missing the point. A happy
or honorable person didn't just happen; something caused the
person to become happy or honorable. *Why* did Eleanor Roosevelt turn out so virtuous? Were there influences that helped her
become virtuous that could be encouraged in other people, too?
Being physically healthy requires effort—you've got to work at
it with proper diet, exercise, and so on. Maybe being mentally
healthy is the result of conscious effort, too.

Of equal importance, the negative intellectual Zeitgeist that
prevailed for most of the twentieth century tended to romanticize mental illness. Psychological conditions were seen as the
consequence of repressive and exploitive Western societies, depression or neurosis as the inevitable response. When someone
loses his or her mind, many academics, writers, and philosophers
assumed, the awful truth about society is revealed. Positive psychology countered instead that a shining truth is revealed when
someone acquires virtue or lives happily. To the professions of
psychology and psychiatry, this thought was a bombshell.

Eventually the name "good life" movement was dropped because it connoted champagne and dancing till dawn. Positive
psychology became the label, and here are some of its findings:

One is that attaining happiness is hard work. The nineteenth-century English essayist John Lubbock wrote, "Happiness is a thing to be practiced, like the violin." Modern research confirms this view. Laura King, a psychologist at the University of Missouri, has found that achieving a positive attitude toward life requires considerable effort: People may slip into unhappiness simply because it is the path of least resistance.[6] (Freud anticipated this when he wrote, "unhappiness is much less difficult to experience" than lofty mental states.) Positive-psychology theorists marvel at studies showing that quadriplegics, as a group, have a higher sense of well-being than lottery winners. The lottery winners, we can guess, were swept up in materialism and betrayed by it, while the quadriplegics had to adjust to their conditions, and in so doing learned to appreciate the fact of being alive. More, quadriplegics must struggle daily—must work for everything they attain—while lottery winners may lay around snapping their fingers and expecting others to deliver contentment to them.

Positive psychology is deeply interested in the evolution of emotions, the very subject Darwin thought ill-explored. Expanding on Darwin's basic notions, Barbara Fredrickson, a psychologist at the University of Michigan, has shown that natural selection might have favored the positive emotions in many ways.[7] Love among families would cause them to nurture children, increasing the odds of passing along DNA; romantic love would cause men to remain with the mothers of their children, providing resources, protecting children, and guarding the mother during the debilitation that accompanies pregnancy and postnatal recovery. Being joyous or outgoing, Fredrickson supposes, would have improved your odds of making friends who would come to your aid during troubles. Stress and wariness may have been favored by natural selection, but the original condition of the human being need not necessarily have been all downbeat.

Positive psychology also contends that you are better off being an optimist than a pessimist. Lisa Aspinwall, a psychologist at the University of Utah, has shown that as a group the optimistic do better in life than the pessimistic, as measured by longevity, earnings, marriage duration, and other indicators.[8] This does not mean become a Pollyanna; optimists, Aspinwall finds, are actually better than pessimists in overcoming negative experiences, because they can bounce back rather than be dragged under.

"Suppose a student got a bad grade in my class," offered Seligman by way of explanation. "A pessimist would say, 'Professors are unfair.' This attitude would only increase the chance of having another unhappy experience with a professor, or discourage the person from trying at all. An optimist would respond to the bad grade by saying, 'Professor Seligman is unfair.' Then I'm the one to blame, rather than assuming the whole world is a fraud, and you can approach the next professor with the hope that he will treat you fairly." Optimists, positive psychology finds, are not trying to dodge or deny the many objectionable aspects of life. Rather, they are employing mental strategies that help overcome the bad and improve the situation. In this thinking, it is in your self-interest to be optimistic.

Optimism can be instilled, partly by training yourself to think positively. Among other things, positive psychologists and other practitioners of cognitive therapy teach patients to beware of the "automatic" negative thoughts that flit through the mind when unhappiness is coming on, and to counter such thoughts. It's common, for example, for those who suffer depression to experience an automatic thought along the lines of "here we go again" whenever something happens that resembles a cause of sadness from the past. Positive psychology teaches to fight the thought "here we go again"; instead, focus on how the new set of circumstances might turn out differently than the prior one.

Anyone who has read any of the "power of positive thinking" volumes, from the originals by Norman Vincent Peale to his many imitators, will recognize such advice. Trying to think positively is common sense, if for no other reason than you can be sure that thinking negatively will accomplish nothing. One reason for the Western depression epidemic may be that contemporary society, awash in media and intellectual negativism, has lost track of the common-sense guidance that an optimistic outlook usually improves your prospects. Positive psychology is attempting to revive this view.

Seligman advocates "learned optimism," that by learning to expect tribulations and occasional blue periods, a person can avoid the sort of discouragement that engenders depression. Beginning in primary school, Seligman thinks, children should be taught to anticipate difficulties in life. That way, when problems occur, as inevitably they will, children will not be traumatized but see their need to deal with the problem as part of the natural course of events. Though positive psychology is positive, it opposes any idealized picture of life; idealized expectations only foster disillusionment, whereas fully anticipating some really bad days now and then may foster a sustainably hopeful outlook. Managing one's approach to life in this way requires, of course, self-control. And another positive psychologist, Roy Baumeister of Case Western Reserve University, has found that self-control is a better predictor of "life outcomes"—career success, well-being—than is IQ.

Today, positive psychology, and most forms of cognitive therapy, are concerned with treatment of the depression epidemic. A depressed person has two basic choices, therapy or medication such as Prozac or similar drugs. Receiving therapy or taking medication for depression both have about the same success rate—two-thirds of people who do either get better, while one-third fail to respond regardless. Many psychologists argue for therapy over medication in many cases. Therapy has no side effects and continues to help once the therapy sessions end, whereas medication only works when being taken.

The financial wrinkle is that just as insurers would rather pay for Ritalin than ADHD therapy, insurers would rather pay for medication for depression than therapy; or will authorize therapy for depression only when the diagnosis includes one of the standard codes for mental illness found in the *Diagnostic and Statistical Manual*. The result is that many either pay for therapy out of their own pockets, to avoid having such an entry on their medical records, or, if they can't afford to pay, receive no help at all. At this writing, psychologists are arguing for legislation and changes in insurance-company policies that would provide treatment for those with depression, and similar mild psychological problems, without stigma.

Extending health care therapeutic coverage to a broader range of mild to moderate psychological problems, such as unipolar depression, would not be without cost, of course. Therapy costs money, and psychologists benefit by recommending it just as pharmaceutical manufacturers benefit by persuading patients to take drugs. But as the West grows both more affluent and more depressed, doesn't an investment in society's psychological well-being make sense?

Today some might say that those who feel bad all the time, or have unfocused anxieties, should keep quiet and tough it out. But a generation ago, physicians thought that those who had failing knees, or chronic back discomfort, or gradually occluding heart arteries, or arthritic joints, or any of a number of unpleasant but not imminently life-threatening ailments should keep quiet and tough it out. Now the premise of medical care for our bodies is that every possible cure and relief from pain should be provided. Shouldn't this same premise extend to relief from pain of our minds and spirits?

If medical knowledge of the future will significantly extend human longevity, as there is reason to hope, it will become ever more important that lives be lived with reasonable well-being and fulfillment, or else why be around a long time merely to feel bad for a long time? This means human beings will require steadily improved understanding of their own psychology.

Evolution had little reason to be concerned about our psyches. Forces of natural selection serve mainly to make a living thing more likely to reproduce, and what may happen in the years afterward, or how a thinking organism may feel about it all, is of small consequence to nature. But these issues are of great consequence to us, to our families, friends, neighbors, and faiths—especially if, as lifespans lengthen, more and more people in the world live most of their lives after the age of reproduction, which is the point at which natural selection stops paying much attention to us.

For the short term, the statistics on modern treatment of depression are encouraging: If you suffer this malady seek help, because there is a two-thirds likelihood you will get better.

For the long term, what does positive psychology tell us about how to reorder our lives? Here are two important points of advice: We should be more grateful, and more forgiving. Religion and folk wisdom have long held these feelings to be meritorious. New research suggests gratitude and forgiveness are in our self-interest.

Chapter 8

....

SELFISH REASONS TO

BECOME A BETTER PERSON

The story is so striking it is hard to believe. Amy Biehl, an idealistic white California college student, wins a Fulbright Scholarship to travel to South Africa to assist the anti-apartheid movement; caught in a 1993 race riot, she is murdered by a black mob. Following years of grief, Amy's parents Linda and Peter gave up their fashionable upper-middle-class California lifestyle and moved to South Africa to try to complete the work their daughter started. The Biehls not only met two of the young men who killed Amy but, learning of the chaotic circumstances of the riot and the heartfelt remorse of the killers, gradually *became friends* with the men who helped murder their daughter. The young men asked if they could atone for their crime by doing public service for a foundation the Biehls established in Amy's name. For two years they worked with Amy's parents daily, and eventually became close enough that they addressed Linda Biehl as "mom."

Few among us could be so forgiving, whatever religions may

teach. Amy Biehl must have been an exceptional person to inspire her parents to transform their lives in her memory; to be capable of such gestures, her parents must be exceptional as well. Most people will never be tested in the way that the Biehls were; in an ideal world, no one ever would. What lingers from the telling of this story is that both the elder Biehls—Peter died of natural causes in 2002—reported that they felt happier and more at peace after forgiving two of their daughter's killers.

The Biehls' experience is an unusually dramatic example of a rule that seems to apply to everyone: Forgiveness is good not just for the person forgiven, but for the person who forgives.

That being forgiving is good for *you*, in addition to the person you forgive, is among the most compelling findings of positive psychology. Research now suggests that those who take a forgiving attitude toward others not only make better friends, neighbors, and coworkers—anyone would guess that—but are themselves happier, healthier people who live longer than others and know more success in life. Are they forgiving because happiness makes them magnanimous, or does forgiving improve their well-being, bringing about the happiness? Studies suggest the latter.[1]

Similarly, positive psychology finds that people who take a grateful attitude toward life, counting their blessings rather than inventorying their complaints, tend to be healthier, happier, and more successful than others. Again it appears to be the sense of gratitude that causes the happiness and health, rather than the other way around.

Such insights are important because Americans and Europeans live in an age in which most aspects of life are improving for most people, yet many feel progressively worse; in parallel, Americans and Europeans live in an age in which the collecting of grievances and holding of grudges is elaborately encouraged, while forgiveness and gratitude are looked down upon as quaint traits of Kansas farm wives from previous centuries.

Trends in the educational, legal, political, and media systems all urge contemporary men and women to view themselves as wronged by various forces real or imagined; to get angry and fight back; to fixate on any harms of which they may have been the target; to search out wrongs about which to become outraged. Americans and Europeans are further encouraged to even the score with those who may or may not have wronged them, using litigation or bad publicity or other means. The recent fads of children filing lawsuits against parents, or parents filing accusations against other parents regarding events between their children on the sports field or at school, are just two examples of this.

Some people actually are victimized, of course, and it is healthy for society if big business and big government institutions, especially, know that people will not just quietly take mistreatment. But perhaps the fact that modern Western culture encourages men and women to nurse grievances reveals something about the progress paradox. We feel bad though things are getting better; various cultural forces encourage us to seek things to feel bad about; people don't know that forgiveness and gratitude may be antidotes to their own acetous feelings.

Most larger social forces are essentially beyond the typical person's control. If you don't like suburban expansion or rap music or the designated-hitter rule or United States foreign policy regarding Ecuador, on a practical basis there is relatively little you can do about these things. Each person can, however, decide for himself or herself what kind of view about life to take.

Cultural, media, and social institutions now urge us to take the negative view. Psychological research is beginning to show that taking the positive view is in our self-interest.

....

The murder of Amy Biehl is an extreme example, but one that shows the dynamic positive psychologists have found in forgiveness studies, which is a relatively new subset of psychological research. Amy's grieving parents faced a choice: They could allow their lives to be burned up in hatred for those who committed the crime and for the place where it happened, or they could forgive. Given the horrible circumstances, no one would have criticized them for taking the first course. But would it have been in the Biehls' self-interest? Forgiving Amy's killers caused the Biehls to become better off. Rather than having their years subsumed in enmity, Amy's parents led important, constructive lives as part of the great South African reconciliation effort; kept Amy's spirit glowing as a living memory; felt hope rather than anger.

In the more routine situations most people face, research shows that being a forgiving person is essential to leading a contented life—for the same reason, that the person who forgives comes out ahead. Even when someone wrongs you, feeling fury or experiencing hate only causes your life to descend into unhappiness and resentment. Then you are the one who suffers, not the person you're angry at. Forgiving, on the other hand, lifts the burden. Perhaps when Buddha, Jesus, Baha'ullah, and other great spiritual figures taught followers to forgive those who sin against them, this wasn't only the pronouncement of holy philosophy—they were giving practical down-to-earth life advice.

Everett Worthington, a professor of psychology at Virginia Commonwealth University and a pioneer in forgiveness research, has found that people who do not forgive the wrongs committed against them tend to have negative indicators of well-being: more stress-related disorders, lower immune-system function, and worse rates of cardiovascular disease than the population as a whole. In effect, by failing to forgive they punish themselves. Unforgiving people also experience higher rates of divorce, which reduces well-being. This is true because married men and women consistently do better on health barometers, especially longevity and incidence of depression, than do the divorced, the separated, or the never-wed.

Marriage isn't right for everyone and some people become trapped in bad or abusive marriages; but, overall, those who wed and stay together are consistently better-off as a group than those who do not marry, or who separate. Positive psychology research shows that the most miserable class of persons in the West is the separated; the second-least-happy, the divorced. As noted in an earlier chapter, all forms of longevity are higher among the married, as the University of Chicago social scientist Linda Waite has found. Being and staying married lowers your risk of dying of cancer as much as being ten years younger.[2] The married as a group are also better off financially than the never-married or those whose marriages fail, partly because two people combining finances have higher effective purchasing power, especially in the housing market.

Those thinkers who have denounced marriage as a creaking social convention should bear in mind that one reason some poor and working-class men and women do not escape poverty is that the lower class has a much higher incidence of divorce than the upper-middle and upper classes. Divorce causes the lower class to lose the benefits of combined finances while being saddled with the sunk costs of lawyers, court fines, dual living arrangements, and so on. It's a fallacy that the expensive parts of town are where the divorces are. Divorces among the well-off surely happen, with special frequency at the very top, where wealthy men can afford to throw wives overboard and essentially purchase someone younger.[3] But, overall, people above the median income are less likely to divorce than people below it. Staying married is one of the success secrets of the well-off.

As Donna Ginther and Madeline Zavodny, two economists at the Federal Reserve Bank of Atlanta, have shown, what's sometimes called the "marriage premium"—the fact that the married have higher average earnings than the unmarried—is not an artifact of employers being willing to pay more to married workers.[4] Marriage, Ginther and Zavodny think, brings about higher earnings because it makes the married healthier, more stable, happier, and more reliable, and thus more valuable in the work force. All this relates to forgiveness, since the willingness to forgive is essential to keeping a marriage together.

People who forgive, Worthington further finds, as a group have fewer episodes of clinical depression and better "social support" than the unforgiving. Social support, a complicated way of saying friends and family, generally is an indicator of well-being. People who are active members of almost any kind of group, from houses of worship to volleyball leagues, tend to live longer and report themselves as happier than solitary people, in part because they make friends who come to their aid in social-support situations. And forgiving people, Worthington finds, are better at making friends than those who carry grudges.[5]

....

While psychology has long studied the coping mechanisms that people use to deal with anger, resentment, and desire for revenge, only recently has forgiveness become a common subject of research. Some of the reluctance to study forgiveness stems, the psychologist Kenneth Pargament of Bowling Green State University supposes, from the assumption that forgiveness can only be motivated by faith. For instance, a study by the University of Maryland found that many therapists would discuss forgiveness with patients exclusively in a religious context, steering clear of the topic with nonreligious patients. This reflects the contemporary intellectual, media, and cultural assumptions that we ought to be nursing our grievances, ever on guard for uncovering new complaints. In a milieu in which victimization is viewed as a desirable state, it might seem that only articles of faith could justify forgiveness.

Yet forgiveness can have either a spiritual or secular basis, and both seem equally effective at improving the life of the person who forgives. One of Pargament's studies, published in the *Journal of Clinical Psychology*, compared three groups of subjects who had been wronged by someone in a significant way and sought counseling.[6] The first group received forgiveness counseling based on religious precepts; the second group received forgiveness counseling that made no mention of faith, simply argued the benefits of forgiving; the third group, which was the control, received conventional anger-management counseling that said nothing about forgiveness. The study found that people in the first and second groups had better outcomes than those in the third, and by about the same margins in each case. That is to say, whether someone forgave for reasons of faith or of secular ethics, the benefits were the same. What mattered was not the reason the person forgave, but simply that he or she decided to forgive.

Here are other results from the new wave of forgiveness research:

- A study at the University of Wisconsin showed that older people are more likely to forgive than the young. This suggests that the ability to forgive is a form of wisdom, learned during the passage through life. Everyone knows teenagers and young adults are, on average, more hot-headed than the mature. This study showed that hot-headedness declines not because people lose the passion of youth but rather because they acquire the wisdom of experience. We don't, on average, become more angry and resentful with each passing year: We become less so. This may help explain one of the other central findings of positive psychology, that, as a group, senior citizens, not the attractive and energetic young, have the highest sense of well-being.

- A study at the University of Northern Iowa of psychological treatment plans for adult victims of childhood incest found that those who went through forgiveness therapy experienced less anxiety and clinical depression than a control group. Gains for the forgiveness group persisted after therapy concluded, an important sign; often those who suffer psychological maladies report improved well-being while receiving therapy, but relapse once therapy ends.

- A study conducted by the Institute for Social Research at the University of Michigan supported the contention that older people are more likely to forgive than the young and also found that older people who forgive have better overall health indicators than those who nurse acrimony. "The benefits of forgiveness seem to increase with age," psychologist Loren Toussaint, the lead researcher, said. That is, an older person who takes a forgiving attitude may be rewarded with fewer stress disorders, longer life, and other health benefits. Young people who take a forgiving attitude toward life don't appear to enjoy better health than the young as a group, but then the overall health of young Western citizens is so good that, other than reducing obesity, it's hard to imagine how medical trends for the young could be improved.

• A study of elderly women, published in the journal *Psychotherapy*, found that those who scored well on a standard test of forgiveness traits had fewer episodes of anxiety or depression compared to those who scored poorly.

Of course, personality traits can never be unbundled from one another for wholly detached analysis. And forgiveness, while readily preached, is less readily practiced. Pargament notes that when men or women first suffer a significant wrong or a tragic loss, it's often pointless to speak of forgiveness: That can only come with time. One study at the University of Miami in Ohio suggested those whose partners had been sexually unfaithful recover faster if they exact some kind of emotional revenge on the guilty party. Thus, gentlemen, do not fool around and then tell your wife or significant other that research shows it is in her self-interest to forgive you.

But if the positive psychology movement is right, men and women should forgive most of the wrongs and offenses they experience in life, not for reasons of religious belief or secular philosophy, although those reasons are admirable, but for the self-interested reason that people who let go of their grievances are better off as a result. And if you make the world a more peaceful place in the course of your self-interested forgiving, that's a nice bonus.

....

The idea that it's in your own self-interest to work toward a positive mental quality such as forgiveness may be a break-through thought. Through the centuries, both faiths and systems of philosophy have made arguments that men and women should walk the gentle path. Many have listened but many more have not, answering simply, "What's in it for me?" If positive psychology can show that when you behave in a kind way, what's in it for you is a happier life, this will create a powerful new incentive for people to emphasize the better parts of their nature. Modern society offers ever more affluence, ever more freedom, and ever longer lives, combined with ever more pressure to be irritable, petulant, and dissatisfied. A new reason to seek the good that is within us all is needed, and that new reason might be the self-interest argument in goodness. Perhaps this can soften the acidic mood of our times.

A second instance where this reasoning may apply is gratitude. We know we're supposed to say thank you, to display humility at certain times; almost everyone at some point feels grateful to have been given a chance to live in a world that is strange and beautiful. The religious feel it essential to express appreciation to their Maker for having been made. But that's about as far as it goes for gratitude, which, it's fair to say, most men and women view as a minor emotion—mostly a form of manners, a civility.

Contemporary Western society abides by the surface forms of gratitude by being unfailingly polite—practically everyone says thank you, even in brief phone conversations with total strangers—but how much *true* gratitude is in our hearts? Though most people in the United States and the European Union have far more in material terms than their forebears just a few generations back, how many of us pause to reflect on how favored we are by history? Though most people in the United States and European Union will live much longer, with far more personal freedom, than their forebears just a few generations back, how many of us feel grateful that we can behold the morning sunrise so often and in such liberty? Don't we spend more time feeling envy over those who have more stuff, or more luck or more looks, than feeling thankfulness that we are not one of the 99 percent of *Homo sapiens* ever to have existed who possessed less and knew less and died much younger?

All this matters not as a moralizing sermon but a matter of self-interest, owing to the findings of positive psychology. "Gratitude research is beginning to suggest that feelings of thankfulness have tremendous positive value in helping people cope with daily problems, especially stress, and to achieve a positive sense of the self," says Robert Emmons of the University of California at Davis. Consider what recent academic studies on this topic have shown:[7]

- People who describe themselves as feeling grateful to others, and either to God or to creation in general, tend to have higher vitality and more optimism, suffer less stress, and experience fewer episodes of clinical depression than the population as a whole. This result holds even when researchers factor out such things as age, health, and income—equalizing for the fact that the young, the well-to-do, or the hale and hearty might have more to be grateful for.
- Grateful people tend to suffer less anxiety about status or the

accumulation of material possessions. Partly because of this, they are more likely to describe themselves as happy or satisfied in life.

- In an experiment with college students, those who kept a "gratitude journal," a weekly record of things they feel grateful for, achieved better physical health, were more optimistic, exercised more regularly, and described themselves as happier than a control group of students who kept no journals but had the same overall measures of health, optimism, and exercise when the experiment began. (Researchers use frequency of exercise as a barometer for general well-being because it is an objective measure that links to subjective qualities; people who exercise three or more times per week tend to experience less stress or depression, even when researchers factor out for health conditions that affect the ability to exercise.) Making a "gratitude journal" may sound corny, but if the result is that it improves your health or happiness, what is corny about that? Simply writing down the many things you have to be thankful for—even if your ledger also includes negative entries, disappointments, and wrongs committed against you, as any accounting inevitably will—helps keep the positive in the forefront of your mind. And this, positive psychology believes, is in your self-interest.

- Grateful people are more spiritually aware and more likely to appreciate the interconnectedness of all life, regardless of whether they belong to specific religions or follow a secular philosophy. Spiritual awareness generally links, in research, to increased chance of happiness, lower stress, and less depression. In turn, the more people who appreciate the interconnectedness of all life, the greater the chance that society as a whole will be a clement place.

To be grateful does not mean to take a naïve view of the world. Emmons notes that, in studies, people who score highly on various indicators of gratefulness also report strong awareness of the bad in their own lives and in society. In fact, some research finds that grateful people are slightly more likely to be cynical than the population as a whole. But the grateful person may achieve the ability to be aware of life's drawbacks and yet thankful to be alive, an attractive combination of views.

Grateful people are not necessarily ones whom the world has showered with gifts. People of modest means, or who have suffered personal tragedies, nevertheless may report themselves as grateful, while the well-to-do, the good-looking, or the celebrated may exhibit little gratitude. "To say we should feel grateful is not to say that everything in our lives is necessarily good," Emmons says. "It just means that if you only think about your disappointments and unsatisfied wants, you may be prone to unhappiness. If you're fully aware of your disappointments but at the same time thankful for the good that has happened and for your chance to live, you may show higher indices of well-being."

Psychologist Dan McAdams of Northwestern University became interested in gratitude in the 1990s when he saw studies suggesting that increasing a person's sense of thankfulness could lead both to lower stress and better "life outcomes," meaning success in career and relationships. "Psychologists have tended to look down their nose at gratitude as little more than a question of having good manners and remembering to say thank you," McAdams says. "But if a sense of thankfulness can turn someone's life from bitter to positive, that makes gratitude an important aspect of psychology," McAdams notes—something that should be taught to students and told to patients.

If modern researchers are coming late to realizing the value of gratitude, philosophers did not. Immanuel Kant described ingratitude as "the essence of vileness." The Roman orator Cicero, born about a century before Jesus, viewed thankfulness to society and to the universe as a virtuous emotion that would counter hubris and allow a person to develop high ethical standards: "Gratitude is not only the greatest of virtues, but the parent of all others," he said.

The eighteenth-century free-market thinker Adam Smith, in his *Theory of Moral Sentiments*, supposed that people who did not feel gratitude were only cheating themselves out of happiness in life. Gratitude, Smith wrote, helps make daily life more agreeable, while ingratitude only generates resentment—and who is the victim of that, Smith asked, except you yourself? Closer to the present, shortly before his death in 1970 the pioneering humanistic psychologist Abraham Maslow wrote that he despaired of the lack of gratitude he saw in society. People's lives were getting better, Maslow wrote, and yet most seem to take their blessings for granted and concentrate on finding new complaints.

If gratitude has value, why aren't men and women today more aware of this? One reason, the psychologist Emmons thinks, is modern emphasis on the self; we don't want to think about our indebtedness to others, whether those alive now or those who came before us. The decline of intellectual respect for faith seems another factor. For at least a generation, serious thinkers have looked down on the idea of gratitude toward God as a rote church doctrine; even a sentimental gratitude toward the universe or toward nature is treated as the residue of primitive superstition. If the universe is just there, a product of mindless deterministic forces, and if mere chemistry gave us life, why should anyone feel thankful for a meaningless molecular coincidence?

Yet religious feelings of gratitude hardly need be seen as belittling. When a person of faith thanks the divine for being granted life, he or she is expressing the joy that comes from knowing, *God wanted me to exist*. When a person who does not believe in God thanks the universe for being granted life, he or she is expressing the joy that comes from knowing, *My life matters*.

As McAdams of Northwestern University notes, "You do not need to hold any particular religious belief to feel gratitude in the cosmic sense for the fact that life is precious and we are fortunate to experience it." Regardless of whether there is a divine being, we can still feel thankful for the knowledge that something must have made us. Thankfulness might counter some of the automatic-negative thoughts that contemporary society seeks to program into our minds.

Finally there is the question of whether we have a duty to feel grateful. Hundreds of generations who came before us lived dire, short lives, in deprivation or hunger, in ignorance or under oppression or during war, and did so partly motivated by the dream that someday there would be men and women who lived long lives in liberty with plenty to eat and without fear of an approaching storm.

Suffering through privation, those who came before us accumulated the knowledge that makes our lives favored; fought the battles that made our lives free; physically built much of what we rely on for our prosperity; and, most important, shaped the ideals of liberty. For all the myriad problems of modern society, we now live in the world our forebears would have wished for us—in many ways, a better place than they dared imagine. For us not to feel grateful is treacherous selfishness.

Failing to feel grateful to those who came before is such a corrosive notion, it must account at some level for part of our bad feelings about the present. The solution—a rebirth of thankfulness—is in our self-interest.

Chapter 9

BEYOND CREDIT CARDS AND SUVS

Advising Americans and Europeans that a happier life might be found in adopting the precepts of positive psychology is at some level like advising people to lose weight. No matter how many scientific studies are stacked on the table proving you are better off shedding a few pounds, many cannot resist the next candy bar, simply because it is there and, maddeningly from the public-health standpoint, so inexpensive and easy to obtain. Similarly there might be a stack of scientific studies demonstrating that a forgiving, grateful, or optimistic worldview is in your best interest. But many people simply can't resist the descent into grievance, in part because negative thinking is "inexpensive" and so easy to obtain.

Forgiveness, gratitude, conviviality, and related mental states are active conditions that require effort to achieve. You can have these worldviews, but you've got to work at it. By contrast, nothing is easier to attain than a bitter outlook on life. Seek happiness and you may or may not find it; seek grievances and you are guaranteed success. In a way, an aggrieved attitude toward life can become a form of comfort—there are people who would feel ill at ease, even angry, if the recriminations they nurse magically disappeared.

Because contemporary Western culture encourages the accumulation of complaints, negative thinking seems to counteract the positive feelings that should be brought on by ever higher living standards and an ever better life for most people: resulting in no net gain of happiness. It's almost as if evolution has so conditioned us to assume the worst—intended us to assume the worst, in order not to succumb in the contest of the fittest—that, subconsciously, society now creates a counterforce, the encouraging of complaint, to discourage any outbreak of general well-being. In survival-of-the-fittest terms, this may make sense even today; assuming the worst was hardly an evolutionary advantage in prehistory alone. Terrorism, for example, finds the wary, easily provoked United States a more imposing foe than it would a happy-go-lucky nation.

Yet the contemporary inclination to achieve affluence and then find it unsatisfying—as Thomas Naylor, a professor emeritus of Duke University, has written, modern families "work themselves to exhaustion to pay for stuff that sits around not being used"[1]—is as bad for us, as a society, as being overweight. We could be, physically, much healthier than we are. We could be, in our minds and spirits, much healthier than we are.

Is the current dynamic inexorable, or can it be changed? The means would have to be not mere exhortation, but some reorganization of values that helps bring the favored-but-discontent men and women of the Western nations the sense of fulfillment so many seem to lack.

One possibility is that Western nations are currently in a stage of overindulgence in many matters, including possessions and grievances, and this stage will simply conclude of its own accord. Modern industrial societies "may need to go through a phase of excess individualism and materialism to achieve the necessary level of prosperity before they can once again discover the benefits of family and friends," Robert Lane has suggested.[2]

Since Western governments began trying to make modern economic policy in the nineteenth century, policies have always focused on maximizing production, on the assumption—surely correct in the past—that producing more of everything is among society's foremost priorities, in order to make ample goods available at ever lower real prices and thereby raise living standards for the typical person. Now the typical person in the West enjoys the long, reasonably healthy, educated, and reasonably comfortable life of which our forebears dreamed; and business, aided by government policy, has been spectacularly successful at maximizing production.

Collapse anxiety hangs over these achievements, engendering subliminal fear that prosperity will end. But assuming the Western system does not collapse, there is a reasonable chance that generations to come will not consider maximizing production the essential goal of government policy, or maximizing acquisition the essential private goal. Building on the prosperity already achieved, generations to come may be in a position to seek somewhat different priorities, such as spiritual growth and emotional well-being.

Such a transformation can only be speculated about since, needless to say, commentators have for centuries been supposing that the end of materialism was just around the corner, and all such forecasts have been wrong. The best-selling book in the United States in the year 1901, a title called *The Simple Life* by Charles Wagner, argued that materialism had run its course and was about to disintegrate, with people gladly returning to a basic agrarian existence. That this book sold well indicates that it reflected a dream many held dear; otherwise, needless to say, *The Simple Life* was totally wrong. The goofiest best-selling book of the sixties, *The Greening of America* by Charles Reich, supposed that all of Western society was about to engage in a leap of consciousness to a placid, pastoral existence in which people would stop caring about possessions. Go to any shopping mall, SUV dealership, or credit-card processing center and you'll know how wide of the mark *The Greening of America* sailed.

Still, there is a rising sense that Western societies have lost their way by too much focus on grab-and-get. George W. Bush said in 2000 that Americans must rediscover that "who we are is more important than what we have." Bush himself may or may not really believe this; numerous of his actions in office have favored the rich, a group whose members often care more about what they have than who they are. But Bush, an astute politician, would not have uttered such a statement unless his instincts told him significant numbers of people were thinking similar thoughts. Campaigning for the Democratic nomination to oppose Bush in the 2000 presidential race, Bill Bradley made a like comment: "There is something going on in the country that is widely felt, and that is people searching for some meaning in their life that is deeper than the material. There is a profound reaction to the materialism of our time and to the hollowness of life if you're only interested in material things." About when these comments were being made, the Reverend Jim Henry, pastor of an evangelical "megachurch" in Orlando, Florida—home of Disney World, one of the epicenters of Western full-bore consumption—told me, "People today find that the things they're buying and turning to are just not fulfilling."

Millions are increasingly uneasy with a life based on working to exhaustion in order to make larger piles of stuff. This suggests that a day when people care less about possessions and status, and "once again discover the benefits of family and friends," is not out of the question.

Could spirituality contribute to such a change? Conventionally it is assumed that the better-off people become, the more shallow and superficial they grow. Certainly, we can all think of examples of people for whom acquiring money has also meant the onset of complete personal vacuity. And in yet another nature's-revenge law, men and women who achieve wealth or celebrity may lose their souls in the process. In many cases, affluence and spiritual awareness seem, as a mathematician would say, inversely related.

Yet does it always have to be this way? As the social critic Andrew Delbanco, a professor of the humanities at Columbia University, has noted,[3] the Western treadmill of consumption leaves us with an "unslaked craving for transcendence," the desire to find larger connections to life and purpose. For some, consumerism has become an opiate. For others, the better-off their lives grow in material terms, the more the chance they will step back and ask, "Is that all there is?" Perhaps the old assumption will turn out to be wrong, and rising prosperity will eventually make Western citizens more spiritual, not less.

Spirituality is a vague term, of course, and there is no escaping that a significant percentage of groups that advocate it have California return addresses. But spiritual awareness is an important goal, regardless of how the term may be used in the marketing of twelve-step tapes. It need not mean participation in a specific religion, although of course spirituality often does mean that. A person who believes the universe is entirely natural in origin could nevertheless be spiritual—attuned to life, grateful to be alive, aware of the web of interconnectedness among fellow human beings.

Adherence to formal religious denominations continues to decline sharply in Western Europe and mildly in the United States. Thirty years ago, 38 percent of Americans attended at least one religious service each week; today only 25 percent do, while the proportion of Americans who attend services occasionally dropped from 30 percent to 16 percent in the same period. The decline is much more pointed in the European Union, where fewer than 10 percent of residents of the United Kingdom, France, or Germany attend a weekly worship service.[4]

Yet though formal adherence to religion may lessen, faith or spiritual awareness may endure or even increase.[5] Today, although Americans are less likely to be in a house of worship on a regular basis, 80 percent say they believe in the existence of a divine power, and 59 percent say faith is "very important" in their lives, up slightly from a generation ago.[6] Research by Wade Clark Roof, a professor of religious studies at the University of California at Santa Barbara, has found a solid two-decade trend of rising interest in spiritual issues in Western nations, particularly in the United States.[7] "What's driving the interest in spirituality is a sense among people that their lives are not properly fulfilling," Roof says.

Whether religious or ethical in origin, increased spiritual awareness would be in our self-interest, for reasons of personal well-being. Surely it would be in society's interest, as spiritual men and women are more likely to acknowledge their obligations to others, contributing time or money or both to life's less fortunate. It is a favorable sign in this regard that for more than a decade in the United States charitable donations have been rising faster than the economy as a whole. In 2002, Americans gave away $241 billion—two-thirds as much as the entire defense budget.[8]

Suppose it turns out that rising standards of living become a force for increased spiritual awareness: first by creating the prosperity in which people have time to contemplate higher questions and care about the less fortunate, second by inspiring people to think there must be more to life than work-and-spend.

Some scholars see such trends in nascent form. Ronald Inglehart, a professor of political science at the University of Michigan, has been saying for a quarter-century that Western obsession with buying and spending at some point will peak and a phase of "post-materialism" will begin in which "a sense of meaning and purpose" is valued more highly than any purchase.[9] (Some men and women the world over already feel purpose matters more than possessions; Inglehart's point is that this might become a common feeling.) Robert Fogel of the University of Chicago has begun to say much the same, projecting the twenty-first century will see another "Great Awakening" of spiritual concerns in American life, as people turn toward questions of higher purpose to escape the emptiness of commuting and shopping.[10] This contention is particularly interesting in Fogel's case; by profession he is an economist, in fact a leading free-market conservative. When free-market conservatives begin to suppose that something beyond the free market is necessary for human happiness, a threshold has come into view.

Both contemporary psychological research and age-old common sense suggest that a feeling of purpose improves a person's experience of life. Whether the sense of purpose must arise from religious faith, or can be derived equally well from ethical philosophy, does not matter for the purposes of this book. If God made us, then clearly our life has meaning; if God did not make us, we can give our lives meaning through our actions. In either case the yearning for meaning is the same.

In the Western nations, most things have gotten better, and yet people have become no happier, in the very period that thinkers and educators have proclaimed life meaningless; movies and other forms of popular entertainment advance nihilistic messages; the news media emphasize the most cynical possible interpretation of every event, while discreetly looking away from reporting on human progress or personal virtue. Is it coincidence that these three dynamics—most things better for most people; emphasis on negativism and meaninglessness; most people no happier—occur simultaneously? Perhaps. More likely, these dynamics are wrapped in a web of cause and effect.

Of course, negativistic views are far from the only ones to which men and women are exposed. Many books, movies, and other forms of popular culture transmit uplifting messages, while much of what flows in one ear and out the other on a daily basis—advertising, sitcoms, traffic reports—has nothing to do with questions of meaning. Still, the modern intellectual assumption of meaninglessness has had a powerful effect on Western culture, both directly on its own terms and indirectly by influencing artists, political leaders, newscasters, teachers, and others. Surely this detracts from the general level of well-being, by causing men and women subconsciously to think their lives without consequence when, so far as we are aware at least, human life is the single most important thing going on anywhere in the fifty billion galaxies of the universe.

Modern thought evinces a strange homage to meaninglessness, as if the absence of significance were a welcome reading of the human prospect. For instance, the Nobel Prize–winning physicist Steven Weinberg concluded an influential 1977 book by declaring, "The more the universe seems comprehensible, the more it also seems pointless."[11] Though Weinberg went on to add that "people can grant significance to life by loving each other," through the years I have seen his "the universe is pointless" quotation cited many dozens of times, usually presented as a hard-science confirmation that life lacks meaning, and never once seen anyone cite his qualifier that love grants significance. Other contemporary thinkers have spoken almost as if enraptured by pointlessness. Richard Dawkins, who holds a chair in public understanding of science at Oxford University, in 1995 said existence is "neither good nor evil, neither kind nor cruel, but simply callous: indifferent to all suffering, lacking all purpose."[12] In 1996 Jessica Mathews, president of the Carnegie Endowment for International Peace, declared that "human life is a cosmic accident with no purpose."[13] Page upon page of similar statements can be found from contemporary writers, artists, professors, and intellectuals.

Of course a declaration that life has "no purpose" begs the rejoinder: Maybe your life is a meaningless cosmic accident, but not mine! Statements such as that existence is "neither good nor evil, neither kind nor cruel" can be objected to on simple grounds of accuracy; the found world in which we live categorically does have good and evil, kindness and cruelty, setting aside how these opposing forces came to be. And one can marvel why some of Western society's most privileged individuals—the holder of an endowed chair at Oxford, the president of an important foundation charged to seek world peace—are so eager to decree humanity pointless.

On its face, existential despair appears self-canceling: If life really is pointless, why bother to get upset about that? Wouldn't getting upset be pointless? What matters here is that by believing their lives to be meaningless, modern thinkers are failing to act in their own self-interest, as the evidence now shows that people who embrace a spiritual view of a purposeful life (regardless of whether this view is derived from religion or from philosophy) are more likely to be happy and to find fulfillment in their one chance at life (regardless of whether that one chance is given by a Maker or by nature). On the larger stage, by promoting the notion that life is meaningless, modern thinkers are failing to serve the interest of society, since anyone who listens to this view is less likely to find fulfillment, as well as less likely to donate money or time to others, or engage in other acts of altruism.

Nihilism, existential despair, and the versions of these views that filter into popular culture may be significant factors in why, though most things are getting better for most people, on the whole we don't feel any better about it. But regardless of whether there is an intellectual validity to conjecture about meaninglessness, on a practical basis negativistic views impede happiness; the hopeful view is simply healthier. If there is a God, we should not be nihilists. If there is no God we should not be nihilists either, since what is gained by inflicting misery on our own spirits?

A positive, spiritual view of the human prospect does not mean we should not be keenly conscious of the multitude of injustices and sorrows in the world. Far, far too many people experience suffering or grief, while everyone experiences problems. The positive, spiritual view, whether derived from faith or from philosophy, simply requires that we believe our lives have purpose, and believe we exist as part of a mainly positive continuum in which future generations may experience even better lives.

Gradually moving beyond materialistic obsession, while discarding fashionable theories of pointlessness in order to reclaim a mainly hopeful view of the human prospect, seem two of the leading challenges facing Western society. These are the sorts of changes men and women must make for themselves, from within, since no law can ever determine what is in our hearts.

But there are also areas where the challenges facing the Western nations, and the globe as a whole, are ones regarding the reform of laws and social structures. That leads to the question: Is there still time to change the world?

Chapter 10

CHANGING OUR WORLD

To say that most aspects of American and European life are getting better for most people should not be misunderstood as a claim that all is well, or even that applause is in order. Deep, structural faults exist in Western countries, especially in the United States, and the persistence of deep faults in a wealthy, successful nation like America deserves the world's opprobrium. Many nations, especially in Africa, are in such urgent straits that they would not be expected to have aspirations much beyond immediate survival. The United States, by contrast, possesses sufficient wealth and power as to have no excuse for not addressing its faults. History may judge America harshly if its extraordinary combination of affluence and freedom is frittered away on private jets for Hollywood stars and vacation villas for CEOs.

One deep structural fault of the United States is lack of universal health insurance. Estimates vary, but about 41 million Americans, about 14 percent of the population, lack any medical coverage, while millions more are underinsured, either through Medicaid—the program for the poor, which is state-administered and unimpressive in some states—or through commercial policies that provide only partial indemnity.

As noted earlier in the book, some Americans lack insurance because they have been irresponsible and haven't obtained it, gambling on health. And the fact that someone does not have insurance does not necessarily mean he or she will lack for care, as most hospital emergency rooms and clinics treat patients in distress regardless of ability to pay. (Federal law more or less requires this; the details don't matter here.) When thinking about the health-insurance problem, it is also important to bear in mind that, just as the claimed rise in American income inequality would not be happening if the United States were not the world's most generous nation when it comes to accepting immigrants, the lack of medical insurance traces mainly to the approximately one million new residents the United States admits each year. According to a 2000 report by the Center for Immigration Studies, a Washington think tank, immigrants are three times as likely to lack health insurance as native-born Americans, and account for almost all the growth in the ranks of the uninsured.[1] Were it not for America's open-door policy, about 9 percent of the nation would lack health insurance, rather than about 14 percent, the Center calculates. America's liberal immigration policy is one of the favors the United States does for the world, and a policy other prosperous nations—all European Union states, Japan, Australia—shun for reasons that run an unattractive gauntlet from selfishness to bigotry. (The European governments that hector the United States need to look in the mirror; America is the most racially open society in the world, while much of Europe still has cultural norms grounded in horror of dark skin.) But to repeat the point that applies to complaints about income inequality, you can't advocate a wide-ranging, liberal immigration policy, then complain about the effects that immigrants have on the social profile. One of those effects is to increase the numbers of Americans without medical insurance. A secondary effect is to increase the price of health care for the 86 percent of Americans who are covered—as their premiums and co-pays must rise to bear the costs of the immigrants and others who lack policies, and come to emergency rooms expecting free treatment.

Nevertheless, the failure of the United States to see that every one of its citizens and legal immigrants has adequate medical insurance remains one of the scandals of our age.

To become ill or be injured is not a moral failing. In most cases, illness or injury are, fundamentally, accidents—and a prosperous, compassionate society must insure all its members against accidents. As the ethicist Norman Daniels has argued, to have a class of persons—mainly the less-well-off—who are more likely to fall ill owing to lack of preventive care, and who may suffer financial ruin from large hospital expenses, decreases social justice. In effect, Daniels maintains, lack of adequate health insurance violates the principle of equal opportunity: You cannot compete in the marketplace if you are sick and this cripples you or your family financially, while a higher-income person in an identical situation would suffer no loss of ability to compete.[2]

Universal health coverage is both a matter of compassion and necessary to preserve the equal opportunity upon which the American ideal is premised. Until there is reasonable health coverage for all, American prosperity is tainted—and the consciences of well-to-do Americans should not be clear. The con-

258 | THE PROGRESS PARADOX

sciences, especially, of American Christians ought not to be clear, as Jesus taught that the circumstances of the least well-off should be the first concern of society. Distressingly few American Christians, particularly those active in politics, behave as though the least well-off were their first concern.

<hr />

Next on the list of deep, structural problems of the West, and especially of the United States, is poverty and near-poverty that persists in societies where millions of people not only have more than they need, but have, in many ways, more than is good for them.

One person in eight in the United States, and larger fractions in the non-Scandinavian nations of the European Union (one in five in the United Kingdom, for example), today lives in poverty by the definitions used by the governments of their nations. Far more are nervously poised on the boundary of poverty, in a condition that might be called "money anguish." Money anguish is the circumstance where each dollar is precious: where a person is not destitute but a single car-repair bill, or a single illness and attendant lost wages, a single plumber's invoice, or other ordinary setback, can drop that person downward into the inability to buy groceries or pay the utilities.

The vast political middle in America and Europe doesn't like to think about poverty anymore: It seems to have been conquered, and anyway no longer affects the majority. Certainly, poverty no longer affects the people who vote—or shop, which is nearly as important a form of expression in modern Western society. But poverty persists no matter how much we wish to believe it a problem of our grandparents' day, while money anguish afflicts huge numbers, including huge numbers of people who are hardworking and frugal. The economist Martin Feldstein was chair of the White House Council of Economic

Advisors during the Ronald Reagan presidency, and carries unimpeachable conservative credentials. What worries him today about the American economy—tax rates? Regulations? Government spending? "What the public should be concerned about is poverty," Feldstein said in 2001.

I'm not going to pause to describe the conditions of rat-infested impoverishment in the inner city, or tar-shack impoverishment in the Appalachian hills. You've heard that before in various appeals from various funds, and may already be conditioned to tune out such unsolicited reminders. I'll simply offer one example. On a spring afternoon in May 2002, in Elizabeth, New Jersey, Theresa LaMarca, twenty-two years old, and Damien Connors, twenty-six years old, scrambled over a security fence, hid behind some railway operations equipment, and then, when Amtrak's Metroliner approached at seventy miles per hour, stepped in front of the train and embraced as it hit them.[3] Just a few years before, Connors and LaMarca had been high-school students glistening with promise. Both lost their ways in life, tried drugs, had trouble holding down jobs and paying bills. They committed suicide on the day they had been evicted from their modest apartment, knowing they would have no place to go at nightfall. A few hundred dollars for rent might have kept these two youths from suicidal despair, and the train that killed them, the Metroliner, existing as it does to rocket the Northeast's well-favored up and down the corridor between Washington and New York City, bore many passengers who had more money than they needed or even knew what to do with.

Now let's consider how American society treats those who do not succumb to despair, and remain determined to work their way out of impoverishment.

The current federal minimum wage, $5.15 an hour, is worth less in real-dollar terms than the minimum wage of 1965, which translates to $7 an hour in current dollars. Opponents of a higher minimum wage say it would cause unemployment, but this effect has not been observed in California,[4] which has a state minimum wage of $6.75 an hour, roughly the same in real-dollar terms as the federal minimum in 1965. Unemployment in California is consistently at or only marginally different from the national average.[5]

An alternative to a significant increase in the federal minimum wage would be a significant increase in the Earned Income Tax Credit, a federal program targeted at the working poor. Though called a credit, the EITC is really a negative tax—at tax time, low-income people who work receive money from the government rather than sending it in. Many economists prefer the Earned Income Tax Credit to a higher minimum wage because the EITC does not discourage hiring: the working poor earn more, but without direct cost to small-business owners and other employers. Of course, the money for the Earned Income Tax Credit has to come from somewhere. A relatively small increase in taxes for the wealthy, whose taxes have fallen in recent years while their earnings keep shooting up, could finance an expanded EITC that would fight poverty. Research by Gary Akerlof, who won the Nobel Prize for economics in 2001, has suggested that a higher Earned Income Tax Credit funded by the well-to-do could reduce poverty and increase fairness with little if any harm to overall employment.

Today's minimum-wage man or woman may, in some respects, experience better living standards than known to middle-class men and women four generations ago, but that constitutes no excuse to accept that millions suffer money anguish in our moment. To say that we shouldn't care about the working poor today because they are better off than many of previous centuries is like saying that if your child is hit by a car he or she shouldn't be taken to the hospital, because in a previous century an injured kid would have died anyway.

More troubling, working a forty-hour week at the current federal minimum wage, taking no time off, translates to less than $11,000 a year. The current Department of Labor poverty line for a family of four is $18,100 per annum. This means a head of household in today's United States can work full-time yet still be impoverished. That simply is not right.

That entry-level wages are too low in the United States is particularly true given the restrained definition of the "poverty line." Few readers of this book would be sanguine about living, with three dependents, on $18,100 per annum. After taxes, that equates to $42 a day to pay all the expenses of four people. Food stamps and housing vouchers might be available, but they would increase your resources only to around $55 per day for all expenses for four people. Statisticians at the Census Bureau believe the poverty line for a family of four should be raised to at least $21,000 per annum, which would increase the share of people defined as impoverished in the United States from 12 percent to about 17 percent—about forty-eight million in total, or one person in six considered poor rather than one person in eight, as under the present definition. One person in six poor, in the most affluent nation in world history, would be a shocking indictment of American society. It is America's current condition.

Life can be a ceaseless financial trial for those just above the minimum-wage line, in the money-anguish zone. Entry-level jobs such as day laborer, nanny, or home health care assistant pay $7 to $8 an hour in big cities, less in small towns, not a living wage in any society that is not cold-hearted. Moreover, in most states, once a person graduates from welfare and begins to work, he or she loses Medicaid benefits, and soon after that loses food stamps and housing assistance. Few employers now provide health insurance to entry-level workers, meaning the very act of going out and attempting to become financially self-sufficient can spell financial calamity for those on the edge who become ill, or have a child or spouse who falls sick.

The working poor are poised between social dependency and self-reliance; America ought to do far more to help them than is done today, offering universal health care coverage and "living wage" laws that would ensure that someone who works forty hours per week is not in poverty. Toleration of poverty and money anguish might be unavoidable if the United States were struggling. But its economy is the envy of the world, and every year the inventory of intractable collective problems (pollution, discrimination, the Cold War) goes down, freeing resources to tackle other social ills. Poverty should be high on the list of ills to tackle.

We should not sentimentalize. Poor people will always face a hard climb in life, must accept hard work under difficult conditions to escape poverty, and sometimes are poor owing to foolish choices made of their own accord. Yet millions of the poor and near-poor in the Western world today do accept a fate of hard labor, and toil ardently—working under conditions the well-off would never dream of tolerating, hacking chickens in rancid slaughterhouses, or lining up on streetcorners to plead for day-laborer's handyman slots at construction sites, or waking children at 4 A.M. to ride predawn buses to low-rent child care so Mom can report to work the breakfast shift at a Burger King. To think that millions of the poor and near-poor could face their fates, and toil ardently, but *not* make enough to rise above the poverty line is inexcusable.

How can the West today hold five hundred million who have

ample money, and perhaps tens of millions who actually have more money than is good for them, yet be a family of nations in which huge numbers toil ardently and still experience wretchedness over small sums?

A minor but perhaps not banal example. When at my downtown office in Washington, D.C., I get lunch at the local outlet of the Au Bon Pain chain, which makes tasty fresh sandwiches. The other day I stepped into the elevator to return to my floor, holding a bag lunch from this bakery. A single mother working as a minimum-wage receptionist in the building stepped on board as well. "Bon Pain!" she said dreamily, eyes focused on my bag. "Their food is *so* delicious, but it's seven dollars to have lunch there and three dollars at McDonald's." I never look at the prices in Au Bon Pain, as I suspect many customers do not. It is one of the leading social achievements of the human saga that the United States has created a society in which more people than lived in all of Europe a century ago now have enough money that they need not think twice about the price of lunch. But the vast contingent of Americans whose blessings include not worrying about inconsequential financial matters forget there remain millions within their country for whom tiny sums are painfully unobtainable. Considering taxes, a person working full-time at the federal minimum would have to spend an *entire day's wages* to buy a $7 Au Bon Pain sandwich combo for lunch each business week. This simply is not right.

Cheaper sandwiches are not the solution. Higher wages are the solution.

Today's mainly well-off Americans and Europeans may be able to turn away from the problems of the poor and near-poor, reasoning: Is it my fault they didn't do well on the SAT? Today's mainly well-off Americans may also turn away from the problems of the poor and near-poor because they know that a $5.15 minimum wage ensures low prices at the supermarket, inexpensive goods at Target and the Gap, hardworking and inexpensive lawn-service and house-cleaning personnel, pizzas delivered cheaply. The fact that vast numbers of Americans live so well is anchored, partly, on penurious wages for the have-nots.

If, as there should be, there were higher wages at the bottom and universal health insurance, this would inevitably raise the price of goods and services purchased by Americans; and, inevitably, subtract at least somewhat from the affluence enjoyed by the many millions of suburbanites who get their houses cleaned and pizzas delivered cheaply. But since many millions of Americans have more than they need, shifting part of society's wealth toward the bottom, via higher wages and universal health insurance, would be in the interest of every person who is not heartless.

Americans should essentially tax themselves, via the prices of goods, by insisting on "living wages" plus universal health insurance. Raising wages at the bottom in order to transfer funds to the poor and money-anguished makes much more sense than increasing taxes and then offering the poor additional entitlements such as welfare. Taxes are already plenty high enough, government already big enough, federal entitlements already too numerous.

If America raised low-level wages, and thereby Americans accepted slightly higher prices, the poor and working poor would be directly rewarded for their labor—the reward coming immediately through the marketplace, not via government. The poor and working poor would also receive their rewards without strings attached, so they could decide for themselves how best to spend their money. Of course, some poor people would make unwise choices with money, just as some people of all social ranks make unwise choices. But economic studies are close to unanimous that, in the main (in the "aggregate," as economists like to say), individuals are the best judges of how to allocate resources. The poor may have much keener understanding of how to stretch a dollar than any government-run program ever could. At any rate, the goal should be to allow the poor to earn reasonable amounts, and then decide for themselves how to use the money. Attaining reasonable amounts, then deciding individually how to use it, is the way in which almost everyone in the moneyed class originally got there.

A new dawn for the poor and the money-anguished should come through the free market via "living wage" laws that raise the American minimum wage to at least $10 an hour. Christians, especially, ought to favor such a reform, since its benefits would be concentrated on the least well-off. As a churchgoing Christian, I feel that American political Christianity should be embarrassed that it spends so much time fulminating about sexual choices and public school textbooks and similar complaints and so little time advocating relief of the suffering of the poor.

Suppose the minimum wage went to $10 and health insurance became universal. Pizzas, sandwiches, house-cleaning, and everything at the Gap and Target would cost slightly more; "in the aggregate," middle-class suburbanites and wealthy political donors would become slightly less affluent. But society would become more just, while the prosperous majority could enjoy their positions with a clearer conscience. Higher wages for the struggling, in return for a clear conscience for the successful, represents an attractive bargain: both a moral necessity and in the self-interest of anyone who is not coldhearted.

After the lack of universal health insurance in the United States and the need for living wages for the poor and near-poor, the third deep fault of the Western system, particularly in the United States but also observed in the European Union, is greed at the top. The free, open character of market economics creates jobs and vibrancy and growth and profit, which are all good. But the free, open character of market economics can be misused to grab gluttonous amounts at the expense of others.

The objection is not to those who acquire riches through legitimate, true free-market choices. If, say, an inventor or an entertainer becomes wealthy because buyers freely choose to purchase his or her invention or CDs or movie tickets, we should hope that person will give some of the gain away, but otherwise be untroubled—as a previous chapter discussed, unequal outcomes per se are not the problem. The structural fault of the Western system is the way its freedom can be misused to lavish the few vast amounts that are either not really earned or far out of proportion to the person's efforts—effectively, stolen.

The most important examples involve CEOs and other top officers of public corporations. Many have begun to live like little pashas and at the expense of the typical person, showering themselves with millions while cutting pay and benefits to those in money anguish. This shows, first, that there exists a serious problem of lack of character among American business executives; no class of individuals engaged in legal pursuits has ever revealed itself to have such low standards and lack of character as American top executives at the turn of the twenty-first century. Lawyers now look good by comparison! This shows, second, that the West generally, and the United States particularly, still stands far from having devised a system that achieves the productive efficiency of free markets while avoiding graft from self-serving business managers.

Kenneth Lay of Enron pocketed $101 million from his lies-based company in the period before its collapse wiped out shareholders and employees. Bernard Ebbers of WorldCom awarded himself $408 million in the months before his lies-based company's cooked books caught fire and wiped out shareholders and employees.[6] L. Dennis Kozlowski of Tyco officially paid himself $350 million, from 1999 to 2002, even as the lies-based Tyco was nosediving from $60 a share to $10 in just six months, essentially wiping out average investors. After his June 2002 resignation, Kozlowski was indicted on charges of defrauding the firm of another $170 million[7] and of realizing a further $430 million by selling company stock without disclosing his trades, as top corporate managers generally must.[8] Adelphia, Global Crossing, and other large corporations were during the same period revealed to be little more than shams for the enrichment of their officers, while the Arthur Andersen accounting firm was revealed to have been based on a corporate philosophy of telling any lie, anytime, so long as the top dogs in suits got money. *The New York Times* said WorldCom "may be the largest accounting fraud in history," with perhaps $11 billion in false bookkeeping entries, intended to swindle shareholders; federal prosecutors accused Kozlowski and other former Tyco executives of running a "criminal enterprise," a phrase that in federal law is generally reserved for mafia indictments.[9] Some European firms, such as Vivendi, were almost as bad.

Yet reach-and-grab by CEOs at presumably respectable firms has been just as shameless as behavior at fraudulent enterprises. In 2000, John Welch of General Electric paid himself $144 million, while also receiving millions of dollars worth of perquisites, such as a company-paid home and a private box in the stadium where the Boston Red Sox play. Even the pro-business *Wall Street Journal* editorial page said Welch's reach-and-grab "makes him seem greedy."[10] When Welch left General Electric in 2001, the firm granted him a pension of $9 million annually, plus lifetime use of a corporate jet, an extravagant Manhattan apartment, and such absurd extras as permission to send his liquor bills to the company.

Hundreds of average General Electric employees were laid off—some of their lives ruined—to fund Welch's carnival of greed. And greed it was in every sense, since Welch avidly grabbed from others but gave almost nothing away. Papers filed by Welch himself in a divorce proceeding declared that he had a net worth of $456 million but donated a mere $3 million annually to charity.[11] This is a miser's sum, since $456 million conservatively invested would yield around $20 million annually, allowing Welch to give away much more while still living in opulence and not touching his principal.

Welch was hardly the only CEO of a presumably upright firm to screw the typical person in order to live as a modern Louis XIV. In 2000, Sanford Weill of Citigroup paid himself $90 million, Reuben Mark of Colgate paid himself $85 million. In 2001, Louis V. Gerstner, Jr., of IBM paid himself $127 million.[12] Thousands of average employees were laid off so that these gluttons could grab more for themselves, cackling as they counted their gold and the poor wept.

Always CEOs protest that they are not deciding their own pay, merely receiving a market-determined number. This is fiction.

In most public firms, a compensation board approves the take of top officers. Some firms do have true outsider boards; in practice, many such panels are a rubber-stamp charade. CEOs sit interchangeably on CEO-pay committees of other companies, and share a mutual interest in running up the bill. Christos Cotsakos, CEO of E*Trade, paid himself $59 million in 2001, even though the firm was unprofitable and its share value was plummeting; the supposedly independent committee that approved this expropriation was composed of three executives from companies that at the time did significant business with E*Trade or had overlapping ownership in the firm. Outraged by Cotsakos's pocket-stuffing, shareholders forced him to resign. But he kept the $59 million he had for intents and purposes stolen, and on his way out the door handed himself an additional $4 million rationalized as a severance bonus.

One bad apple? As Diana Henriques and Geraldine Fabrikant have written, a study of the two thousand largest publicly owned American corporations in the year 2001 found that at least 20 percent had compensation committees "with members who had business ties or other relationships with the chief executive of the company."[13] Some of the supposedly independent committee members were relatives of the CEOs whose pay they supposedly reined in, and some were actually officers of the company itself, choosing their own pay numbers. In 2002, Frank Walsh, Jr., once an official of the supposedly independent compensation committee at the lies-based Tyco, pleaded guilty to taking a secret $20 million payment from the company[14] in exchange for rubber-stamping the hundreds of millions of dollars diverted to himself by indicted former Tyco CEO L. Dennis Kozlowski.

Even genuinely independent corporate pay boards do not necessarily pick numbers truly driven by the market value of an executive. To cite one of many possible examples, it would be hard for Colgate to say with a straight face that it had to pay its CEO, Reuben Mark, $85 million in 2000 because there was not one single comparable executive willing to work for less than $85 million!

Analyzing CEO pay for the National Bureau of Economic Research—a nonpartisan organization whose affiliates include most American winners of the Nobel Prize for economics and most past chairpersons of the president's Council of Economic Advisors—three economists from Harvard, the University of California at Berkeley, and Boston University found that top corporate pay at the end of the twentieth century had nothing to do with the market value of executive talent but was, rather, a form of "rent extraction."[15] Them's fightin' words to economists, for "rent extraction" is the economic activity engaged in by the troll sitting under the bridge. This phrase refers to the parasitic behavior of those who use their position to "extract" largesse for no useful product or labor, harming society in the process. The economies of feudal developing-world nations are hampered by the fact that the upper classes of such countries engage in parasitic rent extraction. To hear this term applied by establishment economists to the behavior of *Fortune 500* managers is not reassuring.

Originally, preposterous CEO paydays were rationalized as rewards for raising shareholder returns. But since about 2000, many *Fortune 500* firms have "restated" prior claims of returns— that is, admitted they lied. Tyco "restated" $382 million in previously claimed profits, confessing that the profit had never existed.[16] More than five hundred corporate-profit restatements occurred between 1999 and 2000, which is dozens of times the historic rate. In other cases, executives granted themselves huge paydays on the pretense that corporate performance had been superb. Gerstner of IBM, for instance, justified his $127 million in 2001 by claiming IBM had been having outstanding years. But during the very period when Gerstner maintained that extraordinary IBM performance justified his awarding himself one of the largest paydays a human being has ever received, many stock analysts considered the company's earnings prosaic, given the loud boom of the time; from 1999 to 2000, for example, IBM net earnings rose only 5 percent. Overall, adjusted for "restatements" and other accounting confessions, the rate of increase in corporate profits in the 1990s was essentially unchanged from the 1980s, while arrogation by top executives skyrocketed.

Yet after deceitful claims are exposed, the CEOs get to keep the cash. Ken Lay retains the millions he made by lying about Enron. Paul Allaire of Xerox picked up $16 million in 1998 and 1999 by cashing out options when the company's stock price was artificially inflated based on announcements of imaginary profits. Later the company "restated," retracting its profit claims and wiping out four-fifths of shareholder value; the Securities and Exchange Commission declared that Xerox under Allaire had engaged in "a wide-ranging, four-year scheme to defraud investors" by lying about earnings.[17] Allaire got to keep the proceeds of his fraud.[18] Gary Winnick, CEO of the lies-based Global Crossing, cashed out stock worth several hundred million dollars in the period before the firm's phony books were revealed. In 2002, the thief-in-chief resigned as the remains of the bankrupt company were sold off for about 1 percent of the asset value Winnick had been claiming in order to pump up stock.[19] The purloined money was Winnick's to keep.

As Sarah Teslik, director of the Council of Institutional Investors, which represents pension funds that hold large blocks of stocks, notes, "If you are a robber who steals from a bank, you go to jail and the money is taken back. If you are a CEO who steals from a company, you get fired, but there is no punishment and you retain the proceeds. Top corporate managers know their deceptions eventually will be revealed. But they also know they will be allowed to keep whatever they steal. It's almost rational for them—steal as fast as you can before you're caught."

Top-manager greed has reached the point that CEOs award themselves enormous amounts even when there is no pretense they have been successful managers. Establishing this premise, in 2000 American CEO pay rose by 22 percent as the broad market declined by 12 percent. The next year, 2001, John Chambers of Cisco Systems paid himself $157 million as his company was *losing* $1 billion. That same year, Edward Whitacre of SBC Communications, one of the Baby Bell offshoots, paid himself $82 million even as his firm's stock price fell for the twelfth consecutive quarter. That same year at AOL Time Warner, joint CEOs Gerald Levin and Steve Case paid themselves $148 million and $128 million, respectively, even as the combined company's valuation was contracting by $56 billion because of the two men's self-serving decisions. Fifty-six billion dollars is almost as much money as disappeared in the collapse of Enron, meaning the AOL Time Warner joint CEOs lavished spectacular amounts on themselves while doing nearly as much harm to typical stockholders as did Enron. And also while doing extensive harm to employees, whose retirement savings crashed and who were laid off in large numbers in order to free up more funds for gluttony at the top.[20]

Many expropriations by corporate officials were linked to the tech-stock boom of the 1990s and its attendant "irrational exuberance." But managers whose corporations had no involvement in the tech runup used the mood of the times to create an assumption that it was only natural for CEOs to be paid preposterous sums regardless of performance. John Snow, head of CSX, the old-industry railroad firm, awarded himself steadily larger sums through the 1990s, even as his company's returns were falling and its stock was trailing the Wall Street runup. For instance, in 2001, as CSX profits fell almost 50 percent from the prior year, Snow nevertheless paid himself $10.1 million. When he left the company in 2002 to join the George W. Bush administration, Snow awarded himself $2.5 million annually for life as a pension, even as CSX was cutting pension benefits for working-class retirees.[21] On becoming an important American government official, John Snow decided he deserved extraordinary wealth for life, while ordinary people who worked for him deserved to be screwed to the wall.

Broadly, in 1980, CEOs of *Fortune 500* corporations averaged 42 times the pay of their workers. By 2000 the multiple was up to 419 times, while the top CEOs in earnings that year cleared an average of $154 million, versus a top average of $3.5 million in 1980—a twentyfold increase, adjusting for inflation.[22] Figures like this show that it was not just the managers of firms such as WorldCom and Global Crossing that were engaged in stealing from shareholders and employees. The *typical* big American firm was engaged in corporate stealing at the top.

And while headlines have gone to abuses by CEOs, abuses by other corporate officers are probably as significant. Traditionally, big firms had a chief executive officer and chief financial officer. During the last decade, it has become common for *Fortune 500* corporations to list a dozen or more executives with the word "chief" in their title, as this word justifies million-plus pay packages. It's a way to expand the number of the favored few at the top at the expense of the hourly money-anguished at the bottom. For instance, at this writing, the management committee of Citigroup had twenty-two officers with the word "chief" in their title, all drawing spectacular pay while health benefits for low-level workers were being cut.

Expropriation at the top of business cannot be attributed to the free choice of shareholders, in the way that wealth conferred by celebrity can be attributed to the free choices of people who buy CDs or movie tickets. Many corporate leaders, such as Ebbers, Lay, and Welch, elaborately concealed the truth about their pay or perquisites because they knew perfectly well what they were doing was wrong.

Economic theory says that the voting power of shareholders, who have an interest in honest management that maximizes results for stockholders rather than for management, would vote out scoundrel CEOs. Or, failing that, boards of directors, whose fiduciary responsibility is to the shareholder rather than to management, would serve as the check against management perfidy. This has not worked in practice. Richard Puntillo, a professor at the University of San Francisco business school, has noted that under U.S. securities law, in theory public corporations have shareholders as their kings, boards of directors as the sword-wielding knights who protect the shareholders, and managers as the vassals who carry out orders. In practice, managers have become kings who lavish upon themselves gold, boards of directors have become fawning courtiers who take coin in return for an uncritical yes-man function, and shareholders have become peasants whose property may be seized at management's whim. Management buys off boards of directors with pay and perks for little or no work, while it may be impractical to expect that large companies could be held accountable by millions of diverse shareholders, most with only a small interest in any particular enterprise.

CEO greed has been important to consider for several reasons. One is that it is likely that the period of brazen expropriation by corporate executives, crooked accounting, and methodical deceit by con-artist Wall Street companies such as Merrill Lynch—a period that began roughly in the mid-1990s—will turn out to explain much of the jump in personal income at the very top that occurred in the same period.

As the Princeton University economist Paul Krugman has noted, in 2000 the top thirteen thousand families in the United States were receiving as much income as the bottom twenty million families.[23] Some of those top thirteen thousand families must have been engaged in the kind of constructive pursuits that it is in society's interest to reward, such as making inventions or marketing useful products. But a good guess might be that a significant fraction of those thirteen thousand high-earnings families were receiving their incomes from corporate expropriation on the parts of the top managers whose pay in the 1990s shot up far beyond what their efforts, achievements, or the market could justify.

Another reason to go over this ground in some detail is that it is such a disappointment to discover that so many corporate leaders lacked character. It's the lack of character among CEOs that seems most disturbing—since many, like Welch or Gerstner, did not actively steal yet clearly felt that the business of American business was to grab for themselves while the needs of the less fortunate and the community be damned. It is not an indictment of market economics that the system produces unequal outcomes, or even extremes of wealth. It is an indictment of market economics that the system produces so many business leaders of low personal character.

The long boom phase that lasted roughly from 1980 to 2000 in the Western nations was sufficiently impressive that free-market advocates could argue that big business really had become a force for social good, and big-business leaders really were motivated by improving society. The CEO and accounting-firm scandals that followed showed things haven't changed much since the Gilded Age. Equally important, the sins of CEOs matter because they violate Pareto Efficiency—the free-market concept that holds that it is fine for one person to become very rich while others do not, so long as that one person does not harm anyone else in the process of acquiring wealth.

The executive who overpays himself is not pulling the money out of the air; he is expropriating it from the firm's employees, all of them much lower paid, or from shareholders. Dozens if not hundreds of American corporate leaders in recent years have jacked up their own earnings while laying off others who need the money much more, cutting health benefits for single parents and minimum-wage workers and picking the pockets of shareholders.

Similarly, when a corporate leader sells for personal gain shares that he or she knows, based on financial information the firm is concealing, to be worth less than the market price, the gain is not coming out of the air: The buyer of that stock is being defrauded. Stock fraud is not a victimless crime. Average people, philanthropies, teachers' pension funds, and so on have bought stocks based on corporate accounting claims that turned out to be lies; the business managers who profited from selling lies-backed stocks belong in jail. Unlike the sort of transaction that makes Person A shamelessly rich while having no effect on Person B— a fair outcome under market economics—corporate lies harm Person B. They seem to harm Persons B through Z, all of society other than business leaders themselves.

During the 1980s, there were extensive business scandals involving insider trading and savings-and-loan associations. Billions of dollars were stolen or lost; Congress responded with new laws, and since that time insider trading and banking abuse have declined as problems.[24] Presumably, new federal laws enacted since the accounting and CEO overpayment scandals will work against a repetition of these abuses. But the lesson learned from the 1980s and 1990s is not heartening, namely, that many captains of the free-market economic system simply are not worthy of society's trust.

Left-wing commentators have long contended that Big Business actively seeks to delude consumers, impoverish workers, and enrich itself at everyone else's expense. Businesses that really try to delude consumers pay the price in failure—consumers are pretty sharp, and though they might fall for a defective or shoddy product once, never twice. Businesses that really try to impoverish workers only undercut their own markets, since, as Henry Ford observed a century ago, business needs the average person to be prosperous in order to have someone to sell to. Yet now it seems confirmed by two decades of scandal that a significant sector of big business—its leadership—is in fact trying to enrich itself by expropriation, rather than in the honorable way, by selling an honest product at an honest price.

We ought to be as angry, today, about business leaders who steal from shareholders and employees as we are angry, in retrospect, about how the royalty of medieval Europe stole from the farmers, merchants, and peasants. The principle—those who already have too much using a privileged position to take from those in need—is the same. Just as the excesses of medieval royalty called into question the integrity of the entire old European system, corporate greed at the top calls into question the integrity of the entire contemporary Western system.

And it calls into question the modern soul. There will always be selfish people, and there will always be greed. Yet the realization that not just a few but many of those at the top of Western society were cackling as they counted their gold and the poor wept tells us we have come nowhere near as far as we thought.

On the eve of the Civil War, Abraham Lincoln said that the United States could never assume its true place as the beacon of hope to the world until it rid itself of a moral outrage, slavery. However hard the struggle, Lincoln declared, in the end the world would be better off because America would become the global ideal—and in the end Americans themselves would be better off because they would no longer suffer from guilty consciences.

Today the issues are different but the equation is the same. America cannot enjoy a clear conscience until it provides health coverage to all, pays a living wage to those at the bottom, and devises a system in which corporate leadership is not based on deceit and greed. These steps are necessary to sustain the role of the United States as the world's ideal. They are also in our self-interest, for the clearing of the American conscience. If everyone within the United States made a decent living and had decent health care, while no corporate leaders were engaged in glorified shoplifting, we could all enjoy our prosperity more. Happiness might rise.

Chapter 11

CHANGING THEIR WORLD

In August 2001, as an American Airlines 777 jetliner arriving from overseas descended toward John F. Kennedy International Airport in New York and lowered its landing gear, the frozen body of a man fell into a marsh beneath the field's approach lanes. The body, believed to be that of a young Nigerian, was buried in a plain wooden casket in City Cemetery, the resting place of New York indigents popularly known as Potter's Field. No one will ever know for certain, but it appears the young man, who carried no identification, had hidden in the wheel well of the jet, hoping to steal into the United States. If, as police speculated, he was from an African village, he might not have known that the air outside a jetliner at cruise altitude may be minus-80 degrees Fahrenheit, and that wheel wells are unheated; they are also not pressurized, rendering breathing almost impossible at a jetliner's cruise altitude. Or the victim might have known these things and climbed into the wheel well anyway, because he was desperate. The unknown man's death

marked the third time since 1997 that the frozen body of someone desperate to enter the United States had fallen from the
wheel wells as a jetliner from overseas lowered its landing gear
on descent toward JFK. In the man's pockets were a few minor
personal effects and a street-vendor's map of Manhattan.

Contemplating this tragedy I thought, first, of the horror the
man must have experienced as the plane's mindless hydraulic
mechanisms drew the landing struts and wheels up to crush him.
Somehow he avoided being crushed—only to realize as the aircraft ascended that it was getting very cold and the air was getting very thin, and he was going to die gasping and shaking.[1]
Then I contemplated what the man's final thoughts might have
been. Fear, of course; regret. Perhaps, at the last, dread that his
own death might consign the rest of his family in his village to a
life of suffering: for the desperation of many trying to reach the
West from the developing world is motivated by their desire to
work extremely hard and to live on the edge here, sending part
of their incomes back home to those even worse off.

Are these terrible falls of frozen corpses from the wheel wells
of jetliners just isolated incidents? In recent years, police have
practically barricaded the marshalling yard in Calais, France,
where the elegant Eurostar train must slow down before it en-
ters the Channel Tunnel to England. Today the Calais marshalling yard for the Channel Tunnel looks like what the
military might erect around a flying-saucer wreckage—barbed
wire, electric fences, armed guards, and police dogs everywhere.
Yet each night as darkness falls desperate men from the developing world, Africans and Pakistanis and Afghans and others,
hide throughout the marshalling yard, sprint toward the Eurostar as it slows for the tunnel, and try to cling to its side as it
accelerates again. They hope to survive until the train bears

them into the United Kingdom, for French law treats illegal immigrants harshly, while England is more liberal. Numerous indigent developing-world men have been killed when they have slipped off the sides or the couplers of Eurostar, then fallen beneath its wheels; the stylish passengers aboard the train may feel a slight bump. Yet the men keep trying, though most must know there is hardly anything on this aerodynamically sleek train to grab hold of. Many are arrested as they dash toward the train and the favored life it represents. If released, they return to dash again. If deported, they try to sneak back into the country and dash again.

For all the legitimate problems people experience in the Western nations, we cannot imagine a world which generates such hopelessness that people will hurl themselves toward moving trains, or climb into the wheel wells of jetliners bound for the sky, in order to have a tiny chance of getting to a place where they can dwell in freedom and earn $5.15 an hour.

Perhaps you've heard of Smoky Mountain, the town-sized garbage landfill in Payatas, outside Manila in the Philippines, that is home to an estimated eighty thousand desperately poor Filipinos who eke out a miserable existence scavenging what others throw away. Eighty thousand people is more than the population of Utica, New York. Entire families have been born at the Smoky Mountain landfill and lived their lives there, amidst squalor, stench, and constant smoke of smoldering trash. In July 2000, about two hundred residents of the Payatas landfill died when a large hill of trash collapsed, burying them under a garbage avalanche.[2]

Perhaps, as well, you've heard of the hundreds of thousands of poor people—not individual homeless men but entire families—who live on the streets of Indian cities. The last time

I was in New Delhi, I retreated in a dazed state to the lulling Western comforts of my hotel after a few hours of walking through impoverished districts where there were not only entire families living homeless on streets, grown men would grab you by the arm and beg for money so that their children wouldn't die.

Perhaps as well you've heard of the extreme poverty in the tar-paper shacks of the hills surrounding Quito, Ecuador, whose population has trebled in a generation; or the homeless living among abandoned half-completed office towers in Dar-es-Salaam, Tanzania; or of impoverished boys swimming in urban-sewage conduits in Karachi, Pakistan; or of children as young as six working fourteen-hour days in dim light, sewing soccer balls for the West's pleasant suburban sports leagues in the global sweatshop city of Sialkot, Pakistan. Of many possible instances of developing-world despair, I mention these because they are places I have been. No one person lives long enough to visit every location of developing-world despair.

Perhaps you've heard that 1.2 billion people in the world live on a dollar or less a day—actually, on $1.08 or less a day, according to the latest calculations.[3] Perhaps as well you've heard of choking air pollution in Mexico City, Jakarta, and parts of China, so thick that people gag even with cloths over their faces, and taxis run with their headlights on at noon on sunny days. Perhaps you've heard that a billion people in the world lack access to clean drinking water, or pay a quarter of their daily income for small amounts of clean water, while most Westerners have potable water in unlimited amounts at trivial cost. Perhaps you've heard that two million developing-world children per year die from diseases borne by unclean drinking water, and 2.2 million developing-world children per year die from respiratory diseases caused by indoor air pollution: mainly from indoor open cooking and heating fires, often indoor fires burning livestock dung. These figures for developing-world pollution-caused childhood deaths represent more annual fatalities than all deaths at all ages from all causes in the United States and European Union combined.[4]

Surely you've heard of the public-health emergency in sub-Saharan Africa, where two-thirds of the world's HIV-positive people reside.[5] While most of the Earth's population is living ever longer even in the poor nations, the life expectancy at birth today in Botswana is twenty-nine years: the shortest life expectancy anywhere on the planet in the last two centuries. Today about a third of sub-Saharan African children are orphans, AIDS, other diseases, or civil conflicts having taken both their parents. In sub-Saharan Africa, the combination of want and public-health emergency leaves many people little hope. How are you supposed to pull yourself out of poverty when you are constantly sick, or caring for others who are sick?

You've heard of such problems and probably do not wish to hear more. Pondering developing-world hardship you may well think, "What can I possibly do about this?" The answer is: a lot, and pretty cheaply, too.

For all its manifold troubles, the great story of the developing world in the postwar era is that most things have gotten better for most people, exactly as is happening in the West. Throughout most of the developing world, incomes are rising, literacy increasing, lifespans lengthening, and women's rights being won, while democracy replaces despotism. This means the trend lines for the developing world are guardedly positive—but, because there are so many living in poverty and despair, there remain challenges by the score. That, in turn, is where you come in.

History has made the United States and the European Union prosperous, powerful, secure, open, confident—stronger, relative to the rest of the world, than any alliance at any other point since nations first arose. History has also left the United States and the European Union, at this moment, with a vague sense of lack of purpose; with millions who complain that their favored existence wants for fulfillment. At the same time, history presents the challenge of 1.2 billion people living on $1.08 or less a day; of an entire region where one-third of children are orphans; of fathers so desperate for work that they dodge police to leap onto the sides of moving trains.

Two generations ago, the nations of the West took on as their challenge the defeat of fascism. One generation ago, the nations of the West took on as their challenge the defeat of Communist tyranny. Two historic challenges; two absolute, unqualified victories. The nations of the West should take on as their next historic challenge the defeat of global despair. Seems impossible? So, once, did the defeats of the Nazis and the Communists. If the United States and European Union were to make a dramatic commitment to ending global despair, their prosperous but discontent citizens could know that they were personally responsible for *saving human lives*. And if that doesn't bring you a sense of fulfillment, then I don't know what will.

The starting point for understanding the tasks facing the developing world, and by extension the Western societies that should make a new commitment to defeat global despair, is that while the poor nations have momentous problems, all is far from lost.

In 1975, the average income in developing nations was $2,125 per capita, stated in current dollars; today it is $4,000.[6] Even when the high incomes of oil states are subtracted from these calculations, per-capita developing-world income is still rising. In 1974, one-third of the world's nations regularly held genuine multiparty elections; today two-thirds do. Global adult literacy was 47 percent in 1970 and is 73 percent today. Global school enrollment for girls has skyrocketed.

In 1975, 1.6 billion people existed at what the United Nations classifies as "medium development," meaning reasonably decent living standards, education, and health care. Today 3.5 billion people enjoy "medium development"—as noted earlier, a stunning increase in the sheer number of human beings who are *not* destitute. Something must have gone right in the developing world for so many human beings to be added so fast and yet most of them to achieve a reasonable standard of living. Whatever impression of universal developing-world misfortune that CNN and the evening newscasts prefer to present, huge numbers of people mainly living better than their parents have been born into developing nations in the postwar era, and credit for the fact that hundreds of millions of them are reasonably well cared-for goes to the developing world itself, which did the hard work.

Yes, each year brings more people living on $1.08 per day, but this is mainly because population growth ensures each year brings more people; the percentage of the global population living in privation is in steady decline. As the Indian economist Surjit Bhalla has written, using $1.08 per day as the definition of impoverishment, "The percentage of poor people in the developing world has declined from 37.4 percent in 1985 to 13.1 percent in 2000."[7] Were it not for global population expansion, the ranks of the impoverished would be in decline. As it is, the ranks of the impoverished are growing more slowly than the population as a whole. "On a world scale the risk, intensity and severity of poverty has fallen more sharply in the past fifty years than in the preceding thousand years," Michael Lipton, a professor at the University of Sussex, in England, has written.

Health care access and health care results have improved everywhere in the world except sub-Saharan Africa. The fact that the global population is growing not because of more births, but because of fewer deaths, demonstrates how rapidly medical care has improved in the developing world. Births per woman are declining in almost every nation. In the 1950s, developing-world women averaged six live births; now the figure is three and still going down. This decline is partly attributed to improved women's access to safe birth-control methods and other forms of reproductive health care; partly to rising women's freedom; and partly to the realization, on the part of developing-world men and women themselves, that smaller family size makes sense in an age when education is the first predictor of success. The almost-universal developing-world fertility decline means global population growth is likely to slow soon, and to end in most developing nations before the crisis point is reached.

As the rate of death declines, even in developing nations it is becoming the norm for people to reach old age. It took about a century and a half, from about 1800 to about 1950, for typical European life expectancy to advance from forty to sixty years. In most of the developing world it took just four decades, from about 1930 to about 1970, to realize the same achievement, though antibiotics and other advances had to be extended to far larger numbers of men and women.

Besides a lesser rate of death in most developing nations,

other health care indicators are mainly positive. Eighty percent of the world's children are today vaccinated against polio, diphtheria, and other diseases; inoculations were rare in the developing world as recently as a generation ago. Smallpox has been eradicated from nature—we worry about smallpox falling into the hands of terrorists, but forget that fifty years ago it was rampant naturally in poor nations—while river blindness, once a scourge of Africa, has been nearly eradicated.

Global hunger is in mild retreat. An estimated eight hundred million people in the world today are malnourished, a heartbreaking figure; but this huge number is driven by population growth. The *percentage* of the globe's people who are malnourished is dropping steadily; more than a billion were malnourished a generation ago, and now the total is smaller though the global population is much larger. In 2002, an estimated nine million people worldwide died of hunger or of illness made materially worse by hunger (undernourished people are more prone to disease than the well-nourished). That number too is heartbreaking, but the essential comparison is that twenty years ago an estimated fifteen million people worldwide died of hunger or of illness made materially worse by hunger[8]—two-thirds more hunger deaths, though twenty years ago there were one-third fewer people alive in the world.

Throughout the postwar era, food production has risen faster than population everywhere except sub-Saharan Africa. The hungry child, a humanitarian outrage of a generation ago, increasingly is the exception outside Africa: For instance, a generation ago 40 percent of Latin American children under age five were underweight, whereas today only 5 percent are. Childhood mortality has declined sharply in large part owing to the decline of childhood malnourishment. Today, 10 percent of children in developing countries die before the age of five; horrible, but down from 28 percent half a century ago. Meanwhile, according to the United Nations Food and Agriculture Organization, the developing world's daily average caloric intake and protein intake both are rising. Figures such as these should not divert attention from the ongoing trouble—the eight hundred million who are malnourished equal about the total populations of North America and Western Europe combined. The point is that moderate declines in malnourishment, occurring during a period of record population growth, suggest that with further effort the underlying dynamic of global hunger can be ended; and, a generation ago, global malnourishment was widely viewed as unsolvable.

Moderate improvement in the overall picture for developing nations is especially significant considering that the poor nations were widely expected to spiral into mass starvation and brutal anarchy. In the 1960s, the Stanford University theorist Paul Ehrlich used Malthusian reasoning—Malthus's main assumption was that it was physically impossible for agricultural output to rise faster than population—to predict widespread global famine, forecasting that by now hundreds of millions would have starved to death, while tens of millions more died in food riots. Moreover, it was a "fantasy" that India could "ever" feed itself, Ehrlich declared, and this was not a fringe view but a sentiment widely endorsed by opinion-makers.[9] Instead, the introduction of high-yield Green Revolution crops proved Malthus's theory, published in 1798, belonged to the eighteenth century alone. India went from harvesting eleven million tons of wheat in the early 1960s to harvesting sixty million tons by the late

1990s, becoming self-sufficient in food production. Except in Africa, most other developing nations did about as well, increasing their agricultural output much more rapidly than their population.

Many other predictions of certain catastrophe were made regarding developing nations. In 1980, a presidential report commissioned by Jimmy Carter, *Global 2000,* forecast that, by the year 2000, mass starvation would be common in the developing world while entire ecosystems collapsed and uncontrollable super-plagues ravaged the globe. Not even the awfulness of African AIDS—or the parallel AIDS emergencies building in China, India, and the former Soviet states—comes close to this expectation. In 1994, my own beloved *Atlantic Monthly* magazine ran a cover story with the chipper headline "The Coming Anarchy," which cheerfully declared that "scarcity, crime, overpopulation, tribalism and disease are rapidly destroying the social fabric of our planet."[10] The article predicted that starvation would wipe out entire regions; that unending general warfare over vanishing resources would make crime and combat indistinguishable; that unstoppable mega-epidemics would lead to mass death resembling that of the Black Plague of the fourteenth century; that much of the developing world would devolve to a Dark Ages system of local warlords and no central government, resulting in a Hobbesian war of all against all.

True, such calamities could be in store—the fact that something has not yet happened hardly means it will not. Yet moderate overall improvements in the developing world happened during a period of unprecedented population increase—the global population has doubled since 1965, an astonishing three billion more human beings added in a single generation, with almost all the increase in the developing world. It was assumed that population growth would swamp all living-standards gains, driving the developing world inexorably backward. Instead, for most people in most developing nations, life has mostly gotten better.

....

Much Western conceptualization of the developing world seems bent on emphasizing the negative, as if to suggest everything is dreadful, dangerous, or mismanaged once one steps outside the industrial sphere run by whites. The hubris here is obvious, even if it is equally obvious that, on the whole, Western nations are significantly nicer places to live than developing nations. A surprising amount of Western expectation about the developing world seems more influenced by Hollywood imaginings of a bleak warlord-run disease-ravaged apocalyptic future, the sort of vision from the *Mad Max* movies and their many imitators, than from study of actual trends.[11]

Some Western imagining of the developing world may ultimately be grounded in collapse anxiety—a hidden fear, especially among the opinion-makers of the United States and European Union, that people are about to exhaust the world's resources and any progress in developing nations will only hasten this outcome. As Chapter Two detailed, there is no reason to believe that any current resource is depleting, other than fresh water in a few nations and groundwater in China. But many in the West seem to *want* to believe that resources are quickly depleting, and therefore the developing world can never dream of living like the West. To believe that resources are quickly depleting is another form of hubris—the West is so strong that in just one century it could empty the larder of the very earth!

Believing resources are running out gives many in the West an excuse to look askance on legitimate developing-world needs.

It's common to hear it said in the United States and European Union, for example, that it would be "inappropriate" for people in developing nations to have living standards like the West: that those many millions joining the middle class in China shouldn't have cars, that Latin America shouldn't have air conditioning, that Africa shouldn't have an electricity grid. Western commentators have suggested that China will bring a resource-exhaustion calamity on itself by attempting to transition from a nation of bicycles to a nation of cars; that the current Chinese government goal of building millions of cars will bankrupt the country while creating terrible scarcity of metals.[12] Under this assumption, Western critics have pressured the World Bank and similar institutions not to lend China funds for its automobile industries. More broadly, the World Bank and similar institutions have been pressured not to lend to developing nations for central power plants, hydroelectric dams, agribusiness-style agriculture, and other means to improved living standards.

Yet China is likely to prove so good at making cars, and there is likely to be enough metal and glass and plastic to manufacture such a profusion of cars, that the real problem for the Beijing authorities will be finding roads and parking places for the hundreds of millions of vehicles China will possess,[13] while paying for the fuel they burn and managing the greenhouse gases and smog they produce. (China could alleviate some of the social cost of cars by pursuing clean engineering, such as the exceptionally low-emission gasoline and diesel engines that have recently become possible and, ultimately, building zero-emission "fuel cell" autos. As for what to do about parking spaces, I haven't the slightest idea.)

Who is the West to say that its citizens should have electricity at the flick of a switch, but the developing world should not?

That its citizens should enjoy the comfort, freedom, and personal security of traveling in private cars while the citizens of China or Indonesia or Venezuela should not? As Peter Goodman wrote in 2002 from Beijing, "A decade ago, China's car industry existed purely to manufacture automobiles for government officials. Today 40 percent of all cars in China are sold to private individuals, and the share of sales to individuals keeps rising."[14] Anything that encourages private, middle-class activity in China is to the good since, as experience in the West has shown, private property and private commerce go hand-in-hand with personal freedom and human rights. People in China need cars so that they can go where they wish, get off the farm, get out from under the boots of the party cadres, graduate into the middle class, and find out that being middle class doesn't make them happy.

The notion that the developing world should go without what the West has is a selfish view on the part of those in the United States and Europe who themselves wouldn't dream of living without central heating, well-stocked supermarkets, jetliner travel to college reunions, and fresh asiago panini. The oft-stated statistic that the United States has 5 percent of the globe's population and consumes 25 percent of current resources does not, as often suggested, mean American resource consumption should go down; the United States could eliminate its resource use, and this would not help the impoverished of the developing world one iota. What this statistic tells us is that resource use outside the Western nations must go up, up, up, in order for more of the world to attain a satisfactory standard of living. For example, in 2001 the World Energy Council estimated at a meeting in Buenos Aires that, considering population growth, to bring everyone in the developing world to the "medium" level of living standards by 2050, global energy production may have to triple—and this estimate assumes breakthroughs in energy efficiency.[15]

Western commentators who say it would be "inappropriate" for developing nations to become like the United States or Europe are reflecting collapse anxiety. They don't want the rest of the world acquiring the ability to command resources on a large scale, though this would raise the standards of living for billions, because they want the world's comforts to themselves. As a rationalization, they tell themselves that everything about the developing world is corrupt, failing, or doomed to spiral into anarchy anyway, so why commit to transferring capital and technology there?

Major escalation in developing-world resource consumption will surely pose many economic challenges, in addition to challenges of environmental protection and of managing social change. But as regards resources at least, it seems possible that eventually everyone will live like Americans and Europeans, with the world containing billions of passenger cars and detached homes, huge numbers of big-box retail stores, and truly, utterly frightening numbers of fast-food restaurants.

The practical and economic obstacles to an entire world living closer to the Western standard are many to say the least: But from the standpoint of fairness it is hard to say why all the world should not aspire to the Western standard. The overall global pattern of mild improvement where calamity was predicted should make us fundamentally optimistic about the developing world. As population growth slows, prospects will grow brighter for more developing-world improvement. Hope of bringing a better life to billions of people, while eradicating material despair, will become realistic. The West should turn its eyes toward the developing world both because this is where the West's next great challenge lies—and because success in meeting that challenge is possible.

At bottom there are two exceptionally powerful reasons why the United States and European Union must make a new commitment to work to end global poverty. The first is that, since much has been given to these lands by history, much is expected of them. Much, especially, will always be expected of the United States. As the Brazilian performer and social critic Caetano Veloso noted in 2002, "In the past there were empires, but most people in the world were not affected by them. When Rome or dynastic China or the caliphs were at their peaks, this had no impact on the majority of people alive in the world; indeed, the majority of people alive at those times might not even have known that Rome or dynastic China or the caliphs existed. Today every person in the world knows about the United States and is affected by the United States. This creates, for the United States, special obligations."[16]

Here is the second reason why the United States and Western Europe must make a new commitment to end global poverty. We must do this because it is right.

Some might presume that the September 11 attacks, and the enmity against America they reflect on the part of some in the developing world, constitute a new global crisis as bad as the predicted crises, such as resource exhaustion, that failed to occur. It is certainly possible that amorphous conflict between the West and developing-world terrorists will become an ongoing predicament for international relations—that there will commence a long-term cycle of sudden destruction in a Western city, followed by bombers circling over some remote region most people had never heard of, followed by relative quiet, followed by something else horrible, followed by more bombers.

But there are also reasons to think that conflict between the West and terror will not shape our future. One is that past cycles of terrorism, such as anarchist terrorism in Europe in the late nineteenth century, or Red fanatic terrorism in Europe and Japan in the 1960s and 1970s, eventually ended of their own accords, with the terrorists having accomplished only the discrediting of their causes.

Another is that U.S. military retaliation against the al-Qaeda network both has diminished it and will discourage recruits. The closest parallel here—and, before September 11, the last attack staged on United States soil—was the Pancho Villa terrorist murders in the town of Columbus, New Mexico, in 1916. General John Pershing led a yearlong "punitive expedition" into Mexico to capture Villa, and never found him. But Pershing smashed Villa's organization, killed many of his foot-soldiers, and, most important, changed the psychology of the Villa movement. As Max Boot, a fellow of the Council on Foreign Relations, has noted, before Pershing's expedition, hundreds of Mexican men joined Villa somewhat on a lark[17]—they could be glamorous revolutionaries opposing the mighty United States, without personal risk. Once aligning with Villa came to be seen as a death sentence, Villa lost the ability to recruit and his organization fell apart. Now, with the United States military striking at al-Qaeda around the world, joining this organization will no longer be a game but an excellent way to get yourself killed by a precision-guided munition; al-Qaeda and similar groups are likely to have a harder time signing up members. There is a real-istic chance this will help al-Qaeda activity slow of its own ac-cord, as has been the pattern with terrorist movements of the past.

Whether September 11 foretells a lasting conflict between the Western and the developing world also depends on breaking that tragic event into its two components. The two blur together in Western thinking, but are quite distinct: the tension between Islam and modernity, and the sense of inferiority that afflicts the Arab states. The tension between Islam and modernity is widely viewed in the West as the motivating cause of September 2001, but what happened was not an attack by Islam against the United States. It was, rather, an attack by Arabs against the United States. Keep this critical distinction in mind.

Tensions between Islam and modernity are best seen through an Islamic lens, focused on something of which the average West-erner is not even aware but that every Muslim schoolchild in the world knows with burning intensity: that a thousand years ago it was the West that was backward and veiled in ignorance while the Islamic world was a citadel of learning, knowledge, and power. Every Islamic schoolchild knows, for example, that a thousand years ago, when Europeans lived in filth and believed the sun revolved around the earth, Muslims lived in splendor and their scholars compiled astonishingly accurate stellar charts whose depictions of the earth's revolution around the sun pre-date Copernicus by three centuries.[18] Then it all unraveled.

Bad enough that across the centuries the balance changed, with the old Ottoman Empire, once Islam's superpower, gradu-ally losing battles both military and economic to the West; bad enough that Western science leapfrogged Islamic science; bad enough that by the nineteenth century, the Ottoman Empire was disintegrating, and every clash with the West led only to some new humiliation. In the twentieth century, disaster happened as the West began occupying Islamic territory. The British took control of much of the Middle East, the Russians essentially annexed old Ottoman lands, Israelis seized Palestine, and, finally, the Americans asserted suzerainty over much of Islam's oil wealth. The current ruling family of Saudi Arabia was essentially picked by American agents and installed with petroleum management in mind, while the modern borders of Iraq were drawn by British agents calculating Western interests rather than local ones: There are many other examples. After the Gulf War of 1991, an ultimate indignity was realized when American troops in large numbers were stationed inside the Arabian peninsula. (Never mind that the Islamic world brought the Gulf War upon itself, one Islamic state invading another.) When Jews say the phrase "Holy Land," they mean Israel; when Christians say this phrase they mean Galilee; when Muslims say "Holy Land," they mean Saudi Arabia. To have Western armies stationed in the Holy Land was, to Islam, as bad as it would be to Jews if Islamic armies made camp inside Tel Aviv, or it would be to Americans if Islamic military bases were scattered around Washington, D.C.— even if the Islamic armies said they were in Israel and Washington solely for the purpose of defending them.

That Islam was once on top and now is not—that Islamic fortunes have declined so much that Western troops build airbases and barracks on Holy Land soil and Muslims lack the strength or will to order them to depart—constitutes "the roots of Muslim rage," in the phrase of the Princeton University scholar of Islam Bernard Lewis.[19]

Why Islam was once on top and then fell behind the West is the cause of endless debate. One reason is overconfidence by the old Muslim rulers; all superpowers of the past have grown complacent and eventually lost ground, a fate against which the United States must guard. Another reason was suspicion of new technology; Islamic resistance to the printing press, banned in much of the Ottoman world during the seventeenth and eighteenth centuries, was ruinous.[20] Lewis has supposed that the turning point occurred during the eighteenth century, when Europe began to assert itself and Islamic thinkers decided this was happening because the Ottoman realm was not being sufficiently true to the traditions of the Islamic Golden Age that peaked about the year 1000. Beginning roughly in the eighteenth century, Ottoman rulers tried to turn back the clock to the eleventh century, when all was right in Islamic eyes; but "one does not move forward by going backward," Lewis has written. In the eleventh century, Islam led the modernist movement for much of the world. By the eighteenth century, Islam was marching in reverse in science, economics, politics, and technology. Islam's fortunes grew steadily worse, until the political face of the faith became so weak its combined armies could not defeat the very small military of Israel, while the Holy Land could not protect itself without admitting infidel legions.

This is a boiled-down and, inevitably, elementary account of Islamic displeasure against the West. Note that this boiled-down account turns on politics and commerce, not religion. Of course there is some religious antagonism among Muslims, Christians, and Jews—some Buddhists and Hindus can't get along, either. But is there a fundamental clash between Islam and the West, so deep and religious in nature the two can never get along? Unlikely. Islam needs a recovery of its power and political self-respect. When these things happen—as they will if the Arab nations face their faults and become democratic—tensions between Islam and modernity will recede.

Having lived in Pakistan and known Muslims in both the Western and Islamic environments, I can attest that while mainstream Islam differs from the Judeo-Christian mainstream on many points—beyond distinctions of theology, much of Islam believes courts and governments should run by religious precept, a concept Christianity and Judaism reject, and Islam and the West sharply disagree on women's rights—overall, Islam as a faith is neither hostile to the West, nor do the majority of Muslims wish the West ill.

Let me offer a few generalizations based on personal experience living in the Islamic world. Most Muslims are good-hearted, peace-loving people, just as are most Christians and Jews. A small minority of Muslims are vicious fanatics. But then the Christian ethos has spawned its share of hideous killers, among them the terrorist Timothy McVeigh, and this tells us nothing about the typical Christian. Most Muslims respect Judeo-Christian beliefs, probably more than most Jews and Christians respect Islamic beliefs. Americans and Europeans tend to forget that Islam views itself as the fruition of Judaism and Christianity, with Abraham and Jesus revered names in Muslim theology. Most Muslims want nothing to do with terrorism or violence, wishing no one harm.

Disagreement with American foreign policy is common in the Islamic world, as is blaming the United States for the plight of the Palestinians; but such things are differences of opinion, and should not be mischaracterized as threats. Pious Muslims, especially, are horrified that a vicious minority has hijacked their beautiful faith and made it something dirty. And most Muslims reject the view of the vicious minority that the Koran requires jihad against the West. "Jihad," in Koranic usage and in most Islamic theology, means a person's individual struggle to find the path toward God in a sinful world. That this word engages an obligation to kill is distinctly a minority view, just as, say, the Seventh-Day Adventist contention that the world is about to end is distinctly a minority view among Christians.

Most Muslims admire the prosperity, power, and creativity of the West. I've never visited anywhere in the Islamic world where Muslims weren't extremely friendly to me as an American and eager to emphasize how they love the United States, just disagree with its foreign policy. Most Muslims long for their societies to become more like the West, at least as regards higher living standards, fairer law, freedom of opportunity, and honest government. (The sense of inferiority that Islam feels toward the West is grounded partly in private shame that the West operates so smoothly and the Islamic world does not.) And an ever increasing number of Muslims admire the West's freedom.

The history of Islam enfolds long periods—some lasting centuries—in which the Muslim world had favorable relations with the West. There were times in the Middle Ages when Jews preferred to live under Islamic rule in north Africa because they were treated better than under Christian rule in Europe. Recent strained relations between the Islamic and Western worlds may prove a temporary condition, especially if the conflict between Israel and the Palestinians is settled.

Roughly one millennium after its founding, and lasting for a few centuries, the Christian world descended into violence and betrayal of its own ideals—through the Crusades, the corrupt papacies of the middle period, and finally the Thirty Years War, during which Catholics and Protestants slaughtered each other. Since that spasm, Christianity has become steadily less violent and more tolerant—more like what the faith's eponym would have wanted. Perhaps it is merely coincidence, but the Islamic fundamentalist wave began roughly one millennium after the founding of Muslim belief, and now has lasted a few centuries. If the Christian example tells anything, Islam's desire to turn back the clock may soon expire.

What might cause it to expire? The advent of freedom in the Arab nations.

If the tension between Islam and modernity is a general problem stitched into the tapestry of long-term trends, and thus one for which solutions can only be gradual, the embarrassing condition of the Arab nations is a specific problem with a specific immediate solution, namely, freedom.

According to the *Arab Human Development Report* published by the United Nations,[21] the world's twenty-two Arab-majority nations have 280 million citizens—about the same as the United States—yet a combined GDP smaller than that of Texas. Other than fossil fuels, the twenty-two Arab-majority states together produce exports worth less than the annual exports from Finland, population five million. Even with money from fossil-fuel sales flowing into many Arab states, per-capita income growth in these nations is slower than in parts of the developing world with few natural resources, notably China and East Asia.

There are many differences of religion, culture, and tradition between the West and the Arab states, but on the current world stage the operative distinction is that the West is free and the Arab nations are dictatorships. Latin America, the former Soviet states, much of Africa, and even China have moved toward democracy in recent decades, and typical people in all these places are better off as a result. The Arab nations remain steadfast in their rule by thugs, tyrants, or corrupt inbreds. Surely this is not because of Islam! At this writing, there was a functioning Islamic democracy in Turkey, which is not an Arab state, while one of the world's largest nations, Indonesia, was holding to a tenuous mix of democracy, Islam, and civic liberty. Along with North Korea and Cuba, the Arab nations stand among the final holdouts of repression of the many by the few. As the United Nations dryly declared in 2002, the Arab world "needs to begin an era of good government."

Why the Arab world is despotic is an issue for cultural historians; regardless, despotism is what makes the Arab world so weak. Despotism crushes the spirit, discourages innovation and entrepreneurship, dampens business, stops the free flow of information on which strong nations and cultures depend, and, in most cases, isn't even particularly good at fielding armies. People cannot be productive if their freedoms are denied and they spend their days quavering before royal-born goons or placating corrupt officials.

The West is strong and the Arab world feeble because the West is free and Arabs live in chains. Someday this lesson will sink in on the Arab nations, if only because there must come a time when the peoples of the Arab states grow tired of being weak, dependent, and pathetic in the eyes of the world.

Freedom will be the solution to the weakness of the Arab states. As Thomas Friedman has noted, owing to globalization and modern communication, "Young Arabs now have a much better sense of where they stand vis-à-vis the world and how far behind they are." This, Friedman supposes, will cause increasing public pressure in Arab nations for government reform.[22] Just imagine if Iraq, a nation with vast petroleum resources, an educated population, and a long tradition of lofty accomplishments, becomes a true democracy. If free, the people of Iraq would make their nation among the most successful in the world, reversing the psychology of Arab inferiority and setting an example for the liberty that must come to all Arab states.

For now, the psychology of Arab inferiority—rooted in lack of freedom and the Arab world's internal shame regarding its cowering position compared to the West—can spawn terrorist fanaticism. This is not because Islam and modernity cannot be reconciled, nor because Arabs and the West cannot coexist. Both advances are possible, and the key to both is the further expansion of human liberty.

....

If tensions between the West and Islam should not prohibit the United States and European Union from a new commitment to the developing world, what, then, need the Western states do?

First, the West should rid itself of one of the central fallacies of contemporary political debate, the canard that foreign aid failed. This false view is now endorsed by conservatives who dislike foreign aid, by the anti-globalization left that dislikes the World Bank and International Monetary Fund, by editorialists who proclaim that since global poverty has not been routed and the many problems of the developing world remain, aid must have failed.

Yet *why* are developing-world indicators slightly positive at a time when they were expected to be sharply negative? The actions of developing-world citizens themselves are the first reason, and the second reason is the benefit of free-market economics: Developing nations with open economic systems have three times the growth rate of those with closed systems. The final reason is Western aid.

If the measure of foreign aid is whether every nation on earth became a middle-class liberal democracy, then aid is a failure. But that is an impossible standard. If the measure is whether life got mildly better for the world's typical citizen, rather than getting much worse as expected, then the roughly $1 trillion that the United States and Europe have given away to the developing world since the end of World War II has had spectacularly good effect. Foreign aid, in fact, has been one of the signal achievements of Western culture, saving many tens of millions of lives.

If foreign aid has actually worked, that sounds like a reason the West ought to give more. Instead the numbers are flowing in the opposite direction. Over the past decade, all industrial nations have reduced aid, as "donor fatigue" has set in and rising social-welfare obligations to retirees increasingly dominate the balance sheets of Western governments. The reduction in foreign aid is coming, as the Nobel Prize–winning economist Joseph Stiglitz noted in 2000, at the very time donor institutions such as the World Bank have finally perfected ways to prevent most aid graft.

America's aid reduction has been most abrupt. The roughly $11 billion for foreign aid in the fiscal 2003 U.S. federal budget is only about one-seventh as much, in inflation-adjusted dollars, as the United States spent on foreign aid during the 1950s, when the country was much less prosperous and had many more domestic problems that required government money. The 2003 amount is lower in absolute dollars—not inflation-adjusted figures—than was spent on international aid during most of the Ronald Reagan administration.[23]

In the years immediately after World War II, when the United States was funding the successful reconstruction of Western Europe under the Marshall Plan, 15 percent of the federal budget went to foreign aid. Today polls show that most Americans think 15 percent of the federal budget goes to foreign aid, and they consider that too high. According to polls, most Americans think foreign aid should consume between 1 percent and 5 percent of the federal budget.[24] But it turns out the United States today devotes only about 0.5 percent of federal spending to foreign aid, barely a tenth the amount many Americans think would be advised.

Measured by national income, the United States today invests just 0.1 percent of GDP on foreign aid—a smaller share of national income than that spent by Portugal—versus an average of 0.24 percent for the OECD nations. True, other OECD nations do not have significant military obligations, because the United States shields them. Japan is usually the world leader in total international development assistance, and Denmark usually the leader in assistance as a share of GDP; both countries exist under the American security umbrella. But while the United States must protect the globe, the United States is also the wealthiest nation on earth. To trail Portugal in an important measure of moral responsibility to the needy should keep even foreign-aid skeptics awake at night. All of sub-Saharan Africa—made wretched by the triple whammy of poor public health, illiteracy, and malnutrition—at this writing receives a mere $1.3 billion annually in U.S. foreign aid. This is about half of what the United States spends for each new attack submarine. America needs military hardware because it must defend the free world.

But can anyone seriously argue that the cost of a submarine, if invested to save millions of lives in Africa, would not be money well spent?

Of course, some developing-world projects financed by Western aid have been white elephants. But those that have focused on health care, education, Green Revolution agriculture, and the provision of basic needs such as clean drinking water have made the world a much better place.

Many opportunities for such projects remain. At least a billion people in the world need clean and affordable drinking water; pipes must be laid, reservoirs built, treatment plants raised. Two billion people in the world have no reliable access to electricity, with electrical generating capacity in India, Pakistan, and Africa being only about one-seventeenth per capita what it is in the United States. For some of these people, the small-scale solar projects beloved by environmentalists will be right;[25] for most, what's needed are the central power generating facilities that environmentalists hate. That two billion people heat or cook indoors using open fires represents one of the leading public-health problems in the world, as it is the world's foremost cause of respiratory disease. Americans file lawsuits to complain of parts per billion of invisible 2.5-micron particles in the air, while two billion people in the world live in homes full of smoke.

And the Green Revolution must come to Africa, the one place where food production has not risen faster than population, accounting for its hunger. Africa is also the one place where subsistence farming remains ubiquitous. Western activists romanticize subsistence farming as "appropriate," but few would last out a day trying to crack parched earth behind an ox-drawn plow; and even when successful, subsistence farming cannot raise the farmer's family above destitution. Africa is the one place in the world where controlled irrigation and fertilizer are not being used on a widespread basis—the latter especially important because African soil is notoriously depleted, owing to this continent not having been glaciated in several ice-age cycles. In a perverse result of ideological environmentalism, most Western governments have stopped offering fertilizer and other Green Revolution farming aid to Africa, owing to scare campaigns led by people who don't understand or don't care that the toxicity of fertilizer—which only replaces that which is naturally found in soil—is a tiny fraction of the toxicity of pesticide.

Norman Borlaug, the Iowa-born plant breeder and Nobel Peace Prize winner who devoted the first half of his illustrious life to the successful fight against starvation in India and Pakistan, has devoted the second half to an unsuccessful effort to convince Western governments that much of the human emergency in Africa could be addressed by a Green Revolution there, too. Borlaug says of the Western commentators and environmental fundraisers who maintain that it would not be "appropriate" for Africa to adopt the Green Revolution, "They've never experienced the physical sensation of hunger. They do their lobbying from comfortable office suites in Washington or Brussels. If they lived just one month amid the misery of the developing world, as I have for fifty years, they'd be crying out for tractors and fertilizer and irrigation canals and be outraged that fashionable elitists back home were trying to deny them these things."[26] The United States could do its next righteous service to the world by teaching Africa our granary-filling methods of farming—farming being, in many respects, what America does better than anything else.

Raising living standards and expanding liberty throughout the developing world will be a many-decades enterprise, in some ways the greatest project ever undertaken by humanity. It will be a project in which the West will play at best a secondary role, as the essential work must be done by developing nations themselves.

But building water systems and power plants, sowing high-yield crops, starting newspapers and publishing houses that print unrestricted commentary: These are the things that Westerners in general, and Americans in particular, are really good at. Why shouldn't the West make a new commitment to help the rest of the world in such endeavors? Helping the many millions of the developing world who look to us for aid—whether helping with money, or technology, or by traveling overseas and getting our fingernails dirty—would not only be a good deed; it would be in our own self-interest, because we would get to feel good about ourselves.

And the price, at least in money terms, may be surprisingly within our means. The Indian economist Surjit Bhalla calculates that "Simple mathematics tell us we can already live in a world without destitution." His studies show that in 2000 there were 455 million people existing at the level of desperation—an average income of 79 cents per day, versus the $1.08 per day that should be the floor even in the poorest nations. This means, Bhalla notes, these people need only to acquire *an extra twenty-nine cents per day* to be released from desperation, and that seems a plausible objective.

Economic growth in developing nations is by far the first choice to provide that extra twenty-nine cents per day, and developing-world economic expansion would be aided if Western nations lowered their trade barriers. One of the disgraces of Western economic policy is that, while the United States and Western Europe demand unfettered access to developing-world markets, both maintain trade barriers designed to keep out developing-world goods. Heavy tariffs are placed by the United States on textiles from the developing world, for example, and these tariffs live on despite the World Trade Organization regime the United States uses to demand full access to the markets of other nations. Laborers from developing nations would live better, and their children have a better chance to ascend into the middle class, if all Western tariffs against developing-world products were dropped.

That would slightly detract from the Western economy, as textiles industries of the West would close. But just as Americans ought to pay slightly higher prices so that the minimum wage could become a living wage, all Western economies ought as well to sacrifice slightly so that developing-world workers can live better. This would increase the degree of justice in the world, at a relatively low price—in fact, it's hard to think of a more cost-effective way to increase global justice. Perhaps 500 million Americans and Europeans literally would not notice the loss of twenty-nine cents per day, where for Bhalla's 455 million destitute in the world, this sum represents the difference between destitution and hope. To transfer such amounts to developing nations via lowered trade barriers is simply the right thing to do.

But suppose that, ultimately, the Western world simply gave twenty-nine cents per day to those 455 million people as aid. What would it cost? Forty-eight billion dollars per year—about one-eighth what the West spends on internal agriculture subsidies, less than a tenth what it spends on military budgets, considerably less than the United States recently allocated to tax cuts for the wealthy. Ending despair in the developing world is not a blue-sky dream. It is something this generation can do, starting right now.

Chapter 12

IT'S NEVER TOO LATE

In the Middle Ages, Europeans dreamed of a utopia called Cockaigne. Said to exist on a distant isle, Cockaigne was a place where unlimited food appeared whenever anyone wished for it. Roast meats, grilled fish, stuffed goose, and fruit pies could be had in any quantity simply by thinking of them; rivers flowed with wine; no matter how often drained, cups magically refilled themselves with beer; some buildings were even made of food.[1] You could sleep as long as you wanted: days on end, if you wished. You could have sex with whomever would agree, as often as you wanted, without pregnancy or any legal complications. Everyone wore clothes made from fine fabrics in bright colors: in the Middle Ages, fine clothing being what the typical person most longed to possess. Everyone's pockets bulged with gold. Most of all no one had to work, for no work needed to be performed. Food grew itself; plates washed themselves; fires tended themselves.

Small wonder that men and women in an age of poverty, drudgery, food shortages, and condemnation of sex dreamed of a realm of drinking, eating, sleeping, free love, and never being called to toil. Musicians of the Middle Ages sang songs of Cockaigne; mothers hushed children to sleep with tales of how they would someday be transported to this land; many must have reflected, bitterly, on how merciless was fate to allow men and women to imagine such a kingdom but never experience it. Historical asterisk? With the exception of exemption from labor and a few details like washing the dishes, hundreds of millions of Americans, Europeans, Canadians, Japanese, and Australians today reside in Cockaigne.

Others have dreamed of different utopias. In his 1516 book that gave the concept its name, Thomas More thought utopia would be a tranquil and modest place. Money would not exist because people would gladly perform fairly pleasant tasks to produce whatever society required, then exchange generously with others. Flashy clothes would not exist; More detested competition over who could afford the rarest fabrics or brightest dyes, and essentially wanted everyone in a school uniform. Unhappiness would not exist; people would lose interest in possessions and status, and in doing so be set free from the cycle of desire. Thomas More wrote *Utopia* as a satire of money-obsessed, fashion-obsessed, gotta-have-it-now sixteenth-century England, and was surprised when readers told him this imaginary land sounded like a place they'd like to live. Needless to say hardly anyone, except the deeply philosophical or devoutly religious, today dwells in the utopia envisioned by More—while all the materialistic obsessions about which More fretted still continue, at perhaps 100,000 times the global GDP.

Still others have imagined cloud nine differently. To the Greek thinker Plato, the essence of a perfect society was political—

small communities of well-educated landholders happily would submit to rule by philosophical guardians who would own nothing themselves, in order to exercise wisdom divorced from self-interest. (Plato would have been horrified at the idea of a CEO setting his own pay number.) To the Roman poet Virgil, humanity should long for a place called Arcadia, a romanticized countryside without violence or disease in which people lived simple lives laboring relatively little because crops never failed, and where everyday life consisted mainly of appreciating nature, music, and poetry. Arcadians would work and farm in the morning, have long naps after a big lunch, spend evenings singing, dancing, and drinking huge quantities of wine; the next morning they would rise at dawn, never with an aching head, to speak a humble prayer of thanks as they beheld the daily miracle of the arriving sun. There would be no princes or rich men and, as important, no one would wish to be a prince or a rich man.

To Rousseau and the many he inspired, utopia would be the abandonment of governments, businesses, churches, and schools for return to a conjectured minimal condition that is naturally good. Everything once actually was Eden, Rousseau believed, until civilization invented the concept of corruption. "Nothing could be more gentle" than the initial noble-savage condition of humankind, Rousseau famously asserted. He lived before the archeological evidence showing that misery, violence, and general warfare were common if not standard aspects of the primal human past.[2]

The inventory of proposed utopias would in itself be a book,[3] with everything from anarchy to absolute social control having been proposed in many flavors. Dystopias—reverse utopias, where everything is awful—have come closer to realization. In the past century alone the Nazis, Soviet Communists, Chinese

Communists, Cambodian Communists, and imperial Japanese created dystopias, though all fell. One aspect of dystopias that seems especially frightful is how desperately hard the Nazis, Communists, and imperial Japanese worked to make their societies as awful as possible. In each case, it was not some outside circumstance (a famine, say, or an enemy attack) that imposed sorrow. Rather, the men and women of the society itself—mostly the men, of course—worked assiduously, even at personal sacrifice, to make their nations awful places to live and to ensure that their friends, neighbors, and own children would be utterly miserable. What this dynamic tells us about human nature we would, perhaps, rather not know.

Yet a dystopia need not be a tyranny. Following the tradition of Thomas More, in 1931 the British writer Aldous Huxley used a depiction of a twenty-fifth-century society to satirize the society of the present; what he imagined was a perfectly voluntary dystopia. His work *Brave New World* foresaw a place where people were so totally obsessed with getting and having that they would submit to social programming, especially by swallowing drugs that erased their personalities. Freed of human individuality, society functions efficiently. Physical luxuries are everywhere, while no one ever suffers any material need. The anti-personality drugs cause people to smile and appear happy. A weirdly affable big-brother organization wants everyone to have a good time; recreation, amusement, and pretty much unlimited sex are available; men or women who seem even slightly sad are immediately contacted and offered a wide range of delights. But the whole "utopia" only works because people have stopped thinking.

Huxley feared that the quest for contentment, rather than military or dictatorial power, would be the ultimate adversary of human freedom. In *Brave New World,* men and women have voluntarily surrendered their personalities in return for always having whatever they want. Some people would, in fact, take that bargain voluntarily, while no one would ever volunteer to live under tyranny. This is the reason Huxley feared contentment as an ultimate danger: People will always fight tyranny, but they might surrender to materialism of their own free will. Writing the book in the late 1920s, during the first Western consumerism boom, Huxley thought he saw the budding signs of runaway materialism. Now the global GDP is a hundred times what it was then.

Asked to outline a utopia today, the typical Western citizen might say the abolition of poverty; a big house and car for everyone, and no money worries; eat and drink what you want without gaining weight; live 150 years; more sex (for men) and more romance (for women); television remote-controls that find themselves; global peace and larger airline seats.

No one can say what the future may hold—nuclear war, new dictatorships, horrible errors of genetic engineering, a comet strike, other things that could go badly wrong. But it is not out of the question that someday the suburban utopia sketched in the above paragraph will more or less come to pass: that everyone in the West, perhaps even everyone in every nation, will have access to whatever material things they require without money anxiety, while living very long lives in slender good health with recreation and romance, and in a world finally at peace.

The arrow of progress already points in these directions. Though readers of this book will not live to see the semi-utopia sketched above, their children's children might. Remember that today's Western life would seem, to our great-grandparents, more or less a utopia. Our relatively near descendants may live in societies that would seem utopian to us, though perhaps it could be argued that world peace is more likely than comfortable airline seats. Economic, medical, and technological arrows of progress, at least, point toward ever-better lives.

If society advances toward what would seem to us utopia, no one should expect this will mean an end to problems. The pattern of history observed so far is that for each problem solved, a new problem arises; it may be that new problems always arise to replace old ones, each generation handing a fresh set of challenges to the next. There is no reason to think this sequence will ever change, barring the arrival on earth of the divine.

A future society that would be utopian by our standards—no rat race for money, no violence, no person knowing material want—surely would continue to have problems. People could still be satisfied or sad; be talented or typical; be liked or disliked; still fail to make the class play or drop the touchdown pass in the big game; still have trouble finding meaning in life; still, surely, experience a broken heart. Even in a physical utopia, our descendants will continue to have complaints. I don't know what their complaints will be; I am certain they will have them, and keenly felt.

And even if what would seem to us utopia is someday achieved, there is no guarantee it will make our descendants happy. Life has gotten dramatically better for almost everyone in the Western world during the past half-century, yet people are no happier. Centuries to come may see life better still, and happiness not increased.

This is a poignant prospect, but otherwise need not concern

us. Absent the arrival of the divine, it is likely there will never be a social order or moment in time, even in a place without want or fear, when human happiness is assured. Happiness must come from within, and money cannot buy it. Whether or not we attain happiness will probably always be unrelated to whether life is getting better.

....

That people will still be complaining in Arcadia should not prevent us from continuing to move one step closer. The world remains a place of want, fear, and injustice. It need not be so.

If the last century of human progress teaches anything, it is that it's never too late to change the world. In our lifetimes "impossible" problems that could "never" be solved—pollution, crime, indigent old age, the Cold War—have declined or disappeared before our eyes. Astonishing reforms and progress have been accomplished more rapidly, and in most cases at lower cost, than anyone dared hope. Endlessly experience teaches that we need not accept what we see out the window; we can make the view one of our choosing.

The reason that the problems of the present—such as developing-world destitution, greenhouse gases, or poverty amidst American plenty—seem "unsolvable" today is simply that we have not yet begun the work of solving them. We should, for it is never too late to change the world. Want can end, and be forgotten; an artificial greenhouse effect can be prevented; even in a world of many billions of souls, there can be a safe and secure place for everyone. It is ours to decide what the future will hold. And if we decide well, the future may hold an ever-better life, about which our descendants will complain.

NOTES

CHAPTER 1

1. In 2001, the GDP of North Korea was estimated at $22 billion. See http://www.countries.com/countries/north_korea.

2. See *Myths of Rich and Poor* by W. Michael Cox and Richard Alm, New York: Basic Books, 2000.

3. See "Gap Between Rich and Poor Found Substantially Wider" by Robert Pear, *The New York Times*, September 5, 1999. The data cited are from the Congressional Budget Office.

4. See, among others, *Why the Working Class Still Matters* by Rudy Teixeira and Joel Rogers, New York: Basic Books, 2000; and *Wealth in America: Trends in Inequality* by Lisa Keister, New York: Cambridge University Press, 2000.

5. See "The Impact of Immigration on the Size and Growth of the Poor Population in the United States" by Steven Camarota, Washington, D.C.: Center for Immigration Studies, 1999.

6. See "Recent Changes in U.S. Family Finances: Evidence from the 1998 and 2001 Survey of Consumer Finances" by Ana Arizcorbe, first author, *Federal Reserve Board Bulletin*, January 2003. Text available online at http://www.federalreserve.gov/pubs/bulletin/2003/03 bulletin.htm#jan.

7. Because immigrants, who work for low wages, tend to depress wages for native-born Americans at the bottom of the ladder, it is possible that banning immigration would impose grave hardships on the poor of other nations seeking entry to the United States, while improving the lot of the native-born poor. Then we are left with the argument of utilitarianism. Should we be concerned only with the American poor, or pursue the greatest good for the greatest number?

8. See "Importing Poverty" by Steven Camarota, Washington, D.C.: Center for Immigration Studies, 2000.

9. See the excellent *The Good Life and Its Discontents* by Robert Samuelson, New York: Random House, 1995.

10. In 2002, health care costs were 14 percent of America's GDP versus 10 percent in 1982.

11. Cost average estimate from the Web site arthroscopy.com.

12. See "Health Spending: How Much Is Too Much?" by David Wessel, *Wall Street Journal*, January 9, 2002.

13. "The Middle of the Middle Class" by Camille Sweeney, *The New York Times Magazine*, June 9, 2002.

14. Such schools include Amherst, Boston University, Grinnell, and Swarthmore. See "Colleges Offer Students Privacy" by Sara Rimer, *The New York Times*, January 27, 2003.

15. Interview with me. Unless a quotation in the text is attributed to a printed source, it comes from an interview with me, and the endnote to this effect will not be repeated. In the interview, Waldie suggested that one reason suburbs have such a bad name is that most writers live in big cities, whence they pen denunciations of the suburbs. Suburbs lack a pool of writers to pen denunciations of cities, putting them behind in the struggle of prestige.

16. Critics of suburbs hate cul-de-sacs because they take up more space than grid street systems; anti-suburb snobs actually write in praise of the notion that people should live in congested, "high-density" circumstances so that the least possible land is used. With land still abundant in the United States—less than 6 percent of the country is "built up," according to the U.S. Geological Survey—this kind of view makes sense only in academia and at Upper East Side cocktail parties.

17. Sweden is second at an average of 11.1 years, then Japan at 10.7 years. See *The State of the Nation* by Derek Bok, Cambridge, Mass.: Harvard University Press, 1996.

18. See *The Rise and Fall of the American Teenager* by Thomas Hine, New York: Harper Perennial, 2000.

19. Polls show that 200 million of America's 284 million people have taken at least one airline trip in the past five years.

20. National Restaurant Association statistic.

21. *The First Measured Century* by Thomas Caplow, Louis Hicks, and Ben Wattenberg, Washington, D.C.: AEI Press, 2001.

22. *Time for Life* by John Robinson and Geoffrey Godbey, State College, Penn.: PSU Press, 1999. Juliet Schor of Boston College estimates that average free time has been declining for Americans, and has engaged in a running duel of statistics with Robinson and Godbey. Most who study the numbers side against Schor and endorse the notion of a rising average for leisure hours, though of course there are many individuals—millions, probably—whose lives are painfully time-stressed. As for Western Europe, it is undisputed that free-time hours are increasing there, since the average workweek has declined throughout the European Union nations during the postwar period.

23. American women, the researchers estimate, perform two-thirds of the nation's housework and four-fifths of its child care, but today have about the same amount of free time as men, owing to fewer work-for-wage hours.

24. "Working Less and Living Longer" by Jesse Ausubel and Arnulf Grubler, *Technological Forecasting and Social Change*, summer 1995.

25. "Biology and Society" by Christopher DeMuth, speech at the American Enterprise Institute, Washington, D.C., October 1998.

26. African American males live shorter lives than white males, but this is true even for well-to-do African American males, suggesting the longevity difference is not primarily a phenomenon of income.

27. This might give Americans a moment of pause. Our system, after all, is denounced for materialism, superficiality, litigiousness, celebrity worship, sexual obsession, media oversimplification, and fixation on faux instant scandals—and we're the strongest, healthiest, freest, and most prosperous nation in the world! Maybe materialism, superficiality, litigiousness, celebrity worship, sexual obsession, media oversimplification, and fixation on faux instant scandals is somehow actually a constructive combination, and other nations of the world should aspire to these things.

28. See *The Optimism Gap* by David Whitman, New York: Walker & Co., 1998.

CHAPTER 2

1. Now is a good time to reread Gibbon's *Decline and Fall of the Roman Empire,* last volume completed in 1788, which contends in part that this ancient realm crumbled because it lost the will to send armies to distant lands and attack enemies before they could gather enough strength to bring destruction to the gates of Rome. The parallel to the current American situation is obvious.

2. Increased security will reduce standards of living marginally, via the price of security itself, some slowing of international commerce, and the "opportunity cost" of time lost standing in metal-detector lines and enduring other checkpoints rather than doing something else. But estimates of the wealth-draining effect of security put the total at less than 1 percent of the Western GDP.

3. See the *Uniform Crime Reports,* published annually by the Federal Bureau of Investigation and found at http://www.fbi.gov/ucr/ucr.htm.

4. "Lowest rate ever" in this sense means since statistics have been kept; it's not a metaphysical judgment. See *America's Children: Key National Indicators of Well-Being 2002,* Federal Interagency Forum on Child and Family Statistics, Washington, D.C.: Government Printing Office, 2002. This report can be accessed online at Childstats.gov.

5. See "The Fall of Murder in New York" by William Rashbaum, *The New York Times,* December 29, 2002.

6. " 'Fort Apache' Precinct Shows Spectacular Crime Drop," *Wall Street Journal,* May 4, 2002.

7. The best source for comparative environmental statistics is the *Leading Index of Environmental Indicators,* an annual analysis of EPA data published by the Pacific Research Institute, a California think tank; these figures are from the 2003 edition.

8. In 2002, New York City also was certified as in compliance with Clean Air Act standards for carbon monoxide, a poison and a lung irritant, also called "winter smog." As recently as the 1970s, New York violated federal carbon monoxide standards dozens of times per year, and the problem was widely viewed as unsolvable. When the New York carbon monoxide problem was solved, *The New York Times* ran this as a small box on page A16. The story, being inconveniently

positive, had to be buried. Any indication that carbon monoxide in New York was increasing would, of course, have gotten the page-one doomsday treatment.

9. See "Green Surprise" by Gregg Easterbrook, *The Atlantic Monthly*, September 2000.

10. Comparative statistics for Los Angeles smog can be viewed online at http://www.aqmd.gov.

11. "Environmental Doomsday?" by Gregg Easterbrook, *Brookings Review*, Spring 2002.

12. *Walden* by Henry Thoreau, published 1854. See *Thoreau's Country*, by David Foster, Cambridge, Mass.: Harvard University Press, 1999, for a fine analysis of what Thoreau thought would happen to the environment versus what actually happened.

13. The gray whale and bald eagle benefited from special laws passed before the Endangered Species Act, but once the Endangered Species Act came along, protection for these creatures was essentially rolled into it.

14. Recent public-opinion surveys on the environment summarized in "America Celebrates Earth Day 1970, for the 31st Time," by Jonathan Rauch, *National Journal*, April 28, 2000. For instance, 57 percent of respondents told the poll company SWR Worldwide that "U.S. environmental conditions are worse today than 30 years ago," while 67 percent said that "despite the Clean Air Act and Clean Water Act, air and water pollution seem to continue to get worse."

15. China has accomplished a Green Revolution miracle of rice production partly by depleting its aquifers at a sprightly pace; groundwater supply may become a serious concern in this nation sooner than anyone would care to think.

16. See "Opportunity Cost" by Gregg Easterbrook, *The New Republic*, May 15, 2000.

17. Cover headline of *Time* magazine, October 10, 1985.

18. "Broken Limits to Life Expectancy," Jim Ooppen and James Vaupel. *Science*, May 10, 2002.

19. Many statistics in this section come from the 2001 edition of *OECD Social Indicators*, an annual analysis published by the Organization for Economic Cooperation and Development in Geneva, Switzerland.

20. See *Human Development Report 2002*, a United Nations publication, Oxford: Cambridge University Press, 2002. Only in parts of Africa, where AIDS is raging and public health poor, is life expectancy declining.

21. See *The Ultimate Resource* by Julian Simon, Princeton: Princeton University Press, 1998. Simon died at the age of sixty-five, denied the full lifespan he considered so essential for others.

22. See "The Population Implosion" by Nicholas Eberstadt, *Foreign Policy*, March 2001.

23. See *One World: The Ethics of Globalization* by Peter Singer, New Haven: Yale University Press, 2002.

24. See Chapter 1, note 17.

25. "Increase of Maximum Life Span in Sweden, 1861–1999," John Wilmoth et al., *Science*, September 29, 2000.

26. See *Annual Report to the Nation on the Status of Cancer*, National Cancer Institute, Washington, D.C.

27. Though America's homicide rate is awful, its suicide rate is low compared to many Western nations—50 percent less than that of France, for example.

28. Building fires have declined by about 40 percent since 1980, though annual on-the-job deaths of firefighters have remained roughly constant at a little under 100 per year nationally. That figure does not incorporate September 11.

29. See "Motor Vehicle Crash Fatality and Injury Estimates for 2002," National Highway Traffic Safety Administration. Available online at http://www-nrd.nhtsa.dot.gov/pdf/nrd-30/NCSA/Rpts/2003/Assess01.pdf.

30. Most research suggests autism is a result of brain-development problems in the womb; as infant mortality declines, more babies who once would have died are saved, living to express their autism and thus resulting in higher incidence of autism. Some graphs show autism rates increasing in sync with prevalence of polio vaccination, and, until the 1990s, polio vaccines contained tiny amounts of a mercury-based preservative called thimerosal. Whether the vaccine link is real was at this writing hotly debated; thimerosal is no longer used in medication.

31. Obesity and its complications are now estimated to kill 280,000 Americans per year, rendering it the second-worst preventable cause

of death after lung cancer caused by smoking. See "The Disease Burden Associated With Overweight and Obesity," Avia Must, first author, *Journal of the American Medical Association*, October 27, 1999.

32. For this reason, my Brookings Institution colleague Jonathan Rauch has long advocated that physicians ought sometimes to advise patients to drink. America's current alcohol consumption, 8.3 liters per adult per annum (calculated at 80 proof, or the strength of vodka), works out to somewhat less than half the amount necessary for the average adult to consume the equivalent of two glasses of wine daily, which many health studies suggest would be ideal. The French drink exactly twice as much per adult—in other words, as a nation they hit the ideal average just about on the head.

33. See *America's Children: Indicators of Well-Being 2002*, Federal Interagency Forum on Child and Family Statistics, Washington, D.C.: Government Printing Office, 2002.

34. See *The Case for Marriage* by Linda Waite and Maggie Gallagher, New York: Doubleday, 2000.

35. "Illegitimate Births Decline Statewide" by Agnes Palazzetti, *Buffalo News*, March 19, 2001.

36. See *The American Paradox* by David Myers, New Haven: Yale University Press, 2000.

37. See *America's Children: Indicators of Well-Being 2002*, Federal Interagency Forum on Child and Family Statistics, Washington, D.C.: Government Printing Office, 2002.

38. See "Declining Rates of Abortion, 1995–2000," Alan Guttmacher Institute, New York, 2002.

39. According to the Centers for Disease Control, there were 1.2 million abortions in the United States in 2000, the lowest total since 1978, though still a huge figure from the standpoint of moral quandary. The CDC also reports that, in 2000, 2 percent of American women had had an abortion, lowest share since 1975.

40. See "Why We Don't Marry" by James Q. Wilson, *City Journal*, winter 2002.

41. Steven Levitt, an economist at the University of Chicago, and John Donahue III, a law professor at Stanford University, have proposed

that about half the crime decline of the 1990s could be attributed to the 1973 *Roe* decision that extended abortion rights nationwide. The reasoning is that, by avoiding unwanted births, abortion reduces the cohort of those most likely to commit crimes—male children from broken homes who are born to unwed mothers, such children being most likely to become criminals regardless of race.

About 1990, when the crime decline began, Levitt and Donahue have pointed out, is sixteen years after access to abortion became common in the United States, and it is at about age sixteen when boys begin to steal and otherwise break the law. Many unwanted boys who would have begun joining the criminal element around the year 1990, Levitt and Donahue contend, simply did not exist, owing to federal legalization of abortion. They note that the five states that legalized abortion before *Roe*—New York, California, Washington, Hawaii, and Alaska—saw their crime declines start sooner than the national decline, in each case the crime drop commencing about sixteen years after access to legal abortion went into effect.

42. See "What Have 17-Year-Olds Known in the Past?" by David Whittington, *American Education Research Journal*, March 1991.

43. See *The State of the Nation* by Derek Bok, Cambridge, Mass.: Harvard University Press, 1996.

44. See *Digest of Education Statistics 1999*, National Center for Education Statistics, Washington, D.C.: Department of Education. Interestingly, though commentators hyperventilated about the SAT score "decline," little was said about the similar ACT achievement test, whose typical scores never declined because nearly all the lower-performing students deciding to join the ranks of test-takers took the SAT, not the ACT.

45. See *National Assessment of Educational Progress*, Department of Education, Washington, D.C.: Government Printing Office, 2000.

46. "Massive IQ Gains in 14 Nations" by James Flynn, *Psychological Bulletin*, June 1987.

47. See *The Blank Slate* by Steven Pinker, New York: Viking, 2002.

48. "Women Rising in Corporate Ranks, Report Says," by Kirsten Downey, *The Washington Post*, November 19, 2002.

49. "Gap Between Pay of Men and Women Smallest on Record" by David Leonhardt, *The New York Times*, February 17, 2003.

50. See, especially, *The Declining Significance of Race* by William Julius Wilson, Chicago: University of Chicago Press, 1980.

51. Black poverty in 2000, the National Urban League found, was 26 percent versus 13 percent overall for that year, leaving an African American about twice as likely to be poor as an American generally. This is about the postwar norm: In the 1960s, about 40 percent of blacks were poor, versus about 20 percent of Americans overall. At any rate, the figures for both categories—African American poverty and overall American poverty—reflect steady, linear decline.

52. During the early 1960s, when welfare was hard to qualify for and viewed as a source of shame in the African American community, about 5 percent of blacks were on state assistance. That figure rose through the 1970s and 1980s as rules were liberalized and the disastrous throw-the-fathers-out clauses were added to welfare, peaking at 11.5 percent of blacks on welfare in 1991. By 2000, the percentage had fallen back to 6.7 percent, not much more than before the 1960s welfare-expansion experiment—now mostly universally viewed, including by many blacks, as bad for blacks—began.

53. *America's Children: Indicators of Well-Being 2002*, Federal Interagency Forum on Child and Family Statistics, Washington, D.C.: Government Printing Office, 2002.

54. "Don't Mess with Welfare Reform Success" by Heather MacDonald, *City Journal*, winter 2002.

55. *The Shape of the River* by William Bowen and Derek Bok, Princeton: Princeton University Press, 1998.

56. For an argument that statistics like these mean African Americans really aren't making up much ground, see *The Anatomy of Racial Inequality* by Glenn Loury, Cambridge, Mass.: Harvard University Press, 2002.

57. The sociologist Christopher Jencks argued in an influential 1972 book, *Inequality*, that even if minority education rose, minority income would never rise, owing to insurmountable barriers of prejudice.

58. "The Best Time Ever to Be Black" by Ellis Cose, *Newsweek*, December 24, 1999.

59. During the 1970s, a lightning-rod issue in American politics was the proposed Humphrey-Hawkins Full Employment Act of 1978, championed by Hubert Humphrey, which would essentially have put any

unemployed person on federal welfare whenever unemployment exceeded 4 percent. Many economists scoffed at 4 percent as an impossible goal that would lead to runaway inflation. In 1999, the United States achieved 4 percent unemployment—without inflation.

60. The CEO lying was awful, but media reports often misrepresented its impact. On an evening newscast I heard an Enron secretary lament that she had been wiped out of the $700,000 in Enron stock that had accumulated in her 401(k) in the previous five years. This figure—surely more than her total income during the period—was strictly a figment of Enron lying, money that we now know she did not deserve in any case. The problem is that Enron executives, who cashed out their options, got to keep the figment money they made through lying.

61. See *One World: The Ethics of Globalization* by Peter Singer, New Haven: Yale University Press, 2002.

62. See "Does Globalization Help the Poor?," Washington, D.C.: International Forum on Globalization, 2002.

63. See *Imagine There's No Country: Poverty, Growth and Inequality in the Developing World* by Surjit Bhalla, Washington, D.C.: Institute for International Economics, 2002.

64. See "Hi I'm in Bangalore But Can't Say So" by Mark Lander, *The New York Times*, March 21, 2001. Reps at the Amazon.com office in Bangalore use assumed names such as "Naomi Morrison" and are instructed to pretend to be in the United States. The company gives them free tapes of U.S. TV shows such as *Friends*, so that they can be current with cultural references and fads.

65. Marx believed that if capital were allowed to move freely among nations, inevitably all workers would be driven to a level of destitution as production shifted to whatever countries had the cheapest labor. This has not happened for a variety of reasons: unions, which are more effective than Marx thought they could be; that many corporations favor educated workers, whereas Marx thought industry would want illiterate drones; and the fact that labor is only one of many cost components in manufacturing, not the be-all-and-end-all Marx theorized.

66. *Nickel and Dimed* by Barbara Ehrenreich, New York: Metropolitan, 2001.

67. See *Current Population Survey 2002*, Bureau of the Census.

68. Figures in this paragraph from the *Human Development Report 2002*, New York: United Nations, 2002.

69. See "Powerhouse H-Bomb Heads for Graveyard" by Walter Pincus, *The Washington Post*, August 8, 2002.

70. World stocks of small arms—especially machine guns and assault rifles—continue to rise, however. According to the Small Arms Survey, produced by a Geneva, Switzerland, organization, there are now at least 550 million military firearms in existence. Some of the world's worst ongoing conflicts, such as ethnic and tribal-warlord violence in Africa and Afghanistan, are driven not by high-tech weapons but by cheap, plentiful assault rifles.

71. *Peace and Conflict in 2001* by Ted Gurr et al., Center for International Development and Conflict Management, University of Maryland.

72. See the *Arab Human Development Report*, New York: United Nations, 2002.

73. For what it's worth, I would cast my vote with those commentators who maintain that England's May 1940 decision to continue fighting Germany was the single greatest event in world political history. At that point the anti-Nazi cause seemed hopeless, and many Britons favored a ceasefire, dangled by Berlin with the incentive that, if England accepted, its cities would not be bombed. Had Great Britain capitulated in 1940, the United States counterattack against German fascism probably could not have happened, and darkness might reign over Europe still. Alternatively, English capitulation in 1940 might have led to general atomic warfare in Europe, as the United States and Soviet Union attempted to defeat Nazism via the ultimate weapon. Both horrible fates were averted by Britain's determination to keep fighting no matter what the cost; a case in which bellicosity on the part of a democracy turned out to benefit the entire world.

74. *Vital Signs 2003*, Worldwatch Institute, New York: W. W. Norton, 2003.

75. *The Injury Chartbook*, Geneva, Switzerland: World Health Organization, 2003.

76. According to the United Nations Department of Peacekeeping Op-

erations, world peacekeeping expenditures, stated in 2000 dollars, averaged around $300 million per annum in the mid-1980s, and have risen steadily to around $3 billion per annum today.

77. For a while, a theory bounced around that the building of McDonald's restaurants would accomplish what no treaty or diplomat ever did, end war: because no two nations that each had a McDonald's had ever fought each other. This hope evaporated when the NATO states bombed Belgrade, capital of a McDonald's nation, over its refusal to stop killing Muslims in Kosovo. But the prospect that democracies will be less hostile than dictatorships remains real.

78. In this regard, it is worth noting that the Ohio State University political scientist John Mueller has argued that it was not nuclear deterrence that prevented the West and Soviet Union from fighting; rather, it was that voters in the West's democracies demanded that their leaders solve the Cold War without bloodshed, and got their wish. See *Retreat from Doomsday* by John Mueller, New York: Basic Books, 1989.

79. Many in the British Isles resisted the World War I draft, though resisters if caught were severely mistreated in prisons. A national scandal was triggered when the poet and soldier Wilfred Owen wrote a famous poem describing English soldiers dying in a gas attack and denouncing as an "old lie" the sentiment *Dulce et decorum est pro patria mori,* or "it is glorious to die for your country," a phrase then taught as writ in British schools. Owen was killed in action just hours before the armistice that ended the war; his death is described in heartbreaking detail in Pat Barker's World War I trilogy, *The Ghost Road.* The final stanza of Owen's poem reads:

> If in some smothering dream, you too could pace
> Behind the wagon that we flung him in,
> And watch the white eyes writhing in his face,
> His hanging face, like a devil's sick of sin,
> If you could hear, at every jolt, the blood
> Come gargling from the froth-corrupted lungs,
> Obscene as cancer, bitter as the cud
> Of vile, incurable sores on innocent tongues,
> My friend, you would not tell with such high zest

> To children ardent for some desperate glory
> The old lie: *Dulce et decorum est*
> *Pro patria mori.*

80. See the report *World Military Spending*, Center for Defense Information, Washington, D.C., 2003.
81. See "Conventional Arms Transfers to Developing Nations," Washington, D.C.: Congressional Research Service, 2002.
82. *The Crime Drop in America* by Alfred Blumstein and Joel Wallman, Cambridge, Mass.: Oxford University Press, 2000. Another good work on this topic is *New York Murder Mystery: The True Story Behind the Crime Crash of the 1990s* by Andrew Karman, New York: NYU Press, 2002.
83. See the excellent, chilling article about cruel mandatory minimums for nonviolent drug offenders, "Reefer Madness" by Eric Schlosser, *The Atlantic Monthly*, August 1994, available online at http://www. theatlantic.com/politics/crime/reefm.htm. Its opening paragraph:

   "In the state of Indiana a person convicted of armed robbery will serve about five years in prison; someone convicted of rape will serve about twelve; and a convicted murderer can expect to spend twenty years behind bars. At the age of thirty-eight Mark Young was arrested at his Indianapolis home for brokering the sale of 700 pounds of marijuana grown on a farm in nearby Morgan County. Young was tried and convicted under federal law. He had never before been charged with drug trafficking. He had no history of violent crime. Young's role in the illegal transaction had been that of a middleman—he never distributed the drugs; he simply introduced two people hoping to sell a large amount of marijuana to three people wishing to buy it. On February 8, 1992, Mark Young was sentenced by Judge Sarah Evans Barker to life imprisonment without possibility of parole."
84. Spoken to Bill Moyers in 1965 and quoted by Moyers in his 2002 eulogy at Gardner's memorial service. See http://www.carnegie.org/sub/docpublications/moyers.html.

CHAPTER 3

1. *Mapping Human History* by Steve Olson, New York: Houghton Mifflin, 2002.

2. As the writer Michael Pollan has noted, as recently as the United States in the late eighteenth century, sugar was for most people an unattainable delicacy. Most children grew up with candy rarely if ever passing their lips, while the primary sweet things the typical person encountered in a lifetime were maple syrup and fruits, accounting for the popularity of apples. See *The Botany of Desire* by Michael Pollan, New York: Random House, 2001.

3. See *Loss of Happiness in Market Democracies* by Robert Lane, New Haven: Yale University Press, 2000.

4. See *The Good Old Days—They Were Terrible!* by Otto Bettmann, New York: Random House, 1974.

5. I'm skipping the 1980s and 1990s since, in my bargain, you must go back to a year before your own birth. Teenage readers, don't take offense.

6. See *The Affluent Society* by John Kenneth Galbraith, New York: Houghton Mifflin, 1958.

7. See *The Good Life and Its Discontents* by Robert Samuelson, New York: Random House, 1995.

8. Each week I buy a $7 bunch of gorgeous fresh flowers from a flower seller on the street corner outside my office in Washington, D.C., and each week marvel that the flowers, flown up from Ecuador, are of such high quality and so inexpensive. It may well be that the Ecuadorian farmers and American street-sellers involved in this enterprise aren't paid enough. But the thought that for $7 you could produce, fly to another continent, and distribute *anything*—even old wadded-up newspaper—continually amazes me.

9. For farm-chemical decline statistics, see *Vital Signs 2001*, the Worldwatch Institute, New York: W. W. Norton, 2001.

10. Seed companies do vary strains annually, as insurance against some disease mutating to attack monoculture. Consumers are partly to blame for agricultural monoculture, since they favor uniform products. The apple business, for example, has shifted toward monoculture as consumers demanded standard size, shape, and color. Apple taste has been the casualty, as some of the best eating-apple strains aren't shiny red or perfectly round.

11. See *Genetically Modified Pest-Protected Plants: Science and Regulation,*

National Research Council, Washington, D.C.: National Academy Press, 2000.

12. Biotechnology is regulated using EPA laws designed for pollution control and FDA rules designed for pharmaceuticals. But biotech isn't really either of these things, and needs its own regulatory premise; Congress has endlessly punted the issue to avoid making hard choices.

13. Car handling power is measured in "gees," or gravities of lateral acceleration. In the 1960s, family cars could manage about .6 gees in a turn, and sports cars up to around .75 gees. Today about .75 gees is the average, with some family cars doing .8 and sports cars much better. Depending on who's behind the wheel, this can translate either into better control and fewer spinouts or more driving like a maniac.

14. See "The Evolution of Transport" by Jesse Ausubel, Cesare Marchetti, and Perrin Meyer, *European Review*, 1998, volume 6, number 2.

15. See *How Much Is Enough?* by Alan Durning, New York: W. W. Norton, 1992.

16. See "The Slow Lane" by John Seabrook, *The New Yorker*, September 2, 2002.

17. Most figures in this section from 2001 hearings of the Transportation Committee of the United States House of Representatives.

18. Studies by Anthony Downs of the Brookings Institution show that bad traffic jams are still mainly confined to the largest cities. The average Washington, D.C., area resident lost seventy-six hours to traffic jams in 1997, or twenty-three minutes per workday, which is a lot. Houston, Los Angeles, and a few other cities also had dreadful numbers. But the overall national figure is an average loss of three minutes per day to traffic.

19. American Public Transportation Association figures.

20. In 2002, a bill to require higher fuel economy from SUVs drew just thirty-eight votes in the Democrat-controlled Senate. In this case, the unholy alliance is that Republicans don't like fuel economy regulation and Democrats don't want to touch the SUV because most SUVs and "light" trucks are built by members of the United Auto Workers.

21. For details on the relationship between rising SUV sales and depen-

dence on Persian Gulf petroleum, see "Pumped Up" by Gregg Easterbrook, *The New Republic,* October 8, 2001.

22. Tables kept by the Insurance Institute for Highway Safety show that SUVs also have average to above-average rates of collision loss, a mark of safety. These can be viewed online at http://www.hwysafety.org/vehicle_ratings/ictl/ictl_util.htm. See also "Are SUVs Immoral?" by Gregg Easterbrook, Beliefnet.com, available online at http://www.beliefnet.com/frameset.asp?pageLoc=/story/85/story_8578 _1.html&boardID=21956.

23. See *Effectiveness and Impact of Corporate Average Fuel Economy Standards,* National Research Council, Washington, D.C., 2002.

24. There are SUV component assembly plants in Maryland. If you follow the SUV debate, you quickly realize that virtually all politicians who speak out for the "right" to drive dangerous, wasteful vehicles hail from states or districts where there is SUV and pickup manufacturing.

25. If this makes you say, "Then I need to be in an SUV to be protected from other SUVs," by this logic we should all drive tractor-trailer trucks. Suppose someone invented a device that made people within homes safer, but increased the chance that bystanders would die—say, a security system with an automated arrow-launcher. Would it be legally all right to install this system and increase the risk to others, so long as the motive was to protect yourself? This is essentially what has been judged to be legally all right about the SUV—that it's okay to buy a type of car that places other people in danger. Yes, we all need to be safe when driving. You're safer in a five-safety-star-rated sedan than in a three-star-rated SUV.

26. *High and Mighty: SUVs, the World's Most Dangerous Vehicles and How They Got That Way* by Keith Bradsher, New York: Public Affairs Books, 2002.

27. Fox had breast cancer. Her HMO denied coverage for a bone-marrow transplant on the grounds that this was an unproven "experimental" therapy. Outrage over Fox's death, following a denial of a claim, skips the fact that she did receive the transplant: the $150,000 necessary for the procedure was raised privately, and Fox died despite the operation. Subsequent research has shown bone-marrow trans-

plants ineffective against breast cancer; today, no doctor would recommend this, as the procedure is not considered efficacious for the condition Fox had. So, in retrospect, Fox's HMO, called HealthNet, was right to say no to the transplant, though since Fox had been led to believe the transplant would work, the denial might have harmed her by causing anguish.

28. Some of the taxes came from the family of four, of course, and these averages are skewed by the fact that most health care spending is concentrated on the elderly. Also, consumers indirectly bear those medical costs paid by business, since, absent these costs, companies could charge less for products and pay more to employees.

29. My father, George, had a Medicare-paid heart-bypass operation at age seventy-six, when he was near death from occluded heart arteries. The Canadian or English national health care systems would have rejected him as a cost-ineffective case and let him die; at this writing he is eighty-four and going strong. His longer life, wonderful to his children, runs up a bill. I estimate that Medicare's decision to fund my dad's heart-bypass cost taxpayers about $85,000 for the operation itself and for nine subsequent years of additional health care including other operations, plus another $150,000 in Social Security benefits he has lived to claim.

30. Pynchon belabors the "second law of thermodynamics" as a metaphor for the existence of scientific proof that life is meaningless. The second law of thermodynamics holds that unless energy is added to a system, the system must inevitably decline to an undifferentiated state—a log can burn into ash, but ashes cannot reassemble themselves into a log. For the universe, Pynchon maintains, this means all existence must end in a cold blur, and if the universe must end in a cold blur, how can it have meaning?

Well, even if the universe ends in a cold blur the process will take thousands of billions of years, and an enterprise lasting thousands of billions of years might be viewed as meaningful even if it ultimately stops; certainly, such an enterprise will seem eternal from the standpoint of mortals. More important, skipped in Pynchon's understanding of the second law is its qualifier: "unless energy is added." Energy in unfathomable amounts came from nowhere during the Big Bang.

Can more energy come from nowhere? This point is currently under debate by physicists, but energy might be continually added to the universe by natural processes now poorly understood, preventing any second-law demise. See the 1998 book *Before the Big Bang* by the physicist Ernest Sternglass, at this writing one of Einstein's last living assistants.

31. The full first stanza of the poem "The Second Coming":

> Things fall apart; the centre cannot hold;
> Mere anarchy is loosed upon the world,
> The blood-dimmed tide is loosed, and everywhere
> The ceremony of innocence is drowned;
> The best lack all conviction, while the worst
> Are full of passionate intensity.

32. *The Coming Plague* by Laurie Garrett, New York: Farrar, Straus & Giroux, 1994.

33. *Betrayal of Trust: The Collapse of Global Public Health* by Laurie Garrett, New York: Dimensions, 2000.

34. See "America the Okay" by Gregg Easterbrook, *The New Republic*, January 4, 1999.

35. Moody's Moody Bible Institute, a leading religious organization in the early-twentieth-century United States, denounced the League of Nations, the New Deal, and other reforms on the grounds that if they made the world a better place, this would only forestall the suffering that must precede Jesus's return. See *The Scandal of the Evangelical Mind* by Mark Noll, Grand Rapids, Mich.: Eerdmans, 1994. An excellent book on the history of bad-is-better thinking among American fundamentalists is *When Time Shall Be No More* by Paul Boyer, Cambridge: Harvard University Press, 1992.

36. Advertising for the December 29, 2002, *Sixty Minutes*.

37. I and many commentators cite *The New York Times* as the bellwether of the American media because it is the most influential paper; also, it sets the agenda for the networks and news magazines, most of which are headquartered in New York City.

38. When the controversy broke, *The Washington Post* also ran a page-one lead story asserting arsenic protection had been canceled and call-

ing the decision "shocking." When the strict arsenic rule went into effect, *Post* editors saw fit to place the news on page A31.

39. See *America's Renewable Resources,* Kenneth Frederick and Roger
Sedjo, editors, Washington, D.C.: Resources for the Future, 1991.

40. Dennis Avery, an agriculture analyst and former Department of Agriculture official, estimates that, since 1950, high-yield farming has prevented the plowing up of twenty million square miles of land
worldwide. The earth has about sixteen million square miles of forest,
meaning, Avery thinks, "In effect we saved every square mile of forest
on the planet." See "The Greening of Biotech" by Jonathan Rauch,
The Atlantic Monthly, March 2003.

41. Steve Taylor of the University of Nebraska, a food-safety researcher
whose studies documented the presence of the allergen, notes that
eventually genetic engineering should be able to remove allergen
genes from foods. This is, after all, what food companies have a
financial incentive to do, since allergy-free peanuts and similar products should be a hit in the marketplace.

42. See *Arsenic in Drinking Water,* National Research Council, Washington, D.C.: National Academy of Sciences Press, 1999. I calculated the
one-in-three-million estimate by taking the NRC risk figure for a lifetime of water-with-arsenic consumption, then factoring in that only
about 10 percent of American drinking water contains arsenic, and
also factoring in that because Americans move, most will not spend a
lifetime drinking water in the areas where arsenic is found. For details
of the calculation, see "Everything You Know About the Bush Environmental Record Is Wrong" by Gregg Easterbrook, Washington,
D.C.: AEI-Brookings Institution Joint Center for Regulatory Studies,
2002.

43. Estimates vary, but worst-case numbers for permanent harm caused
by vaccine are a few dozen cases per annum in the United States. By
contrast, at least five hundred children under the age of fourteen are
killed annually in the United States when cars strike them along
streets or at intersections; most deaths occur after dark, and most victims are wearing dark-colored clothing. Yet the very slight risk caused
by vaccines has become hugely controversial among parents, pediatricians, and tort lawyers seeking profit. Meanwhile, have you ever

heard anyone so much as mention the risk of children wearing dark-colored clothing at night? See various statistics on these points compiled by the National Safe Kids Campaign, online at safekids.org.

44. In 1999, the FBI, which has jurisdiction over kidnappings, logged ninety-three cases of children kidnapped by strangers (that is, not involved in custody disputes) versus an average of about three hundred per year in the 1980s. Ninety-three kidnappings in a year is plenty bad enough, but nowhere near what is popularly imagined. See "Abduction of Kids By Strangers Is Rare and Getting Rarer" by David Crary, *Minneapolis Star-Tribune,* July 28, 2002.

45. For a profile of George Gerbner and a detailed analysis of studies of media violence, see "The Man Who Counts the Killings" by Scott Stossel, *The Atlantic Monthly,* May 1997. Available online at http://www.theatlantic.com/issues/97may/gerbner.htm.

46. *Ibid.*

47. Disney's Miramax film division is to blame for, among others, *Scream* and *Pulp Fiction.* The former depicted stabbing friends and teachers to death as a trendy, amusing sport; the latter glamorized two hitmen. The Columbine High killers, who murdered their own friends, are said to have been big fans of *Scream.* The Disney PG movie *Mighty Joe Young* begins with a scene of a girl watching her mother murdered; at the conclusion, it's twenty years later and the murderer has come back to kill the heroine, too, pointing a gun in her face and saying, "Now join your mother in hell." This in a Disney *children's* movie.

48. See "Watch and Learn" by Gregg Easterbrook, *The New Republic,* May 17, 1999.

49. See "The Effects of Media Violence in Society" by Craig Anderson and Brad Bushman, *Science,* March 29, 2002.

50. See "Natural Born Excess" by Gregg Easterbrook, *The Washington Post,* September 18, 1994. Hollywood also misrepresents the extent of serial killing. In the AOL Time Warner movie *Natural Born Killers,* the two serial murderers the film presents as glamorous antiheroes are depicted as killing more than seventy-five people. According to the FBI's National Center for the Analysis of Violent Crime, the worst serial killer ever, John Wayne Gacy, killed thirty-three people. Isn't the realistic figure bad enough?

51. See "Stats Say Cops Not Trigger Happy" by Donna de la Cruz, Associated Press, February 21, 2000.

52. *Ibid.* That year, 1999, was the year of the killing of the innocent Amadou Diallo by New York police, a horrifying event. But Diallo's death was depicted in the media as a common sort of thing, when in fact police killings of the innocent are both rare and in decline. During the crime wave of the 1980s, New York police killed an average of forty people per year; today they kill an average of about ten people annually. Almost all of those slain by New York police have criminal records or had raised weapons.

53. I live in Washington and am around its federal buildings regularly; my wife is a foreign service officer, so I've been around a few embassies, too. I have yet to observe an American government official arriving anywhere in a limousine.

CHAPTER 4

1. See "Navels, Nipples Get Attention at Surgeons' Offices," *Wall Street Journal*, August 1, 2002.

2. Women's fashion in 2002 also favored the "perky" nipple visible through clothes, and though this effect can be obtained by not wearing a bra, most women aren't comfortable without bras, so alternatives were required. One was offered by a firm called BodyPerks, which sold discreet plastic aureole enhancers that could be slipped into the bra cup. BodyPerks advertised in women's magazines—"now also available in mocha," proclaimed one ad—and became a hot sales item after the one-track-mind heroines of the television show *Sex and the City* wore them for an episode and got lots of hot guy action. But BodyPerks don't work with swimsuits or once your clothes have fallen to the floor. Enter cosmetic surgery for the nipple, to insert an enhancing disk for that frisky look twenty-four-seven, or to correct imperfections, achieving symmetry and sex appeal. Nipple augmentation did not take off as much as navel improvement, but cosmetic surgeons reported decent business here, too, despite an $8,000-to-$10,000 price tag, again paid solely by the patient.

3. See "Roses by Other Names," Cynthia Crossen, *Wall Street Journal*, June 29, 2001.

4. My thanks to Anand Giriharadas for research on this point.

5. The quote is from Rousseau's *Second Discourse*, also called the *Discourse on the Origins and Basis of Inequality Among Men.*

6. Rochester's population is about 220,000.

7. See "Look at All Their Stuff," *Wall Street Journal*, January 7, 2000.

8. See "Wowing Them with Excess in the Hamptons," *The New York Times*, July 18, 2000.

9. *All* the projected American population increase is expected to come from immigration; the fertility rate of native-born American women is today almost exactly 2.3, which is the "replacement rate" of zero population growth.

10. For example, children of families with incomes from $70,000 to $80,000 average 1,041 on the SATs; add another $10,000 to the family income and the score average jumps to 1,068. At the extremes, children from families earning less than $10,000 average a total score of 859, which is only somewhat better than guessing, while those from families earning more than $100,000 average 1,123, which means "Hello, good college." See the *Annual Report of the College Board*, New York: The College Board, 2001.

11. The $953 average annual charitable donation by American adults represents a significant fraction of after-tax income. The average annual donation is $380 in France, $275 in the Netherlands. See *Vital Signs 2002*, the Worldwatch Institute, New York: W. W. Norton, 2002.

12. See *The Costs of Living* by Barry Schwartz, New York: W. W. Norton, 1994.

13. My house, I am forced to confess, has four televisions.

14. None of my family's four TVs are in a kid's bedroom; this I can say in my defense. But more than once I have walked through the house and found each of my three kids in a different room watching a different show on each of three TVs.

15. See a useful "Motley Fool" analysis of credit-card debt at http://www.fool.com/credit/credit.htm.

16. See *The Overspent American* by Juliet Schor, New York: Basic Books, 1998.

17. See "Closet Craving" by Jura Konicus, *The Washington Post*, January 31, 2002.

18. See "Leaving It to the Professionals" by Caitlin Flanagan, *The Atlantic Monthly*, March 2002.

19. See *Beside Still Waters* by Gregg Easterbrook, New York: William Morrow, 1998.

20. For amusing examples of simultaneous finger-wagging about materialism in others combined with shallow cravings by the writer, see *Consuming Desires: Consumption, Culture and the Pursuit of Happiness*, Roger Rosenblatt, editor, New York: Houghton Mifflin, 1999. The book is a collection of essays denouncing materialism, but numerous contributors essentially argue that everyone else should be deprived, though not them. The environmental activist Stephanie Mills, for example, stridently denounces sprawl and other people's desires for detached homes, then notes she owns the thirty acres around her home so that she doesn't have to be disturbed by seeing the comings and goings of neighbors. Thirty acres devoted solely to a single person's home! If everyone demanded this, the entire nation would need to be paved over. (Average home lot size in the United States is one-quarter of an acre.)

21. See *Lead Us Into Temptation* by James Twitchell, New York: Columbia University Press, 1999.

22. See "The Disease Burden Associated with Overweight and Obesity," Avia Must, first author, *Journal of the American Medical Association*, October 27, 1999.

23. See "Prevalence and Trends in Obesity Among American Adults," Katherine Flegal, lead author, *Journal of the American Medical Association*, October 9, 2002. The problem is worst among African American women, 55 percent of whom are now obese and 15 percent of whom are morbidly obese, which usually means heavier than 350 pounds.

24. See "The Spread of the Obesity Epidemic in the United States, 1991–1998," Ali Mokdad, first author, *Journal of the American Medical Association*, October 27, 1999.

25. See "Walking Compared with Vigorous Exercise for the Prevention of Cardiovascular Events in Women," JoAnn Manson, lead author, *New England Journal of Medicine*, September 5, 2002.

26. See "Rubens Was Right" by Paul Campos, *The New Republic*, January 13, 2002.

27. See *The State of the World 2002*, Lester Brown, editor, New York: W. W. Norton, 2002.

28. "Big Reasons Why We Eat More than We Want" by Shannon Brownlee, *The Washington Post*, December 29, 2002.

29. "The Evolution of Transport" by Jesse Ausubel, Cesare Marchetti, and Perrin Meyer, *European Review*, 1998, volume 6, number 2.

30. In 1998, 1999, and 2001, more pedestrians were killed by speeding cars in Montgomery County, Maryland, where Bethesda is located, than there were homicides.

31. See "Decline in Physical Activity in Girls During Adolescence," Sue Kimm, lead author, *New England Journal of Medicine*, September 5, 2002.

32. See "The Evolution of Transport," above.

33. See the United Nations' *Human Development Report 2001*, New York: Oxford University Press, 2002.

34. That a third of the *Forbes 400* got their wealth through inheritance should concern policy-makers, considering that inherited wealth is the converse of a free and open system, and considering that the federal estate tax is scheduled to expire in 2009. A prominent reason the United States has a more vibrant economy than Western Europe is that fewer assets are inherited. America has fewer idle rich than Europe, fewer entrenched big-money families devoting their efforts to stopping change; most people who have big money in the United States got it by working, doing, or creating. A reason fewer assets are inherited in the United States than in the European Union is America's effective estate tax. Abolishing it might alter this balance.

   The estate tax is paid only by the wealthy, as it is imposed on less than 2 percent of estates, meaning 98 of 100 people's heirs never pay any estate tax. Currently, the first $1.5 million of an estate is exempt from tax; the exemption is scheduled to rise in stages to $3.5 million in 2010. Because small farms are almost never worth enough to trigger the estate tax, the notion that estate taxes cause families to lose their farms is urban legend. The primary problem facing most family farms is debt for operating loans; often the family farmer owns valuable land but has modest net worth, and it is net worth that triggers the estate tax. Neil Harl, an agricultural economist at Iowa State University whose specialty is the study of family farms, says he has never come across any real-world example of a family farm lost owing to estate taxation.

Political pressure against the estate tax comes exclusively from the very rich, as the heirs of the very rich are the only ones who pay this assessment. The estate tax exists not so much to raise money for government as to prevent wealth from gradually accumulating in favored groups. That a third of the *Forbes 400* got their riches through intergenerational accumulation, rather than by doing any work of value to society, is disturbing enough, since it happened during a period when there was an estate tax. (The estate-tax top rate is presently 39 percent, meaning that a zillionaire still leaves more than half a zillion to his or her heirs.) If the estate tax is repealed in 2009, accumulation of wealth will begin to accelerate, creating in the United States an ever larger group of idle rich whose main interest in life is preserving the status quo. The goal of the estate tax is to prevent the economy and social structure of the United States from becoming the economy and social structure of Europe—a goal of considerable benefit to everyone except the idle rich.

35. See *The End of History and the Last Man* by Francis Fukuyama, New York: Free Press, 1992.

36. See *The Blank Slate* by Stephen Pinker, New York: Viking, 2002.

37. See *Something for Nothing: Luck in America* by Jackson Lears, New York: Viking, 2003.

38. Pareto's name is unknown outside economics; economists are uncomfortable with him because he wrote ultranationalistic pamphlets later used by the 1930s Italian fascist movement.

39. See *The End of Equality* by Mickey Kaus, New York: Basic Books, 1992.

40. See *Middletown Families* by Theodore Caplow, lead author, New York: Bantam Books, 1983.

41. See "Five and a Half Utopias," Steven Weinberg, *The Atlantic Monthly,* January 2000.

42. This quotation brings to mind the heart-rending Willa Cather short story "Paul's Case," in which a man who has lived in near-poverty all his life embezzles from a bank, enjoys unlimited luxury for one week,

and then commits suicide, feeling there is no point in living a life of longing for what others have.

CHAPTER 5

1. *The Loss of Happiness in Market Democracies* by Robert Lane, New Haven: Yale University Press, 2000.
2. See "The Epidemiology of Major Depressive Disorder: Results from the National Comorbidity Survey Replication (NCS-R)," Ronald Kessler, et al., *Journal of the American Medical Association*, June 18, 2003.
3. *Happiness Is a Serious Problem* by Dennis Prager, New York: Dimensions, 1999.
4. See *The Pursuit of Happiness* by David Myers, New York: Avon Books, 1993.
5. Per-capita income statistics by state may be read online at http://niip.wsu.edu/unitedstates/comuspdf/rycpcius.pdf.
6. See "One Nation Slightly Divisible," David Brooks, *The Atlantic Monthly*, December 2001.
7. See *Peace Is Every Step* by Thich Nhat Hanh, New York: Bantam Books, 1992.
8. See *Happiness and Hardship* by Carol Graham and Stefano Pettinato, Washington: Brookings Institution press, 2002.
9. See "Will Globalization Make You Happy?" by Robert Wright, *Foreign Policy*, January 2000.
10. *A General Theory of Love* by Thomas Lewis, Fari Amini, and Richard Lannon, New York: Random House, 2000.
11. See *Social Indicators 2001*, Geneva: Organization for Economic Cooperation and Development, 2001.
12. See *The Biophilia Hypothesis* by E. O. Wilson, New York: Island Press, 1993.
13. See *Loss of Happiness in Market Democracies*, above.
14. See *A General Theory*, above.
15. "Prevalence, Correlates and Course of Minor Depression and Major Depression in the National Comorbidity Study," Ronald Kessler, et al., *Journal of Affective Disorders*, Summer 1997.

16. See *The Churching of America* by Roger Finke and Rodney Stark, New Brunswick: Rutgers University Press, 1994.
17. See "Do You Need a Pill to Stop Shopping?" by Anne Marie Chaker, *Wall Street Journal*, January 2, 2003. Celexa is a "selective seratonin reuptake inhibitor," chemically similar to Prozac and Zoloft. Possibly other SSRI drugs such as Prozac and Zoloft work against the shopping impulse, too. So far only Celexa has been studied for this use.

CHAPTER 6

1. *The Moral Animal: Evolutionary Psychology and Everyday Life* by Robert Wright, New York: Vintage Books, 1994.
2. In the "prehistoric" societies that still exist today, such as Amazon River tribes, some 60 percent of males die by violence. See *Constant Battles: The Myth of the Noble Savage and a Peaceful Past* by Steven LeBlanc with Katherine Register, New York: St. Martin's Press, 2003. See also a book by the anthropologist Robert Edgerton, *Sick Societies: Challenging the Myth of Primitive Harmony*, New York: Free Press, 1992.
3. See *The Pursuit of Happiness* by David Myers, New York: Avon Books, 1993.
4. See "The Truth About the Lawyers" by Ralph Nader, *Slate*, March 2, 2002.
5. See "The Family Dinner Is Alive and Well" by Karlyn Bowman, *The New York Times*, August 25, 1999.
6. See *The First Measured Century* by Theodore Caplow et al., Washington, D.C.: AEI Press, 2000.
7. *The Promise of Sleep* by William Dement, New York: Delacorte, 1998.
8. See "Psychotropic Practice Patterns for Youth" by Julie Zito, et al., *Archives of Pediatrics and Adolescent Medicine*, January 2003.
9. See "Clinics Offer Controversial Heart Treatment" by Thomas Burton, *Wall Street Journal*, October 14, 2002.
10. "Mindfulness and Its Role in Psychological Well-Being" by Kirk Brown and Richard Ryan, *Journal of Personal and Social Psychology*, April 2003.

11. See her highly readable book *The Balance Within: The Science Connecting Health and Emotions* by Esther Sternberg, New York: W.H. Freedman, 1999.

12. See *Technology and the Character of Contemporary Life* by Albert Borgmann, Chicago: University of Chicago Press, 1984.

13. See, mainly, Heidegger's 1927 book *Being and Time*.

CHAPTER 7

1. The quotation is from *Conversations of Socrates*.

2. Also, psychology of the time sought to identify geniuses, who would be selected out of normal life and given special privileges. Finding geniuses remained a concern of psychology roughly through the early twentieth century, when psychologists helped design the Army standardized testing that paved the way for the SAT and the IQ test. Today it is generally felt that geniuses can fend for themselves and are more likely to be creative if not treated in any special way.

3. From *Civilization and Its Discontents*, 1930.

4. *Raising America: Experts, Parents and a Century of Advice About Children* by Ann Hulbert, New York: Knopf, 2003.

5. See *Psychology, Sixth Edition,* by David Myers, New York: Worth Publishers, 2001.

6. "Why Happiness Is Good for You" by Laura King, *Prevention and Treatment,* March 2000, American Psychological Association.

7. "Cultivating Positive Emotions to Optimize Happiness and Well-Being" by Barbara Fredrickson, *Prevention and Treatment,* March 2000, American Psychological Association.

8. "Understanding How Optimism Works" by Lisa Aspinwall, first author, in *Optimism and Pessimism, Theory and Practice*, E. C. Chang, editor, Washington, D.C.: American Psychological Association, 2001.

CHAPTER 8

1. "Interpersonal Forgiving in Close Relationships" by M. E. McCullough, et al., *Journal of Personality and Social Psychology,* Autumn 1997.

2. See *The Case for Marriage* by Linda Waite and Maggie Gallagher,

New York: Doubleday, 2000. It's worth noting that this book, a compendium of arguments why most people are better off married, was initially to be published by Harvard University Press. Some Harvard faculty members lobbied furiously to prevent the book's publication, although Waite is an eminent academic at the University of Chicago. Harvard University Press ultimately refused to publish the book, because its board felt it was antifeminist to suggest that women are better off married than single; though if data shows women are better off married, shouldn't they be given that information and trusted to make up their own minds? The story ended happily when *The Case for Marriage* was snapped up by a major publisher, but Harvard University Press should feel abashed about this attempt at Orwellian censorship.

3. Of members of the 1999 *Forbes 400* list of the nation's richest individuals, almost all of whom were men, 72 percent had been divorced at least once, a far higher proportion than among the population as a whole. See *Class Warfare in America* by Charles Kelly, San Francisco: David & David, 2000.

4. "Is the Male Marriage Premium Due to Selection?" by Donna Ginther and Madeline Zavodny, working paper of the Federal Reserve Bank. Available online at http://econpapers.hhs.se/paper/fipfedawp/97-5.htm.

5. Details of his work can be found in *Dimensions of Forgiveness* by Everett Worthington, Philadelphia: Templeton Press, 1998. Another useful book is *The Forgiving Self* by Robert Karen, New York: Doubleday, 2001, in which a clinical psychologist describes case histories of patients whose lives improved when they learned to forgive wrongs large or small.

6. "Forgiveness and Romantic Relationships" by Kenneth Pargament, et al., *Journal of Clinical Psychology*, Winter 2002.

7. See "Rx for Life: Gratitude" by Gregg Easterbrook, available online at http://www.beliefnet.com/frameset.asp?pageLoc=/story/51/story_5111_1.html&boardID=7159.

CHAPTER 9

1. See *Affluenza* by Thomas Naylor, San Francisco: Berrett-Koehler, 2001.

2. See *Loss of Happiness in Market Democracies* by Robert Lane, New Haven: Yale University Press, 2000.

3. See *The Real American Dream* by Andrew Delbanco, Cambridge: Harvard University Press, 2000.

4. See "The Morality Gap in American Politics" by Thomas Byrne Edsall, *The Atlantic Monthly,* January 2003. Despite declines in the percentage of Americans who attend services every week, by the measure of regular presence at worship services, the United States remains the most religious nation in the world, surpassing Saudi Arabia and easily surpassing Israel.

5. Studies by Benton Johnson, professor of sociology at the University of Oregon, have found that rising levels of education do not associate with declining belief. In the United States, people holding doctorate degrees are more likely to be atheists than the population as a whole, but below the doctoral level, belief in God or divine agency is approximately the same for all education strata. Fundamentalists, Johnson has found, as a group are just as well-educated as members of the mainstream liberal denominations, while college graduates are as likely to believe in the existence of God as are those who did not attend college.

6. By contrast, only 21 percent of Germans today say religion is "very important" to them, and only 21 percent of Italians say this, though Italy is the home nation of the Roman Catholic denomination. See "Religion Among Wealthy Nations," a 2002 report by the Pew Research Center in Washington, D.C., available online at http://people-press.org/reports/display.php3?ReportID=167.

7. See *A Generation of Seekers* by Wade Clark Roof, San Francisco: Harper San Francisco, 1994.

8. Source: the American Association of Fundraising Counsel, whose annual report *United States Giving* can be viewed online at www.aafrc.org/trust/charts.html.

9. See *Culture Shift in Advanced Industrial Societies* by Ronald Inglehart, Princeton: Princeton University Press, 1990.

10. See *The Fourth Great Awakening and the Future of Egalitarianism* by Robert Fogel, Chicago: University of Chicago Press, 2000.

11. See *The First Three Minutes* by Steven Weinberg, New York: Basic Books, 1977.

12. See *River Out of Eden* by Richard Dawkins, New York: Basic Books, 1995.

13. See "Evolution and Creationism" by Jessica Mathews, *The Washington Post*, April 12, 1996.

CHAPTER 10

1. See "Without Coverage: Immigration's Impact on the Size and Growth of the Population Lacking Health Insurance" by Steven A. Camarota, Washington: Center for Immigration Studies, 2000.

2. See *Just Health Care* by Norman Daniels, Cambridge, England: Cambridge University Press, 1985.

3. See "Family Says Drugs Tortured Couple Killed by Train" by Maria Newman, *The New York Times*, May 5, 2002.

4. Opponents of a higher minimum wage also sometimes note that not everyone making the minimum depends on it; teenagers flipping burgers after school are trying to earn money for clothes and cars, not to run a household. The teenager problem is easily solved by having a lower minimum wage for those under eighteen.

5. At this writing, for example, unemployment in California was 6.2 percent, versus 6 percent nationally.

6. Ebbers's windfall came in the form of a forgiven loan, which is not meaningfully different from a grant of cash. After the WorldCom bankruptcy, Ebbers said that he would repay the loan, but then failed to make the promised payments. A June 2003 report commissioned by WorldCom's own post-bankruptcy directors declared that the company under Ebbers engaged in "significant fraud." A 2002 report by the Washington advocacy group United for a Fair Economy found that from 1999 to 2001, CEOs of companies under investigation for accounting fraud paid themselves an average of 70 percent more than CEOs of the *Fortune 500* as a whole. See "CEOs Who Cook the Books Earn More," available online at http://www.ufenet.org/press/2002/EE2002_pr.html.

7. See "Top Tyco Executives Charged With $600 Million Fraud Scheme" by Andrew Sorkin, *The New York Times*, September 13, 2002. Misuses of shareholder funds by Kozlowski were alleged to include billing Tyco for a $5,000 shower curtain for a personal apartment

and $110,000 for thirteen personal days in the presidential suite of the Savoy Hotel in London. Fraud by Kozlowski, prosecutors have alleged, included using company funds to buy $64 million worth of lavish homes and Manhattan apartments in his own name, to buy a yacht, and to stage a spectacular $2 million birthday party for his wife. Any lower-level clerical worker who embezzled a small fraction of such sums would spend many years in jail; if convicted, what will this CEO's penalty be? Two other Tyco executives were also indicted for what amounted to embezzlement. An SEC report on Tyco abuses can be read online at http://www.sec.gov/Archives/edgar/data/833444/000095013002008787/d8k.htm.

8. SEC regulations require that top corporate officers disclose their sales of the company's own shares because such sales often occur just before share prices turn down. Investors have a right to know that the company's management is betting on a downturn. Had Kozlowski disclosed his $430 million in alleged illicit sales, investors would have realized this meant Tyco's CEO knew a collapse was coming; in turn, the company stock price would have fallen, and Kozlowski's gain been much less.

Though SEC regulations require disclosures by top officers of public corporations, it's generally up to the corporation to define its "top" people. Most *Fortune 500* companies require twenty to thirty top staffers to disclose their trades, but some, such as Disney and DuPont, only require this of a few people, which has the effect of letting managers just below the top tier profit from manipulated stock-price runups without scrutiny.

Overpay in cash and stock of managers just below the ranks of CEOs, again at the expense of workers and shareholders, is also a problem. For instance, when Enron laid off thousands of employees before its 2001 bankruptcy, it paid non-managers an average severance of $13,500; that same year, the firm's top 140 executives just below the CEO/CFO level were paid an average of $5.3 million.

9. "Corporate Scandals, A User's Guide," *The New York Times*, May 11, 2003; "Tyco's Bad Odor," *Wall Street Journal*, May 1, 2003.

10. See "Jack's Booty," unsigned editorial, *Wall Street Journal*, September 12, 2002. Upon retirement, Welch was allowed to keep several mil-

lion dollars' per year worth of perks in perpetuity, plus was given a consulting contract that pays him $2,150 an hour to offer General Electric advice. Following public criticism, Welch gave up some of the retirement benefits.

11. See "Here's the Retirement Jack Welch Built" by Rachel Emma Silverman, *Wall Street Journal*, October 31, 2002. Welch's own divorce filing says he needs $366,114 a month for "basic living expenses" and $8,982 a month for food and beverages.

12. The big numbers in most of these payday figures come from stock grants or the exercise of stock options. CEOs endlessly protest that their stock paydays shouldn't count because the money does not come directly from operating income as salary. But any exercised option dilutes the value of existing shares held by stockholders, and also represents a share that the company could not itself sell to raise equity—this is the reason stock exists in the first place—and thus the gain comes out of the company's coffers.

CEOs also assert that it is unfair to ascribe to them big paydays when they cash several years' worth of accumulated options in a single year. But since they also claim that the book value of awarded options should not be counted as gain in the year the options are received, how else to do the accounting? If stock gains were scored the way CEOs prefer—not projected for the future when awarded, and then discounted as past due when cashed—total pay to CEOs would *never* be toted up.

13. See "Deciding on Executive Pay: Lack of Independence Seen" by Diana Henriques and Geraldine Fabrikant, *The New York Times*, December 18, 2002.

14. Most large sums paid to officers of public corporations must be disclosed to the Securities and Exchange Commission.

15. See "Managerial Power and Rent Extraction in the Design of Executive Compensation" by Lucian Arye Bebchuk, Jesse M. Fried, and David I. Walker, NBER Working Paper 9068, available online at http://papers.nber.org/papers/W9068.

16. See "Tyco Relies on an Unusual Definition of 'Cash Flow' " by Alex Berenson, *The New York Times*, December 31, 2002.

17. See "Panel Members Attract Scrutiny" by Jonathan Weil, *Wall Street*

Journal, December 9, 2002. Amazingly, even *after* Xerox under Paul Allaire's leadership was denounced by the SEC for deliberately defrauding investors, Allaire was named to head the audit committee at Lucent.

18. Ultimately the Securities and Exchange Commission order cost Allaire $1 million, allowing him to keep the other $15 million, and found that Xerox, under Allaire, had issued $1.4 billion in fictitious claims of profit—the fabrications used to justify the huge payments to Allaire and several other top Xerox managers. Details of the SEC decree may be read online at http://www.sec.gov/litigation/complaints/lr18174.htm.

On paper, the SEC appeared to order that Allaire forfeit $5.2 million of the sum he obtained by fraud, which still allowed him to keep the bulk of his ill-gotten gains. But Xerox said that by contract the company or its insurers would pay all but $1 million of the judgment against Allaire, while also paying his legal fees. Thus Xerox stockholders were victimized twice—once when Allaire and other top managers engaged in "securities fraud and aiding and abetting Xerox's violations of the reporting, books and records and internal control provisions of the federal securities law" (the SEC's words) and again when they had to cover the fines resulting from the law-breaking. Allaire, the CEO, walked away whistling with almost everything he in effect stole. Don't think that other CEOs failed to notice that you can engage in "securities fraud," become rich, and be allowed to keep most of the proceeds.

Note to readers: I owned no stock in any of the corporations whose managers' actions this book objects to.

19. See "Global Crossing Chairman Resigns After Sales of Assets" by Simon Romero, *The New York Times*, December 31, 2002.

20. There have been CEO lying and overpayment scandals in the European Union, too, though none as stark as America's.

21. See "Executive Pensions Eclipse Years on Job" by Felicity Barringer, *The New York Times*, December 17, 2002.

22. See "Greed Isn't Good" by Gregg Easterbrook, *The New Republic*, July 7, 2002.

23. See "How the Permissive Capitalism of the Boom Destroyed Ameri-

can Equality" by Paul Krugman, *The New York Times Magazine*, October 20, 2002.

24. Kozlowski, of Tyco, was not accused of insider trading, rather of failing to disclose trades to the SEC as required. At this writing, only the Martha Stewart case involved an accusation of insider trading, and the sums at issue were comparatively small.

CHAPTER 11

1. See "Body Falls From Airliner," *The New York Times*, August 9, 2001.
2. See "Landslide at Manila Dump Kills 200," *The New York Times*, July 18, 2000.
3. See *World Development Indicators*, Washington, D.C.: World Bank, 2001.
4. See "World Poverty and Hunger: The Challenge for Science" by Ismail Serageldin, *Science*, April 5, 2002.
5. At this writing, there were thirty times more HIV-positive people in Africa as in the United States, and that figure was expected to keep rising indefinitely.
6. See *Human Development Report 2002*, New York: United Nations Development Programme, 2002. Unless otherwise cited, statistics in this chapter come from that document, and the footnote to this effect will not be repeated.
7. See *Imagine There's No Country: Poverty, Growth and Inequality in the Era of Globalization* by Surjit Bhalla, Washington, D.C.: Institute for International Economics, 2002.
8. This is a representative number, not a figure chosen from a bad year. Global deaths from hunger have been declining on a roughly linear basis for about three decades, even though population is rising.
9. See Ehrlich's 1969 doomsday treatise *The Population Bomb*; also another doomsday best-seller of the 1960s, *Famine 1975!*, by Paul and William Paddock.
10. See "The Coming Anarchy" by Robert Kaplan, *The Atlantic Monthly*, February 1994.
11. Quasi-apocalyptic futures of busted cars and people living in squa-

lor after some general calamity have become conventions of science-fiction movies in part because they are cheap to film: the main costumes are old ripped clothes.

12. World automobile production in 2002 was about 41 million passenger cars; world bicycle production was about 100 million, with about half of the world's bicycles built in China. See *Vital Signs 2003*, the Worldwatch Institute, New York: W. W. Norton, 2002.

13. Currently, China builds about three million cars per annum. Output is expected to double no later than 2010, at which point China would be the world's number-two producer of cars, behind the United States but ahead of Japan.

14. See "Car Loans Fueling China's Independence from Agriculture" by Peter Goodman, *The Washington Post*, January 8, 2003.

15. Detailed estimates of year-2050 global energy needs may be found online at http://www.worldenergy.org/wec-geis/edc/scenario.asp.

16. Caetano Veloso interviewed on the PBS-TV show *Newshour*, December 27, 2002.

17. See *Savage Wars of Peace: Small Wars and the Rise of American Power* by Max Boot, New York: Basic Books, 2002.

18. For details on the achievements of Islamic research during the Christian Dark Ages, see *Lost Discoveries: The Ancient Roots of Modern Science* by Dick Teresi, New York: Simon & Schuster, 2003.

19. See "The Roots of Muslim Rage" by Bernard Lewis, *The Atlantic Monthly*, September 1990, which a decade before September 11 warned of "a surge of hatred" by Islamic hard-liners against the United States.

20. See *What Went Wrong: The Clash Between Islam and Modernity* by Bernard Lewis, New York: Oxford University Press, 2002.

21. See the *Arab Human Development Report*, New York: United Nations, 2002.

22. See "After the Storm" by Thomas Friedman, *The New York Times*, January 8, 2003.

23. The effective figure is smaller still, since about $4 billion of the $11 billion foreign-aid budget goes to Israel and Egypt in what is officially called development aid but is for all intents and purposes an annual payment to ensure observation of the treaty that ended the 1973 Israel-Egypt war.

24. See "The Case for Foreign Aid" by Gregg Easterbrook, *The New Republic*, July 29, 2002.

25. See "Bright Lights, Small Villages" by Nicholas Thompson and Ricardo Bayon, *Washington Monthly*, December 2002, for a convincing argument that small-scale solar power would work and be surprisingly affordable in many developing-world villages.

26. See "Forgotten Benefactor of Humanity" by Gregg Easterbrook, *The Atlantic Monthly*, January 1997.

CHAPTER 12

1. See *Dreaming of Cockaigne* by Herman Pleij, New York: Columbia University Press, 2001.

2. See *Constant Battles: The Myth of the Noble Savage and a Peaceful Past* by Steven LeBlanc with Katherine Register, New York: St. Martin's Press, 2003.

3. See *Utopian Thought in the Western World* by Frank Manuel and Fritzie Manuel, Cambridge: Harvard University Press, 1979. See also *Utopia: The Search for the Ideal Society*, edited by Roland Schaer and others, New York: Oxford University Press, 2000. The latter's 385 pages are essentially an inventory of hypothesized utopias.

ACKNOWLEDGMENTS

For the realization of this volume, thanks are due to many friends, colleagues, and editors: Rev. Susan Andrews, John Berryman, Julie Bosman, Michael Carlisle, Gina Centrello, Matthew Cooper, Bryan Curtis, Christopher DeMuth, James Fallows, Henry Ferris, Garance Franke-Ruta, Anand Giriharadas, Malcolm Gladwell, Ann Godoff, Erica Goode, Rev. Andrew Greeley, Tedd Habberfield, David Hendrickson, Jonathan Jao, Jonathan Karp, Leon Kass, Charles Lane, Toby Lester, Robert Litan, Jynne Martin, Jeremy McCarter, Dan Menaker, Scott Moyers, Cullen Murphy, Martin Peretz, Thomas Perry, Charles Peters, Jonathan Rauch, Rebecca Rimel, Hope Roberts, Marc Romano, Reihan Salam, Robert Samuelson, Sally Satel, Laura Sheahen, Joshua Wolf Shenk, Allison Silver, Anne Simpkinson, Benjamin Soskis, Anke Steinecke, Mark Steinmeyer, Strobe Talbott, Michelle Tessler, Lawrence Urbano, Steven Waldman, David Whitman, William Whitworth, Leon Wieseltier, Veronica Windholz, Robert Wright, and Marcia Yablon; to my brothers, Frank and Neil Easterbrook; to Michael Kelly, 1957–2003; and to my wife, Nan Kennelly.

I wish to thank the Smith Richardson Foundation, of Westport, Connecticut, for supporting some of the research for this book and the Brookings Institution of Washington, D.C., for sponsoring that research.

INDEX

depression: bipolar or "manic,"
164–65, 214; clinical, 164,
181, 214–15, 233, 235, 238;
and consumerism, 185–86;
cost of, 181; in developing
nations, 165; and drugs, 185,
225; and exercise, 239; and
forgiveness, 233, 235, 236;
and gender, 201; and
gratitude, 238; increase in,
163–66, 181; and marriage,
232; and psychology, 223,
224, 225, 226; reasons for
increase in, 182–86; treatment
for, 225, 226; unipolar, 164,
165, 181, 182–86, 201, 225
Descartes, René, 196
developing nations: change in,
279–310, 317; conflict beteen
West and, 296; and everyday
life in past, 82; foreign aid for,
303–7; and global economics,
63–65, 67; and globalization,
68–69, 73; and "medium
development," 285; moral
responsibility toward,
294–310; negativism about,
290; population in, 285–86,
287, 289–90, 292–93, 306;
and progress, 85; Western
imagining of, 290; and West's
commitment to ending global
despair, 284–310. See also
specific topic
"device paradigm," 208–9
dictatorships, 36, 302, 315
Die Hard (films), 115
Diener, Edward, 168–70, 173, 216
diet, 196, 204. See also food;
nutrition
disease, 48–49, 83, 102–3, 220–21,
282, 283, 287, 289, 306, 313
Ditton, Jason, 113
divorce, 35, 51–52, 179, 232, 233
DNA, 56, 108–9, 110, 189, 222
domestic economics, 60–62

domestic violence, 38
dorms, college, 17
Double Gulp soda, 149
drugs: and ADHD, 198, 199; and
ambivalence about health
care, 95, 96, 98–99; and
average people are better off,
13–14; and brain, 178; and
consumerism, 185; cost of, 95,
98–99; and depression, 185,
225; in developing nations,
286; and emotions, 178;
generic, 98–99; illegal, 35, 51,
75; prescription, 14, 95;
psychotropic, 201–2; and
stress, 196, 198, 199, 201–2;
and utopias, 314
Druning, Alan, 90
drunk driving, 77
dystopias, 313–14

E*Trade, 269
Earned Income Tax Credit (EITC),
260
Ebbers, Bernard, 267, 274
Eberstadt, Nicholas, 47
economy/economics: and crime,
75; in developing nations,
308–9; domestic, 60–62; and
economics-of-children
analysis, 73; global, 62–68;
and globalization, 72–73; and
happiness, 176; and Islam,
298; market, 67; and
oversupply, 67–68; and
practically everything is
getting better, 60–68, 72–73;
and reasons why things are
better, 75; shortage, 61; and
utopias, 316; and war, 72
education: and average people are
better off, 20–21, 24–25, 31;
in developing nations, 285,
286, 306; and equality, 58–59,
158; and everyday life in past,
82, 83; and globalization, 69;

spirituality, 249–50; and
    utopias, 313
self-serving, 105
Seligman, Martin, 182–86, 220,
    223, 224
Seneca, 169
senior citizens, 13–14, 38, 50, 83,
    96–97, 112, 115, 181, 235,
    317. *See also* Medicare
sentencing: mandatory-minimum,
    74–75
September 11, 2001, 34, 36–37,
    38, 60, 61, 116, 294, 295,
    296
serial killings, 114–15
7-Eleven stores, 149
sex, 53–54, 83, 177, 200, 311,
    312, 315
Sharper Image, 126–27
shredders, 134
"silent floors," 132
Simon, Julian, 46
"simplification," 144–45
Singer, Peter, 47, 62–63
single parents, 52–53
Sixty Minutes (CBS-TV), 106
sleep, 195, 196–97, 198, 311, 312
small towns, 82, 207–8
Smerick, Peter, 114
Smith, Adam, 139, 241
Smith, Will, 116
smog, 42–43, 44, 291
smoking, 35, 51
Smoky Mountain (Philippines),
    281
Snow, John, 272
snowmobiles, 7
social class, 78, 156–57, 233
Social Security, 46
social welfare, 155–56
Socrates, 214
The Sorrows of Young Werther
    (Goethe), 214–15
soul, modern, 277–78
Soviet Union, 176, 289, 302
soybeans, 110

Speedpass, 193–94
Spengler, Oswald, 101–2
spirituality, 146, 211, 239, 246,
    248–54
sports, 40
sprawl, 129–30, 131
Spruce Creek (Daytona Beach,
    Florida), 5
Stael, Madame de, 215
standard of living: and average
    people are better off, 8–9,
    12–13, 31–32; and call-and-
    raise-the-Joneses, 141; in
    developing nations, 290, 291,
    292–93, 308; and divorce, 52;
    and domestic economics, 60;
    and everyday life in past, 82,
    83; and faults of system in
    West, 160–62; and fear of
    death, 209; and fulfillment,
    246; Galbraith's views about,
    84; and global economics, 67;
    and globalization, 69; and
    happiness, 176, 180; and
    intelligence, 56; and Islam and
    West, 300; and living alone,
    13; and "medium
    development," 285; and
    positive psychology, 245;
    public opinion about, 32; and
    purpose of life, 205; and
    spirituality, 250; and stress,
    189; and wages, 260–61; and
    waking up from American
    Dream, 186; and why good
    news scares people, 84
Sternberg, Esther, 203–5
Stigler, George, 66
Stiglitz, Joseph, 304
stock fraud, 276
stock market, 22, 60
storage, 142–43
stress: and anxiety, 192, 200–201;
    and brain, 193; and choice,
    200–203; and diet, 196; and
    drugs, 196, 198, 199, 201–2;

Printed in the United States
by Baker & Taylor Publisher Services